The Spaces of Justice

The Fairleigh Dickinson University Press Series in Law, Culture, and the Humanities

Series Editor: Caroline Joan "Kay" S. Picart, MPhil (Cantab), PhD, JD, Esquire Attorney at Law; Adjunct Professor, FAMU College of Law; former English and HUM professor, FSU

The Fairleigh Dickinson University Press Series in Law, Culture, and the Humanities publishes scholarly works in which the field of Law intersects with, among others, Film, Criminology, Sociology, Communication, Critical/ Cultural Studies, Literature, History, Philosophy, and the Humanities.

On the Web at http://www.fdu.edu/fdupress

Publications

Peter Robson and Johnny Rodger, *The Spaces of Justice: The Architecture of the Scottish Court* (2017)

Doran Larson, *Witness in the Era of Mass Incarceration: Discovering the Ethical Prison* (2017)

Raymond J. McKoski, *Judges in Street Clothes: Acting Ethically Off-the-Bench* (2017)

H. Lowell Brown, *The American Constitutional Tradition: Colonial Charters, Covenants, and Revolutionary State Constitutions 1578–1786* (2017)

Arua Oko Omaka, *The Biafran Humanitarian Crisis, 1967–1970: International Human Rights and Joint Church Aid* (2016)

Marouf A. Hasian, Jr., *Representing Ebola: Culture, Law, and Public Discourse about the 2013–2015 West Africa Ebola Outbreak* (2016)

Jacqueline O'Connor, *Law and Sexuality in Tennessee Williams's America* (2016)

Caroline Joan "Kay" S. Picart, Michael Hviid Jacobsen, and Cecil E. Greek, *Framing Law and Crime: An Interdisciplinary Anthology* (2016)

Caroline Joan "Kay" S. Picart, *Law In and As Culture: Intellectual Property, Minority Rights, and the Rights of Indigenous Peoples* (2016)

The Spaces of Justice

The Architecture of the Scottish Court

Peter Robson and Johnny Rodger

FAIRLEIGH DICKINSON UNIVERSITY PRESS
Madison • Teaneck

Published by Fairleigh Dickinson University Press
Copublished by The Rowman & Littlefield Publishing Group, Inc.
4501 Forbes Boulevard, Suite 200, Lanham, Maryland 20706
www.rowman.com

Unit A, Whitacre Mews, 26-34 Stannary Street, London SE11 4AB

British Library Cataloguing in Publication Information Available

Library of Congress Cataloging-in-Publication Data

Library of Congress Control Number: 2017946966
ISBN 978-1-68393-088-4 (cloth : alk. paper)
ISBN 978-1-68393-089-1 (electronic)

Printed in the United States of America

Contents

Acknowledgments

We are much indebted for the kindness, generosity and sheer hard work of many individuals and institutions in helping us both research and prepare the material in this volume. We would like to thank the *Royal Society of Edinburgh* for funding the fieldwork which allowed us to research and gather materials from courthouses across Scotland. We are also very grateful for the courteousness and goodwill that was shown us by employees of the *Scottish Court Service* (Scottish Courts and Tribunal Service from April 1, 2015) again across Scotland and with particular thanks to Richard Jones for his willingness to share his specialized knowledge, for his ready provision of materials, and for the telling advice which he was always eager to offer us. The staff at all the courts across Scotland were unfailingly generous, with their time and assistance ensuring our task of visiting every court was a rewarding engagement. Many others have given us great help, including Sarah Alvi, John Blackie, Vivian Carvalho, Miles Glendinning, Louise Horne, Brian Knox, Angus MacDonald, Linda Mulcahy, Robert Paton, Alan and Shona Percival, Niamh Thomson, and the staff at Sarti's. Special thanks also must go to the team at Fairleigh Dickinson University Press, especially Caroline Picart, for their interest in this project and assistance in bringing it to fulfilment. Finally, we'd like to make public our immense gratitude for the patience and support of our respective partners and families while we obsessed with this work.

Introduction

This study examines the nature and development of the places where the administration of law unfolds in Scotland. It discusses where these places are, when they were put there and why, who designed them, and how they operate. Coming from different academic backgrounds, the two writers did nonetheless share an initial perception of the material to be studied. That untutored perception may indeed be widespread. Namely, that, the places for dispensing justice were, like the town halls of Scotland, impressive monuments to the civic pride of the Victorian age. They seemed to represent the stability of an established, mature judicial system that had developed in a recognizable form since the founding of the Court of Session in the early sixteenth century. Our interest in taking these observations beyond the impressionistic was fired by the work on the architecture of justice by Resnik, Curtis, Graham, and Mulcahy. These authors surveyed a range of buildings in which justice was conducted to provide overviews of court facilities in the United States and in England and Wales, and the significance and symbolism of these spaces. Fascinating though this work was, there was no reference to Scotland or its justice system. We were keen to discover how the spaces of justice had emerged in our own distinct jurisdiction. The Scottish legal system has coexisted for over three centuries alongside the English and Welsh legal system, which is ten times larger, while sharing the same supreme civil court and a joint legislature. The pressure to rationalize and conform to English practice in the letter of the law has long been a feature of Scottish legal life, although not as we note, one of the built environment.

This work, then, focuses on the status and condition of the Scottish courthouse. As the principal space in which justice is enacted in Scotland, we examine the types of courthouses that exist, the styles of architecture, the interior organization, the history of the courthouse buildings, the current plans for change to the extent and situation of the courthouses, and the future of the courthouse in Scotland. The book is written at a time of momentous change in the Scottish court system. Several court buildings have recently been closed, and we are on the cusp of a major regional and administrative reorganization. To understand that change, who or what is driving it, why it is happening, and what the effects of the change are, we need to view it at several levels. At its widest possible level we can see it as an inevitable part of a global phenomenon, where, as two American scholars recently put it:

> As the end of the twentieth century approached, many courts systems focused on "long range planning" or "futures" projects sparked by anticipation of the new millennium coupled with anxiety about the "quiet crisis" of aging facilities in poor condition that were required to respond to a growth in caseloads and prison populations. In long established countries, extant facilities were criticized for providing an insufficient number of courtrooms, inadequate rooms ("undersized and windowless") for staff, too few holding cells for detainees, and too limited citizen services, "compromised" by congested waiting rooms and corridors.[1]

The extent to which these global conditions apply is encountered in a localized variant and confronted in turn by the range of policies and initiatives available in the Scottish, British, and European political and legal systems, which are examined in some detail. A range of other, more particular contexts in which the Scottish courthouse is encountered—including the historical relationship and status of the law alongside other pillars of Scottish life and culture such as religion, art, literature, and education as well as the specificities of Scottish geography and the role of the law and the judicial system in local civic life—are analyzed here in our attempt to get a critical hold on the phenomenon and its vicissitudes in Scottish life.

We thus start by examining the range of views of and engagements with the courthouse, comprising the professional and intellectual experience of court personnel, the civic view in the engagement of the law with urban and local life, and the version of "the court" encountered in popular culture: the building, its history, and its processes. We outline the history of the Scottish court system and how it shifted from ad hoc and temporary use of various sites for the dispensing of justice to purpose-built courts. We note changes in the types of jurisdiction it has and has had, and how, through its various evolutions and types of courts, the sheriff court came to be the principal local form. It may seem counterintuitive, however, that before we recount that history of the development of the Scottish court, and the emergence of the modern court, we discuss the most up-to-date proposals for change in the Scottish court system and the likely effects of these changes on the future of that system. How, it might be asked, can the reader comprehend the real significance of the changes proposed for the system before they have been brought to a full understanding of how that system works and how it has developed through time? It is our contention that it is precisely in this moment of great change that such a survey of the most recent changes is invaluable. The history and development of the system should not be read just through eyes of curiosity for its value as a historical and legal idiosyncrasy but also through the lens of the proposed changes so these changes can be assessed in relation to how they relate to the current system as it has developed. It is the moment of change that confers a greater significance on that history.

The changes proposed had their origins in a governmental initiative, which subsequently worked its way through judicial and administrative reports and recommendations. The sources and paths of the far-reaching recommendations are traced here and likely civic and legal effects are predicted where possible. The guiding principle of the enterprise appears to have been that reform of a largely nineteenth-century built heritage in the court system was overdue and that a major rationalization would mean closure of many courthouses and a regional reorganization of the administration of justice. These changes also sought to account for several changes in the nature of the resolution of conflict through litigation, with which we conclude our study.

To provide a rounded picture of the system we examine the extent of the built estate of the Scottish court system and what factors were central in its major phases of development in the nineteenth century. We then examine the specific styles of architecture adopted and how these styles relate to broader issues in Scottish society. We go on to note its civic situation and its artistic and symbolic worth. We then examine how the symbolism of justice, which we initially encountered in the recognizably "justice" focused buildings in Scottish streets, seems to lack expression in the form of statues and artworks. We suggest why this might be so and note the links with other jurisdictions and their iconography with which we are familiar.

We conclude by assessing the wider factors at work in determining the likely future of these traditional dedicated Scottish court buildings. These factors are, as mentioned, centered around changes in the nature of the resolution of conflict through litigation. The pressures include technological changes and the shift from a paper-based to a digital system and "virtual" courtrooms. They may also be seen as a response to changes in the economics of litigation, with specialization and globalization impacting on future practice in the courts and tribunals. We also note the kinds of changes envisaged in England and Wales as indicators of possible developments with an eye to the reduction of public expenditure. The relevant factors also include the impact of various alternatives, such as mediation and other forms of alternative dispute resolution. We conclude with an assessment of the likely effects of the changes on the current system and on its civic context, and the possibility of an improved and more efficient system of justice in Scotland. What seemed a stable and unchanging aspect of Scottish civic life is undergoing rapid change in both its location and the nature of its future operation. The system, which has hardly altered in external form over the past century, will in a few years' time, be unrecognizable to current users. There are, as we indicate, good reasons to welcome some of these changes in terms of the accessibility and transparency of the justice process. Regretfully, however, it does not seem as though the opportunity is being taken, as elsewhere, for infusing into the justice apparatus of the future any tangible expression of the values that a justice system could embody. Nonetheless, as we finally conclude, the loss of an attractive architectural setting could be regarded as a price worth paying for an improvement in the legal process.

Note

1. Judith Resnik and Dennis Curtis, *Representing Justice: Invention, Controversy, and Rights in City-States and Democratic Courtrooms* (New Haven, CT: Yale University Press, 2011), 193.

CHAPTER ONE

Justice—Personnel, Procedure, and Places

This study examines the development of the law courts in Scotland—where they are, when they were put there and why, and how they operate and their architecture. The buildings in which the business of justice is conducted have, traditionally, occupied a prominent place in the streetscape of over fifty Scottish towns and cities. A countrywide survey of these buildings reveals a set of distinctive and imposing structures dedicated to the conduct of court business. Within those buildings is found a very particular set of interior spaces fashioned to order, contain, and direct the participation of the various parties present in the processes of justice. Our study looks at the emergence of this national network of courthouses. It examines their civic location and use, the development of both an exterior and interior architecture and design to fit the purposes of the process, and the consequences for this network of courthouses given the changes in train for the Scottish court system and the move to a much smaller cohort of "justice centers."

Introduction

Given the centrality of courts and litigation to the legal process it might seem surprising that legal scholars have come to consider the courtroom only recently. Why lawyers have paid little attention to their surroundings needs to be explored in detail. It is best understood in the context of what legal education has been focused on and the relationship between legal practitioners and legal scholars. Practicing lawyers have always been principally concerned with what answers the legal system will provide for their clients. Whether this achieves any abstract notion of justice is for the moment, at least, of less import. Their core interest is in the application of the law, and the method of legal training for centuries was by observing and doing. Legal training from its professionalization in universities in the nineteenth century was similarly centered on the legal solution.[1] This concern with the "letter of the law" has been described as "doctrinal."[2] It has been decried by reforming scholars as ignoring the justice goals of the legal system and enshrining the status quo. At its worst, this focus on what the rules of any given system produce runs the risk of producing blind obedience to the rules of the state without any concern for justice. The result has been in the recent past legal actors operating within systems like those of Nazi Germany, apartheid South Africa, and Stalin's Russia and conferring a spurious legitimacy on those regimes. In the immediate post–World War II, this produced new formulations of a version of natural law as a test bed for legitimacy in the work of writers like Radbruch and Fuller. Radbruch sought to devise a fresh basis for natural law to address the issue of lawful but immoral regimes like that of the Nazis in Germany.[3] Fuller, for his part, sought to produce a series of tests against which to measure whether laws could be termed lawful in terms of their procedural content.[4] Others like Kelsen[5] and Hart[6] resisted the temptation to erect such standards and preferred more oblique approaches to the nature of law.

The Focus on the Personnel of the Law

There have always been challenges to this kind of positivist perspective. There is a long tradition of counterposing natural law as a standard against which to judge humanly created or state law.[7] In fairness, as Fine pointed out, notions of an ultimate standard of "natural law" have often been used as a cloak to protect the interests of the powerful.[8] While these debates are the very essence of jurisprudence and the philosophy of law,[9] the focus in scholarship has shifted to a concern with the day-to-day reality of law's power.[10] What the police actually do and how they operate was one of the first concerns in the opening of legal scholarship[11] and the move away from a focus on the rules in the books to law's practice. The various actors concerned with the law's operation and its impact on people have been examined over the past fifty years, from the police to the judiciary[12] and the legislative process.[13]

In the context of the courts in Scotland there have been studies on the jury in Scotland,[14] as well as on how the process of nonprofessional, or "lay," justice works. Bankowski, Hutton, and McManus looked at the personnel of the Scottish lower criminal courts, the then district courts.[15] They examined the people who had become lay judges and how they perceived their role.

One aspect of the judicial task that they did not address, however, was the locations where this work took place.

The Procedure of Justice

This understandable focus on those operating the systems of applied justice overlooked one important factor. The legal operators were operating a system that was not actually of their making. The police did not outline their own powers nor the judges decide what issues should be brought before the courts. Thus, while the early focus of sociolegal work was on the personnel and the impact of their background and ideology on how they operated, there have also been examinations of the structures and systems in place. These examinations have been both functional as well as sociological. Those working within the legal system have sought to make their work more efficient and effective through examining the procedural and professional constraints on their daily lives. Over the years reports have been commissioned and studies undertaken in Scotland into both the machinery of the law and its operation in practice. These reports have included the operation of the sheriff courts in the 1960s,[16] the civil justice system,[17] and the criminal justice system.[18] The operation of various pieces of legislation have come under scrutiny ranging from the prosecution of sexual crimes[19] to the operation of the protection of the matrimonial home[20] to the rules relating to harassment.[21] All these reports had at their heart an interest in whether the systems as they operated and the rules as they were being interpreted and applied by the police and the courts were achieving justice. The concerns, then, of sociologists and criminologists with the reality of the legal system are linked with the interests and focus of practitioners in a very direct way although they may be expressed in different language. Our examination of the spaces of justice builds on work carried out in the past that noted, for instance, that early decisions on matrimonial interdicts often took place not in the courts but in the cramped and highly unsuitable chambers of the judges.[22] These issues of the operation of specific sets of rules, though, are laid to one side in our current study, important though they are in their individual contexts. We seek to expand on the observations of the early writers on law in its social context and see what can be learned from the spaces in which these activities take place.

The Places of Justice

The work on personnel and procedure, as noted, contained references to the impact of the location of legal procedures for the realization of justice. Hence, there is a link between the operation of the legal system and justice and the interests of scholars examining where the law is carried out daily, in the courts and tribunals. Although it has been suggested that democracy is buttressed using courts and the adjudication process,[23] the judicial process has often been utilized by those with scant regard for democratic principles. Instead, it has been used to provide a form of legitimation of state violence.[24]

Sometimes, the purposes of these exhibitions of judicial toughness had an explicit political goal. Hence, in England, in the wake of the Monmouth Rebellion to overthrow King James VII in 1685, there was a series of trials of those involved in the rising. These trials were presided over by Lord George Jeffreys in the West Country. Almost two thousand were condemned to death, with over four hundred hanged. Yet many of these sentences were commuted to transportation for life to the West Indies. Some of those condemned were also drawn and quartered and their remains displayed around the country as a warning to others minded to rebelling against the Crown.[25] Equally disposed to play a political role was Scots lawyer Robert MacQueen. As Lord Braxfield he achieved a notoriety in Scotland in the eighteenth century because of the harsh way he dealt with those who appeared before him, most famously in telling an accused person that "Ye're a vera clever chiel, man, but ye wad be nane the waur o' a hanging" [You are a very smart fellow but you'd be none the worse for being hanged].[26] He is also reported as asserting that as far as political trials were concerned his role was clear. When consulted on the advisability of a political prosecution, his usual reply is said to have been, "Bring me the prisoners, and I will find you the law."[27] Lord Cockburn, an eminent judge himself, commented on the conduct of Braxfield in the trials for sedition of Muir, Skirving, Margarot, and others in 1793 and 1794, to the effect that Braxfield was the Judge Jeffreys of Scotland.[28]

There exists, then, a long tradition of a range of benevolent tyrants using the theater of law to create both fear and the illusion of legitimacy through the appearance of an even-handed process applicable to all. Hay wrote of the way in which the assize courts on circuit in eighteenth-century England provided a vision of the social order that sought to transcend class interest. By showing that the rigors of the law applied to all, this order could be worthy of respect since it did not favor those of good backgrounds any more than the wretched and poor who were its principal victims.[29]

Such overt terror tactics have featured less in the modern era after the abolition of public executions in 1868.[30] In the twentieth century the methods of maintaining the hegemony of the rich and powerful has been subtler.[31] One of the pioneering texts in British sociolegal studies had as part of its focus the way in which the structures of the courts impacted on the nature of the justice. In her study of the local justice that was most likely to be encountered by members of the public, Carlen presented the world of the magistrates' courts in England.[32] One of the factors that helped make this process particularly alienating was the physical layout of the courtrooms. The bench was located with a commanding view of the whole courtroom from a lofty position.[33] These kinds of observations about courtroom design form part of the broad context that we wish to examine in our assessment of the spaces of Scottish justice. We want now to highlight the major thrust of the scholarship in which our analysis is located. We outline very briefly the issues that those who have examined courtrooms have found of interest in their own jurisdictions. The focus on justice in the courts has been on both a global comparative basis[34] and a localized basis.[35] We look at the principal works in turn.

International Courtroom Scholarship: The Intersection between Images of Justice and the Effectiveness of Law

In a wide-ranging exploration of images of justice and legal practice, the range of issues addressed by Resnik and Curtis in *Representing Justice*[36] is extensive and provides a valuable point from which to reflect on the Scottish experience. Starting from the point of the ubiquity and dominance of justice as a recognized virtue that can be appealed to universally, they explore the provenance and prominence of the iconography of Lady Justice. Whether it be commercial or political, "this remnant of Renaissance iconography"[37]—the clothed statue of Justice with her sword and scales—is readily deployed to a public that understands immediately her significance and what she symbolizes. Although their study draws on no Scottish material, as we demonstrate, Scotland also finds a prominent place for this virtue in civic and commercial life. The local courts in a range of American states deploy the Justice statue as the signifier for a courthouse: "One way to denote that a building housed a court was to display a statue of Justice—often set at the top of a tower or turret."[38]

As we note, however, this is a feature very rarely encountered on or around courthouses in Scotland (see chapter 6), an anomaly that provoked our interest in pursuing the Scottish project. The impressive variety of examples from around the world that Resnik and Curtis display suggest a universality to their themes, which we considered worthwhile measuring against our own local setting. They also go on to explore why it is that the other "virtues"—Temperance, Fortitude, Prudence, Wisdom, or Charity—are absent from law and political theory (see chapter 6), which we advert to in the context of Scottish civic architecture (see chapter 6), although it is less germane to our concerns with projected changes in the administration of justice in Scotland. The absence, too, of contemporary material on the consequences, challenges, and failures of the justice system[39] is a theme that we note as being different in the context of Scotland.

The concern of Resnik and Curtis "to show how the practice of adjudication helped to shape democratic norms about government's relationship to the public"[40] is an area we reflect on the context of the shift from local control and decision making about the appropriate kinds of centers of justice to the centralized model that now dominates in practice as well as in theory in Scotland (see chapter 4). This and the changes in the kinds of issues coming before the courts and the development of alternative practices like alternative dispute resolution, mediation/conciliation, and administrative tribunals are issues that Resnik and Curtis address in the context of the United States.[41] These are themes that resonate with our experience and debates in Scotland and that we explore in our study (see chapter 7).

Although more descriptive in style, the survey of English courts until 1914 by Graham[42] set out "to establish, when, how and why English trials came to be housed in purpose-built accommodation."[43] Graham urges a note of caution when she suggests that "in the case of law courts . . . buildings grew out of procedures" rather than the reverse.[44] This certainly chimes in with the experience in Scotland with the move from written to oral pleading in the nineteenth century changing the demands and spaces required by the burgeoning sheriff courts (see chapter 3). Graham observes that the architectural developments in England "reflected particular and sometimes fortuitous circumstances."[45] This is something that is reflected in our survey of the program of building and types of building style favored in the nineteenth century in Scotland (see chapter 5). Again, although principally a survey of how the purpose-built courtroom buildings developed until 1914, Graham is concerned with issues of the efficiency of these nineteenth-century buildings and how the demands placed on their use change over time. She asks whether they consider the importance of user friendliness and notes that this is something to be addressed.[46] Interestingly, she was pessimistic about this becoming an issue in the English context, in the light of the completion in 2002 of an "extensive program of rationalization and rebuilding."[47] It is, however, something that is at the forefront of Scottish policymaking in the post-Gill era (see chapter 7).

Similar issues are encountered more recently in Mulcahy's work. In her examination of the English court system and its development,[48] she explores the impact of the courthouse and courtroom on those affected by it. She is interested in examining the political significance of the purpose-built law courts of England between 1790 and 1840 and whether they can be seen as sites of containment rather than progress.[49] Another of her themes is the role of the public in the trial and the way the physical layout of the courtroom, as it has developed, has changed this.[50] These are issues that we take up in the Scottish context (see chapter 5). Like other writers in the field, from Resnik and Curtis to Graham, Mulcahy too is keen to engage with the future for justice in the courts with the changes from advances in technology,[51] and we also take the opportunity to discuss such implications for Scotland (see chapter 7).

Beyond Courtroom Studies

There are also several germane areas where scholars' works shed a more indirect light on these concerns with images of justice and the effectiveness of law. Given the situation of Scottish courthouses in towns and cities of strategic local and regional importance the work of urban and spatial theorists offers particularly effective and rewarding analyses for this work. Urban studies have a direct focus on justice and the nature of the city, and some writers have developed a different emphasis on the "space" of justice in general rather than the places in which the justice process takes place.

The concept of "spatial justice" has been much discussed by recent urban theorists.[52] Spatial justice is conceived as an aspect of social justice and at its simplest level concerns the equitable spatial distribution of access to needs like health, employment, and transport. A discussion of this last aspect, for example, can be seen in Edward Soja's extended analysis in *Seeking Spatial Justice* of the fight by the Bus Riders Union of Los Angeles to gain a more just distribution of transport finance toward funding bus travel in that metropolitan area.[53] In that case of city funds being allocated either toward the development of a light rail network in middle class areas or to an arguably more vital bus network reaching out to marginalized and impoverished working class areas to give them access to the city, the concept of spatial justice can be seen in the context of a sociospatial dialectic where, as the philosopher Henri Lefebvre put it, "space is political and ideological. It is a product literally filled with ideologies."[54]

While this concept of space as a political and ideological product has a universal application, it has had a particularly significant role when invoked at the level of the urban, as noted in Soja's Bus Riders Union study. Accordingly, the urban application of the concept may have a special relevance to the civic and localized situation of Scottish courthouses under discussion in this work. Indeed, one notion of Lefebvre's, the "Right to the City,"[55] subsequently also developed by David Harvey,[56] concerns the demand that through participation in the creation of (political and ideological) space in the city, and the right to appropriate it for their own just ends, citizens can transform and renew their "access to urban life."[57]

One important question in our work about spatial justice is that of the fairness and equity of allocation of legal and judicial services, such that there is no discrimination against citizens in terms of the quality of their access to and participation in the civil and criminal justice processes. This is important in the light of the changes proposed by the Scottish Court Service, and already under way, to the number, function, and distribution of courthouses in towns and cities around the country (see chapter 7).

In a critique aimed at a more microlevel of space and design of actual spaces in courthouses, we might also find useful approaches in the behaviorist-oriented theories of an earlier generation of urban theorists. In the wake of the post–World War II rebuilding of Europe and America's decrepit and often bomb-destroyed cities, there arose a critique of modernist architecture and urban planning in terms of its effect on social behavior. Writers like Jane Jacobs, Oscar Newman, and Alan Lipman examined and exposed how the new architecture and the new urban planning of that era effected a breakdown of cogent spatial mechanisms that influenced people's understandings of space and their behavior in it. Newman's "defensible space" theory seeks to understand why with the design of the modern era, the physical environment (his study examines New York City Public Housing Projects) became less easy to control or to make safe. Newman suggests that with the "breakdown of building tradition, through the rapid evolution of new techniques," then "the wisdom of ages is lost."[58] Accordingly he describes his theory thus:

> Defensible space is a surrogate term for the range of mechanisms—real and symbolic barriers, strongly defining areas of influence and improved opportunities for surveillance—that combine to bring an environment under the control of its residents.[59]

In the "traditional" nineteenth-century courtroom in Scotland, as described in chapter 5, there existed just such a series of "real and symbolic barriers" that defined "areas of influence" and "opportunities for surveillance." For example, the low timber barrier, known as the "bar," which separates the public gallery from the well of the court, represents a "symbolic" barrier because any able-bodied citizen could easily climb or leap over or even just open the gate to let themselves through to the center of the action. Yet, for the reasonable and responsible member of the public, this "symbolic barrier" marks out territory in the courtroom into which they must not stray unless they are specifically invited to do so.

As pointed out elsewhere in this work, the clear majority of Scottish courthouses in use when our survey began in 2013 were built before the age of architectural modernism, mainly in the nineteenth century. Even those courtrooms built or renovated more recently, however, including Glasgow, Edinburgh, and Airdrie sheriff courts, still conform to the nineteenth-century model, with minimal variations, which thus employ a type of "defensible space" in terms of the legibility of the fixtures and fittings and barriers that inform the users which space it is legitimate for them to use and in what way.

There are however, a few aspects of modern design where the defensible space critique can be employed to highlight design concerns. The recent tendency to fit glass panels atop the barriers separating the public from the well of the court, doubling their height, has effectively transformed these barriers from "symbolic" to "real" ones. This means there is now a physical obstacle enforcing separation between the public and the court proceedings, rather than a recognized, conventional, and legibly symbolic barrier. We might wonder whether this new design thus violates a historic and civil accord between the court and the public and replaces it with physical authority? Does it represent a violation of the civil integrity of the public, an assault on their "right to the city" in terms of their outright exclusion from the decision concerning the creation and use of space, in this case a formerly tacit assent that the well of the court be used only for the process?

The critique could also, however, be usefully applied to understand the failings of some of the modern design of the courthouse in general, for example the entrances hidden, down below the public street level, and obscured by shrubbery, as at both the modern courts in Airdrie and Dunfermline (see the Gazetteer). Both these entrances might present a danger for the antagonistic parties involved in any court process, as the approach to the building is obscured from public view, and thus unprotected by the casual observation and surveillance of passersby.[60]

Urban theories can, then, be applied to gain understanding and to analyze questions of accessibility and democracy, and to critique both the physical situation of the legal infrastructure in existing settlements and the given range of possibilities for human relations in the designed spaces within and around the courtroom and the court building. Beyond that application, however, there is also at the heart of this study an acknowledgment of the fundamental and even constitutive role the law has in the establishment of the urban realm itself. The legal and judicial system is not simply something that supplements an existent urban context; it is always already engaged as an integral part of any urban system. For legal philosopher Andreas Philippopoulos-Mihalopoulos, there is a "continuum between law and city" where the two are even "co-extensive and indeed tautological."[61] He goes on to explain in everyday terms, writing

> In the city, law's presence is magnified to a deafening extent—so much so that one no longer feels its presence: planning restrictions, environmental regulations, zoning, social control, borders between private, public and restricted access areas, pavements, roads, traffic lights, metro barriers, flow of people, headscarves at schools, hoods in shopping malls, power architecture and landscaping, are just a few of the urban legal moments. In the city, law's presence is concentrated and overt, in close contact with the production, consumption and disposal processes, intensified due to physical proximity. The city remains the great testing ground for law, its loudspeaker and its gaming table. And in turn, the law is the city's measure, the (in)flexible metallic ruler that makes its presence felt through inches and centimetres of propinquity and distance, determining identity and difference. Law is the regulator of spaces between places, connecting and severing urban beings, urban objects, urban desires and fears, amongst themselves and with whatever is imagined to be outside the urban.[62]

In demonstrating just such a "coextensive" and constitutive role of the law in the urban realm, we describe in chapter 5 the physical centrality of the courthouse to the institutions of the nineteenth- and early twentieth-century urban settlement: the council chambers, the police station, the library, the main street, the principal town square, and so on. We also note below, in the Gazetteer, the civic pageantry that marks both the annual opening of the High Court—as at Glasgow until at least the 1960s—and the inauguration of a sheriff court—as at Lerwick in 1876 (see Gazetteer). The cross section of civil bodies, their officers and members that were involved at the celebrations in the Shetland town, is remarkable. We draw attention, furthermore, to how, for one local historian, the establishment of the infrastructure and offices of the law created the very foundation for the first urban settlement on the Hebridean island of North Uist (Lochmaddy; see chapter 5).

Law and Popular Culture

Much of what scholars have written about in relation to the rise of the courtroom and the notions of justice expressed in urban development depends on the spaces in which the justice system operates and the form these take. It is within popular culture that we find these visions of justice and its embodiment given form. When Resnik and Curtis ask why the modern figure of Justice is so readily recognizable across the world to a variety of audiences, we would suggest that this stems from the impact of popular culture. It is the image of law and justice from film and television that in the twenty-first century people recognize and relate to. They may laud it, decry it, and mock its absence, as Resnik and Curtis demonstrate,[63] but it is recognized. We draw on the rich tradition of work on law and popular culture for why this is so. From Macaulay[64] and Friedman[65] to Sherwin[66] and Asimow et al.[67] there is a broad consensus that in the modern age what the public know about law and the legal process stems principally from the media. Our expectations of the reality of the justice system as well as our hopes for its future portrayal are bound up in the images from the entertainment industry. This both confirms and reinforces what we think applied justice looks like and what it should look like.

From the iconic 1950s' film *12 Angry Men* to more recent films like *Philadelphia* and *The Judge* along with TV portrayals of the justice system like *The Defenders*, *The Good Wife*, and *Boston Legal*, popular culture also adds in a version of what the public can expect when they encounter the justice system in the courtroom. The signal that we are entering into the formal world of justice has become a standard signifier.[68] It may open a film concerned principally with a trial as we find in the panning shots at the start of the jury-focused film *12 Angry Men* or the gay discrimination case *Philadelphia*, or most recently *The Judge*. In these typical instances we see the key cinematic symbols of justice—the towering Greek columns or Gothic façade of the courthouse. The move into "formal legal" mode may occur at a later stage during a legal drama as we see in the antihanging drama *Eight O'Clock Walk*.[69] Here, after the crime has been committed and the suspect arrested, we move to the trial by looking down from the heights of Pomeroy's statue of Justice atop the Old Bailey in London. Even where the trial is not a central part of the film, this external shot of the courthouse is how we expect to encounter the law's majesty. In *Wild Things*,[70] the columns of the Florida courthouse again open what we think is the rape trial of a young teacher but which turns out to be a prelude to a multitwisting extortion and revenge thriller.

The other signifier of law and its pomp is the majestic internal appearance of the courtroom. Magnificent wooden benches and soaring ceilings are the order of the day whether it is *Witness for the Prosecution*, *The Accused*, *A Civil Action*, or any of the aforementioned films.[71] These images of Greek-style temples of justice are not limited to the work of the Hollywood dream factories. Although there have been limited opportunities for Scottish justice to be portrayed, nonetheless, when Scottish justice has been portrayed on screen, the same rules apply. The external shots of the start and end of the trial in *Madeleine*[72] show steps running up to a double row of Greek columns in the David Lean production. This was a device to emphasize the baying crowds at both the start of her trial and at the end with her controversial release, the charges having been found not proven.[73] The High Court of Justiciary at the time was located within Parliament House and lacks a grand "cinematic" entrance.

As we shall see, this is not to say that these images are always a travesty of reality, but rather that popular culture provides us with a version of what to expect from courts and courtrooms. In the cases of the various portrayals of Scottish justice that we find in popular culture, the representations are striking for their accuracy. In *Madeleine*, for instance, the version of the High Court of Justiciary shown in the film, which is shown below, is a faithful reproduction of the general layout of Robert Reid's High Court of Justiciary.[74] The major physical difference is the claustrophobic low ceiling beneath which the Lords of Justiciary sit. The rest, though, corresponds to where the witnesses gave their evidence standing opposite the Scottish fifteen-man jury.[75] The principal nonphysical difference between reality and the film version was the use of the peripatetic counsel addressing the jury in the style encountered in most American films. Counsel in Scotland speak from a fixed location and do not walk around the courtroom. That apart, this vision of a Scottish courtroom corresponded to what Madeleine Smith would have experienced before her long sojourn in America.[76]

At a more modest level the portrayals of courtrooms in both the Greyfriars Bobby films show us what to expect in the lower criminal courts in Scotland. The Burgh Court, presided over by Baillie and Lord Provost in Walt Disney's *Greyfriars Bobby*[77] is an accurate version of an Edinburgh courtroom of the 1870s with its high-set bench, witness stand location, and public benches. The more recent version of the story, *The Adventures of Greyfriars Bobby*,[78] while adopting a similar storyline, shows a grander courtroom building using the exterior of the baroque Usher Hall in Edinburgh and an ecclesiastical interior resembling none of the Scottish courtrooms that we have observed, except as far as it featured a raised public gallery.

In television, too, we have a variety of courtroom settings provided in a range of different programs. They range from fictional dramas and procedurals to reality entertainment, and in the United States, actual trials on television. Like film, the dominant material in terms of quantity has been from America. There have, over the past fifty years, however, been almost fifty series of one form or another purporting to show applied justice in Britain.[79]

The few Scottish series produced have encompassed the range of different forms noted above. In terms of the local sheriff court, in the 1970s' *Sutherland's Law*, centered on the work of a prosecutor of crime, the procurator fiscal, is a rural setting in Scotland.[80] The program emphasized the extra-courtroom investigative activities that a fiscal has in theory. Alongside these investigations and crime solving there were courtroom scenes. From this we learned that Scottish sheriff courts can be modest affairs. The 1980s' Dominic Rossi, the lawyer protagonist of *The Justice Game*,[81] who practiced his skills in Glasgow, was based on an amalgam of Glasgow lawyers Joe Beltrami and Paul Laverty.[82] The nature of the storyline, however, meant that our view of Scottish courts was limited to external shots of the modern marble wall relief outside the Glasgow Sheriff Court. The most ambitious and wide-ranging visual examination of Scottish legal practice came in the Edinburgh-set series *The Advocates* from the 1990s.[83] This stressed the investigative role of lawyers, rather than their work in court, but did utilize the actual interiors of the Edinburgh High Court, including using the atmospheric Parliament Hall with its hammerbeam ceiling, stained glass window, and steady flow of ambulant lawyers. Exterior shots of the Court of Session were also featured in what provided a very faithful version of the Scottish court experience. Nothing in the titles of the production, however, indicated that this was how things are in the Scottish courts or that cooperation of the authorities had been provided to allow for this authenticity.

There have also been two versions of reality TV looking at the practice of law in Scotland. The first version involved an actual trial in the sheriff court of a man charged with theft of a bus from a bus garage. Unfortunately, this pioneering piece of television suffered from the same restrictions as those seen in the widely shown Rodney King trial.[84] The jury and the public could not be shown. So although shot in a Glasgow Sheriff Court, the viewing audience get no sense of the courtroom. The same limitations were in place in a six-part series that looked at a range of Scottish courts in 1993.

In the twenty-first century, however, television cameras have been allowed into Scottish courts on several occasions.[85] The retrial of Nat Fraser for the murder of his wife, Arlene, in 1998 was filmed by Channel 4 in 2012 and shown as *The Murder Trial* the following year. In 2012, legal history was made when David Gilroy became the first convicted killer to have his sentencing filmed for TV.[86] In 2015, liberal politician Alistair Carmichael was accused of electoral misconduct by four of his constituents in seeking to secure his own election. He had denied leaking a memorandum from the Scottish First Minister, Nicola Sturgeon, purporting to indicate her desire for a Tory election victory. After the election he admitted he had leaked the memorandum. In view of the public interest in the proceedings, the judges decided to allow television cameras to broadcast live from the High Court for the first time.[87]

Finally, the short-lived reality entertainment show *The People's Court* was shown in 2005[88] with a studio setting in the style of a cut-down "Judge Judy" operation and with similar civil disputes of low monetary value.[89] The height that is seen in the courtroom of Judge Sheindlin is replaced by a more modest bench, and the studio is less elaborate. In fairness, it was not unlike many of the smaller courts that we have come across in modern Scotland (see the appendix). Unlike *Judge Judy*, however, it did not resonate with Scottish audiences and lasted a single twelve-episode series.

While these local examples are variable in their images, it is clear that there has, over the years, been a wealth of images of justice settings—American, English, and Scottish—to inform our notions of what a court building looks like from the outside and what to expect inside. As we have noted, in Scotland, while there is a standard version that applies to most Scottish courts and courtrooms, the reality varies and principally for pragmatic reasons.

This is in no sense blaming any of the producers of films or television images of courts. Their task is not to engage in a civic education process but to convey as simply—and in some cases—as cheaply as possible that the justice process is in play. Whether in the twenty-first century we should worry, whether our actual experience as litigants, accused, witnesses, or jurors does not correspond to what we imagine it will be, is a matter for debate. Perhaps the stark lighting and cheap seats of the Tribunal Service are to be preferred to the majesty of the judicial bench and the elaborate woodcarvings of the courtroom furniture. This is an issue we address in our discussions of the future of the courts. After all, the courts are, as Resnik and Curtis suggest, often simply the settings for the exercise of power, cloaked in the language of legality.[90]

Notes

1. Peter Robson, *Housing and Judiciary* (Glasgow: University of Strathclyde, 1979), 24–60.
2. S. Halliday, *Introduction to the Study of Law* (Edinburgh: W. Green, 2012), chapter 1.
3. G. Radbruch, "Rechtsphilosophie," in *Gesamtausgabe*, vol. 1, ed. A. Kaufmann (Heidelberg: C. E. Müller Verlag, 1987).
4. Lon Fuller, *The Morality of Law* (New Haven, CT: Yale University Press, 1969).
5. H. Kelsen, *The Pure Theory of Law* (Berkeley: University of California Press, 1960).
6. H. Hart, *The Concept of Law* (Oxford: Clarendon, 1961).

7. Thomas Aquinas, *Summa Theologiae* (Oxford: Oxford University Press, 2014; originally published Paris, 1273).

8. Bob Fine, *Democracy and the Rule of Law* (Caldwell, NJ: Blackburn Press, 2002).

9. J. Finnis, *Natural Law and Natural Rights* (Oxford: Oxford University Press, 1980); M. Freeman, ed., *Lloyd's Introduction to Jurisprudence* (London: Sweet and Maxwell, 2014).

10. R. Cotterrell, *The Sociology of Law* (Oxford: Oxford University Press, 2005).

11. J. Skolnick, *Justice without Trial* (Berkeley, CA: Wiley, 1966).

12. J. Griffith, *The Politics of the Judiciary* (London: Fontana, 1975); P. Robson and P. Watchman, eds., *Justice, Lord Denning and the Constitution* (Farnborough: Gower, 1981); A. Paterson, *The Law Lords* (Oxford: Socio-Legal Studies, 1980); A. Paterson, *Final Judgment: The Last Law Lords and the Supreme Court* (Oxford: Hart, 2013)—the thrust of this work is encapsulated in the French Canadian T-shirt slogan *Le bon avocat connait la loi, le grand avocat connait le juge*, which, stripped of connotations of cronyism, sums up the significance of the findings of the American Realist and jurimetrics approaches to legal scholarship. Judgments and decisions of the courts are molded by the politics of the judges. When you know these predilections, then it is easier to explain past and predict future developments.

13. N. Gunningham, *Pollution, Social Interest and the Law* (London: Martin Robertson, 1974).

14. I. Willock, *The Origins and the Development of the Jury in Scotland* (Edinburgh: Stair Society, 1964).

15. Z. Bankowski, N. Hutton, and J. McManus, *Lay Justice* (Edinburgh: Edinburgh University Press, 1987).

16. Lord Grant, *The Sheriff Court* (Edinburgh: Scottish Home and Health Department and HMSO, 1967).

17. Lord Gill, *Report of the Scottish Civil Courts Review* (Edinburgh: Scottish Civil Courts Review, 2009).

18. Lord Carloway, *The Carloway Review* (2010), www.gov.scot/About/Review/CarlowayReview.

19. Michele Burman, Lynn Jamieson, Jan Nicholson, and Oona Brooks, *Impact of Aspects of the Law of Evidence in Sexual Offence Trials: An Evaluation Study* (Edinburgh: Scottish Government Social Research, 2007).

20. A. Jackson, M. Robertson, and P. Robson, *The Operation of the Matrimonial Homes (Family Protection) (Scotland) Act 1981* (Edinburgh: Scottish Office, 1988).

21. K. Cavanagh, C. Connelly, and J. Scoular, *An Evaluation of the Protection from Abuse (Scotland) Act 2001* (Edinburgh: Scottish Executive, 2003).

22. Marie Robertson and Peter Robson, *The Matrimonial Homes (Family Protection) (Scotland) Act 1981: The First Six Months* (Glasgow: University of Strathclyde, 1983).

23. Judith Resnik and Dennis Curtis, *Representing Justice: Invention, Controversy, and Rights in City-States and Democratic Courtrooms* (New Haven, CT: Yale University Press, 2011), 14.

24. Resnik and Curtis, *Representing Justice*, 12.

25. H. Montgomery Hyde, *Judge Jeffreys* (London: Butterworth, 1948).

26. J. Lockhart, *Memoirs of the Life of Sir Walter Scott* (Cambridge: Cambridge University Press, 1846), 425.

27. Lord Cockburn, *Memorials of His Time* (Edinburgh: Blackie, 1856), i, 87.

28. Cockburn, *Memorials of His Time*, 116.

29. Douglas Hay, Peter Linebaugh, John Rule, E. P. Thompson, and Cal Winslow, eds., *Albion's Fatal Tree: Crime and Society in Eighteenth-Century England* (London: Pantheon, 1975).

30. The last public hanging in Scotland took place in Dumfries of a mother of four, Mary Timney, for murder of a neighbor. http://www.heraldscotland.com/news/12360663.Great_day_out_at_the_gallows/.

31. Lord Goddard in the trial of Derek Bentley and Christopher Craig—see *Let Him Have It* (1990) where the words and actions of the judge are taken directly from the trial transcript.

32. P. Carlen, *Magistrates' Justice* (London: Martin Robertson, 1976), 21–24.

33. Carlen, *Magistrates' Justice*.

34. Resnik and Curtis, *Representing Justice*, 1–17; see also Judith Resnik, Dennis Curtis, and Allison Tait, *Constructing Courts: Architecture, the Ideology of Judging, and the Public Sphere* (Dordrecht: Springer, 2014), for a concise overview of these themes.

35. Clare Graham, *Ordering Law: An Architectural and Social History of the English Law Court to 1914* (Farnborough: Ashgate, 2003); Linda Mulcahy, *Legal Architecture: Justice, Due Process and the Place of Law* (London: Routledge, 2011).

36. Resnik and Curtis, *Representing Justice*, 1–17.

37. Resnik and Curtis, *Representing Justice*, 1.

38. Resnik and Curtis, op cit. at 137 and figs. 96 and 97, color plate 28.

39. Resnik and Curtis, *Representing Justice*, 13.

40. Resnik and Curtis, *Representing Justice*, 14.

41. Resnik and Curtis, *Representing Justice*, 16–17.

42. Graham, *Ordering Law*.

43. Graham, *Ordering Law*, 2.

44. Graham, *Ordering Law*, 3.

45. Graham, *Ordering Law*, 3.

46. Graham, *Ordering Law*, 4.

47. Graham, *Ordering Law*, 4.

48. Mulcahy, *Legal Architecture*; Linda Mulcahy, "Back to the Future? The Challenge of the Past for the Courthouses of Tomorrow," in *Architecture and Justice*, ed. N. Temple, J. Simon, and R. Tobe (Farnborough: Ashgate, 2013).

49. Mulcahy, *Legal Architecture*, 9 and 21–27.

50. Ibid., 10.

51. Ibid., 11 and Chapter 8.

52. See, for example, the writings of Henri Lefebvre, David Harvey, and Edward Soja.

53. Edward Soja, *Seeking Spatial Justice* (Minneapolis: University of Minnesota, 2010).

54. Henri Lefebvre, "Reflections on the Politics of Space," trans. M. Enders, *Antipode* 8 (1976): 30–37, at 31.

55. Henri Lefebvre, *Le Droit a la Ville* (Paris: Anthropos, 1968).

56. Harvey, David. "The Right to the City." *New Left Review* 53 (2008): 23–40.

57. Henri Lefebvre, *Writings on Cities* (Cambridge, MA: Blackwell, 1996), 158.

58. Oscar Newman, *Defensible Space* (London: Architectural Press, 1973), 5.

59. Newman, *Defensible Space*, 3.

60. It is notable that most courts in Scotland are entered by a door or portico at street level. Very few have the dramatic sets of open, public stairways leading up to a portico as seen in some courthouses in the United States for example. The modern sheriff court at Falkirk is one exception to this rule, as is Forfar sheriff court, sitting above its baroque stairway to the street, and also the nineteenth-century sheriff court at Lerwick, with its path across an open garden leading to its front door. The design at Airdrie and Dunfermline sheriff courts has indeed moved in the opposite direction of the open, public-spirited design of the American court by lowering the entrance below the street level and obscuring it behind bushes and trees.

61. Andreas Philipopoulos-Mihalopoulos, ed., *Law and the City* (London, Routledge, 2007), 7.

62. Philippopoulos-Mihalopoulos, *Law and the City*, 9.

63. Resnik and Curtis, *Representing Justice*, 1–17.

64. Stuart Macaulay, "Images of Law in Everyday Life: The Lessons of School, Entertainment and Spectator Sports," *Law and Society Review* 21 (1987): 185.

65. Lawrence Friedman, "Law, Lawyers and Popular Culture," *Yale Law Journal* 98 (1989): 1579.

66. Richard Sherwin, *When Law Goes Pop* (Chicago: University of Chicago Press, 2000).

67. M. Asimow, S. Greenfield, G. Jorge, S. Machura, G. Osborn, P. Robson, C. Sharp, and R. Sockloskie, "Perceptions of Lawyers: A Transnational Study of Student Views on the Image of Law and Lawyers," *International Journal of the Legal Profession* 12 (2005): 407–36.

68. S. Greenfield, G. Osborn, and P. Robson, *Film and the Law: The Cinema of Justice* (Oxford: Hart, 2010), 54; contrast with the two series centered on corporate law and away from the courtroom—*Trust* (2003) and *Suits* (2011–), where the equivalent visual focus is on the towering shiny glass offices of the financial sectors of London and New York, respectively—see Peter Robson, "The Portrayal of the Corporate Lawyer on TV: The US and British Models from *L.A. Law* to *Trust* and *Suits*," *Journal of the Oxford Centre for Socio-Legal Studies* 1, no. 3 (2017).

69. 1953 (Lance Comfort).

70. 1998 (John McNaughton).

71. The harsh lighting, low ceilings, and simple chairs of the two-minute courtroom scene in *Erin Brockovich* (2000) (Steven Soderbergh) are the only hint that some forensic business is conducted in less august surroundings.

72. 1949 (David Lean).

73. John Wilson, *Not Proven* (London: Secker and Warburg, 1960).

74. W. Douglas Cullen, *Parliament House: A Short History and Guide* (Edinburgh: Scottish Courts Administration, 1992), 36.

75. Women did not qualify for jury service until the removal of the legal bar under The Sex Disqualification (Removal) Act 1919.

76. She moved immediately to London to escape attention, marrying and having two children in the 1860s. She moved to the United States in 1889, remarried, and died in 1928.

77. 1961 (Don Chaffey).

78. 2005 (John Henderson).

79. Peter Robson, "Lawyers and the Legal System on TV: The British Experience," *International Journal of Law in Context* 2, no. 4 (2007): 333–62.

80. Glendarroch—played by Oban, with McCaig's Folly prominent. See *McCaig v Trustees of University of Glasgow* 1907 SC 231 and *McCaig's Trustees v Kirk Session of the United Free Church of Lismore* 1915 SC 426—fine examples of a judiciary imbued with the spirit of Calvinism.

81. BBC (1989).

82. Interview with the producer, Peter Broughan, November 2006.

83. *The Advocates* ran to two seasons in 1991 and 1992.

84. Elaine Rapping, *Law and Justice: As Seen on TV* (New York: New York University Press, 2003).

85. The somber and technical work of the Supreme Court is now shown live on the Internet and has featured several Scottish cases, including *Macklin v HMA* (on the limited role of the Supreme Court in relation to Scottish criminal cases) and *Trump International Golf Club v The Scottish Ministers* (unsuccessful challenge to the wind turbines off the coast of the Trump Aberdeen golf development allowed by the Scottish government); available on the Supreme Court website: www.supremcourt.uk.

86. http://www.scotsman.com/what-s-on/tv-radio/tv-cameras-to-be-allowed-in-scottish-court-rooms-1-3672116#ixzz3pDi46jnT.

87. Cahal Milmo, "Alistair Carmichael is on trial live on TV over the leaked Nicola Sturgeon memo - but it's less than riveting viewing," September 7, 2015. http://www.independent.co.uk/news/uk/politics/alistair-carmichael-is-on-trial-live-on-tv-over-the-leaked-nicola-sturgeon-memo-but-its-less-than-10490504.html.

88. Robson, "Lawyers and the Legal System on TV: The British Experience."

89. STV, *The People's Court* (2005).

90. Resnik and Curtis, *Representing Justice*.

CHAPTER TWO

The Courtroom in Context

Justice is conceived throughout history as something played out in set spatial contexts, between people, their territory, and their property and objects. One of the earliest images of justice being enacted, from the Akkadian period five thousand years ago, shows a place where a legal hearing is effectively a drama performed between persons coming together across a social hierarchy, with goods and assigned roles, specific rights and approaches, meeting and engaging with the mechanism of the law[1] (figure 2.1). Equally, in what is arguably the most influential and foundational book of the Western philosophical tradition, *The Republic*, written in the fourth century BCE, Plato discusses how justice would be found in a specifically prospective place, an ideal city, and the discussion plays out as a dialogue between various people in an existing city: Athens.

Twenty-First-Century Scotland

There is always and necessarily a consideration of space when the concept of justice is invoked. Thus, a study of the places, fixtures, fittings, and symbols that surround, embellish, and stage the enactment of justice in any judicial system will always bring insight into the hosting civilization and its mores. This has never been truer than in contemporary Scotland. The Scottish justice system is currently undergoing major changes as to where and how justice is provided. Following a request in February 2007 from the then Scottish Minister for Justice, Cathy Jamieson, that a review of the civil court system

Figure 2.1. The Akkadian god Samas as a dispenser of justice, circa 2350–2100 BCE. Original pen sketch by Pat Donald after Tess Rickard's drawing from an original seal in the British Museum, first published in *Gods, Demons and Symbols of Ancient Mesopotamia*, by J. Black and A. Green.

be undertaken,[2] several consultations have been carried out, and reviews, responses, and recommendations published into not only the civil but also the criminal court system.[3]

The aim of the review was to make "recommendations for changes with a view to improving access to civil justice in Scotland, promoting early resolution of disputes, making the best use of resources, and ensuring that cases are dealt with in ways which are proportionate to the value, importance and complexity of the issues raised."[4] This flexibility and wide-ranging set of criteria for change provide the context in which a massive sea change in the spaces available for justice in Scotland has taken place. The Consultation Paper, in relation to the structure and jurisdiction of the civil courts, sought to focus discussion on twenty-four questions including asking "whether the current division of the sheriff court into distinct geographical jurisdictions presents difficulties or does it have advantages."[5] The issue of a major review of the context was absent at this stage. It emerged more obliquely in the Introduction to Lord Gill's 2009 *Report of the Scottish Civil Courts Review* when he noted that

> The basic structure of civil jurisdictions in the Scottish courts remains much as it was in the late nineteenth century. Meanwhile, fast moving changes in the social and economic life of Scotland in recent decades have left us with a structure of civil justice that is seriously failing the nation. Reform is long overdue.[6]

This report made 206 recommendations. The precise nature of many of the proposed changes to procedure do not concern this study. Many, though, had implications for the places where justice is practiced, including the ending of the use of part-time judges,[7] a new sheriff appeal court,[8] locating a specialist personal injury court for the whole of Scotland in Edinburgh sheriff court,[9] and rationalizing the boundaries of the sheriffdoms.[10] The initial report's suggestions, in terms of the impact on accommodation, appeared limited. The newly recommended "district judges"[11] and sheriffs "would be accommodated in existing sheriff court and JP court estate. When the volume of business would not justify there being a resident district judge on a full time basis, a single district judge might cover more than one court."[12] Of importance for any study of the various courts in different sheriffdoms was the rejection of the notion of a national sheriff court or sheriffs having all-Scotland jurisdiction. Rather, Gill recommended that there should be a review to rationalize the boundaries of the sheriffdoms with those of other public authorities.[13]

There was an initial response from the Scottish government, which broadly welcomed the proposals and in particular the six principles under which Gill believed that the system of civil justice should work.

> It should be fair in its procedures and working practices
> It should be apt to secure justice in the outcome of disputes
> It should be accessible to all and sensitive to the needs of those who use it
> It should encourage early resolution of disputes and deal with cases as quickly and with as much economy as is consistent with justice
> It should make effective and efficient use of its resources, allocating them to cases proportionately to the importance and value of the issues at stake
> It should have regard to the effective and efficient application of the resources of others[14]

The Scottish government accepted much of the Gill Report's technical recommendations on case management,[15] multiparty actions,[16] judicial review,[17] and district judges[18] while reserving their position on the cost and funding of litigation.[19] As far as the broader question of access to justice was concerned, they "strongly agree(d) that securing access to justice must be a key aim of the civil justice system"[20] but noted that in a "period of unprecedented pressure on public finances"[21] that it was "necessary to prioritize, to co-ordinate expenditure more efficiently, and to be innovative in identifying opportunities to secure justice in new, cheaper ways."[22]

After further consultation[23] and responses,[24] progress in relation to the major reforms has continued on the matters referred to already, such as a new judicial tier in the sheriff court with district judges,[25] a specialist personal injury court,[26] and procedural changes.[27] Other issues have also been progressed including moving civil business from the Court of Session[28] and improving the judicial review procedure.[29] All have an indirect impact on the location of the reformed services. Direct change proposals, however, emerged in 2013, from the body with the task of managing most of the buildings in which much of the law and justice are dispensed in Scotland,[30] the Scottish Court Service.

Shaping Scotland's Court Services

In 2013, the Scottish Court Service published a response and a plan to house the results of the reforms.[31] Their plan has profound and widespread consequences for the spatial distribution of justice in Scotland, for access to justice and for the places where that justice is delivered. At the time when the Scottish Court Service response was published, it was true to say that the built heritage of the structures within which the judicial proceedings were taking place in Scotland was largely Victorian. Besides three High Court buildings[32] and seven stand-alone justice of the peace courts,[33] there were forty-nine sheriff courthouses across the country at the beginning of 2013,[34] of which over forty had been built originally in the nineteenth century (although many of them had undergone interior renovation and/or had more modern extensions added). The long-term plan now—to take place over a ten-year period—was to reduce the number of mainland sheriff courthouses to sixteen (with also five island courts—Stornoway, Lochmaddy, Kirkwall, Lerwick, and Portree), which would correspond to sixteen justice centers situated in the main population centers of the country. The document states that

> We are in no doubt that the optimal model in the longer term is for purpose built justice centres in key strategic population centres, including the Borders, Fife, Lanarkshire and the Highlands to complement the existing high quality courts that we already have in many of Scotland's cities.[35]

In the shorter term, however, the Scottish Court Service, recommended that some sheriff courts be closed over the period 2014–2015, and that the circuit of High Court business around the country to available and appropriate sheriff courts be reduced:

> Our recommendations include High Court Cases being heard predominantly in three dedicated centres, the closure of 10 Sheriff Courts (including 9 justice of the peace courts), the closure of 7 justice of the peace courts and a move towards 16 specialist jury centres over a longer 10 year period.[36]

High Court cases would be heard in Edinburgh, Glasgow, and Aberdeen. The sixteen centers planned long term for shrieval justice were to be Glasgow, Aberdeen, Inverness, Edinburgh, Livingston, Paisley, Dumbarton, Kilmarnock, Airdrie, Hamilton, Ayr, Dumfries, Perth, Dundee, Falkirk, and Dunfermline. The sheriff courts to be closed over the years 2014–2015 were designated as Dornoch, Duns, Kirkcudbright, Peebles, Rothesay, Cupar, Dingwall, Arbroath, Haddington, and Stonehaven. All these closures duly took place and the buildings have been put to other uses.[37]

The spatial consequences of these actions were wide ranging and have serious socioeconomic effects reaching beyond those intended for and felt in the judicial system. One only needs to examine, for example, the broad cross section of the population involved in the celebrations at the opening of Lerwick sheriff courthouse in 1876 (see the appendix), to appreciate the significance attached by citizens in general to the appointment of their town as the seat of a sheriffdom. The Scottish Court Service showed itself aware that many consider its actions as a major intervention in the workings of the built environment—the "community's heritage and civic identity"—of several small Scottish towns. Their report highlights that many correspondents to their consultation "commented on the potential impact on the local economy and heritage,"[38] but the report rejects this claim noting that they "found little evidence to support the claims." About the access to justice, the question of both the "impact on court users" and "impact on the quality of legal services and Administration of Justice," the Scottish Court Service claimed that "in total only around 5% of overall court business will move to another court, which in most cases will be a distance of less than 20 miles."[39]

While there is undoubtedly a move toward further centralization and rationalization in the court system, driven to a large extent by financial considerations,[40] there is simultaneously an element of dispersal of court business. As we noted the Gill Report proposed for the lowest value of claim needed for a case to gain access to the Court of Session to be raised from £5,000 to £150,000 and for a new local sheriff appeal court to be introduced along with "district judges."[41] This would add to the business at sheriff court level rather than adding to the already stretched Court of Session and High Court. There is a concern about how far people can be expected to travel as either litigants or witnesses in the government's paper on access to justice.

> Subject to the efficient disposal of business, it is desirable that criminal justice be delivered locally. Quite apart from the convenience of witnesses and the interest of victims, this engages the local community in the administration of justice, including providing the opportunity to serve as justices or jurors. What

> is involved in the delivery of criminal justice "locally" may vary with the level of jurisdiction being exercised.[42]

Implicit in Lord Gill's assertion about "fast moving changes" in Scottish life is of course the fact that the whole notion of the "local" is very different now from that which was the case in the nineteenth century. That notion is indeed something that has changed throughout history, and will continue to change. It is highly unlikely that a litigant will arrive at the courthouse nowadays with his prized but perhaps ill-gotten goat in his arms, as seen in figure 2.1. Instead, a video of the goat prancing around its pen might be shown, while a veterinary surgeon testifies as an expert witness to its bestial constitution and its genetic provenance. Just so, the Scottish Court Service points out "both transport and media information services are vastly different from the Victorian period when many of the current courts were built."[43]

The conflict between two of Lord Gill's six principles that should determine how a justice system should operate is always likely to give rise to discord, and as we shall see this is not a modern issue. How to provide a system that is "accessible to all and sensitive to the needs of those who use it" at the same time as making "effective use and efficient use of its resources, allocating them to cases proportionately to the importance and value of the issues at stake,"[44] involves disadvantaging some citizens and some areas. Which citizens and which areas do best in this political process depends on who is able to marshal power and influence most effectively. We can see how this operated in the past with court developments, closures and "rationalization" a constant feature of the Scottish legal scene over the past two centuries since courts in fixed locations became the norm.

There is great scope at this pivotal period in the history of Scottish justice for taking stock of both the existing and newly closed court facilities, and how their urban, territorial, architectural, interior, and symbolic operations have sustained and affected the delivery of justice. We also pay attention to the newer forms of justice available to both business and individuals in the form of mediation as well as the growth in the past seventy years of administrative tribunals that affect the lives and incomes of an increasing number of citizens. It is thus the intention of this work to examine a wider range of historical roots and cultural ramifications of the spatial distribution of justice and the changes planned for its administration than have been possible or practical in the reports and consultations published—and cited here—by the legal profession and official government and administrative bodies.

Appendix

Key

Bold standard: court where a justice center has been identified

Bold underlined: court in the Islands that will continue

Standard: court open in 2016 but will be closed in next decade

BOLD: closed court and year of closure before the Gill Review

Italics: court closed after the Gill Report

Aberdeen, **Airdrie**, Alloa, ***Arbroath*** (May 2014), **Ayr**

Banff

Campbeltown, *Cupar* (May 2014), **CROMARTY** (1934)

Dingwall (2015), ***Dornoch*** (November 2013), **Dumbarton**, **Dumfries**, **Dundee**, **Dunfermline**, Dunoon, ***Duns*** (January 2015), **DUNBLANE** (1975)

Edinburgh, Elgin

Falkirk, Forfar, Fort William

Glasgow, Greenock

Haddington (January 2015); **Hamilton**

Jedburgh

Inverness, **INVERARY** (1954)

Kilmarnock, Kirkcaldy, ***Kirkcudbright*** (November 2013), **Kirkwall**, **KINROSS** (1975)

Lanark, **Lerwick**, ***Linlithgow***, **Livingston**, **Lochmaddy**, **LEITH** (1920)

NAIRN (1977)

Oban

Paisley, ***Peebles*** (January 2015), **Perth**, Peterhead, **Portree**

Rothesay (November 2013)

Selkirk, ***Stonehaven*** (2013), **Stornoway**, Stirling, Stranraer

Tain, **TOBERMORY** (1905)

Wick, **WIGTOWN** (1975)

Notes

1. Jeremy Black and Anthony Green, *Gods, Demons, and Symbols of Ancient Mesopotamia: An Illustrated Dictionary* (London: University of Texas Press and the Trustees of the British Museum, 1992), Mesopotamian Scales Akkadian Period, circa 2350–2100 BCE.

2. Lord Gill, *Report of the Scottish Civil Courts Review* (Edinburgh: Scottish Civil Courts Review, 2009), 1.

3. These include Lord Gill's *Report of the Scottish Civil Courts Review*; Sheriff Bowen's *Review of Sheriff and Jury Procedure* (Edward F. Bowen, *Review of Sheriff*

and Jury Procedure [Edinburgh: Independent Review of Sheriff and Jury Procedure, 2010]; Lord Carloway's *The Carloway Review* (Lord Carloway, *The Carloway Review* [2010], www.gov.scot/About/Review/CarlowayReview); Judicial Office for Scotland, *Principles for Provision of Access to Justice* (2012), www.scotcourts.gov.uk/docs/default-source/scs-consultation-court-structures/statement_of_principles.pdf; Scottish Court Service, *Shaping Scotland's Court Services* (2013), www.scotcourts.gov.uk/docs/default-source/scs-consultation-court-structures/response_to_the_consultation_and_recommendationspdf.pdf; and Scottish Government, *Making Justice Work: Courts Reform (Scotland) Bill—A Consultation Paper* (Edinburgh: Scottish Government, 2013).

4. Lord Gill, *Scottish Civil Courts Review: A Consultation Paper* (2007), www.scotcourts.gov.uk/docs/default-source/civil-courts-reform/scccompleter-(2)7CDD54ABAE89.pdf?sfvrsn=2, 1.

5. Gill, *Scottish Civil Courts Review: A Consultation Paper*, question 13, 42.

6. Gill, *Report of the Scottish Civil Courts Review*, i.

7. Gill, *Scottish Civil Courts Review: A Consultation Paper*, recommendation 1, 245.

8. Gill, *Scottish Civil Courts Review: A Consultation Paper*, recommendation 8, 245.

9. Gill, *Scottish Civil Courts Review: A Consultation Paper*, recommendation 32, 248.

10. Gill, *Scottish Civil Courts Review: A Consultation Paper*, recommendation 36, 249.

11. Gill, *Scottish Civil Courts Review: A Consultation Paper*, recommendation 37, 249, sitting in the sheriff court hearing "summary criminal business and civil claims of modest value."

12. Gill, *Scottish Civil Courts Review: A Consultation Paper*, recommendation 43, 249.

13. Gill, *Scottish Civil Courts Review: A Consultation Paper*, recommendation 36, 249.

14. Scottish Government, *Scottish Government Response to the Report and Recommendations of the Scottish Civil Courts Review* (Edinburgh: Scottish Government, 2010), www.scotcourts.gov.uk/docs/default-source/civil-courts-reform/scottish-government-response-to-the-report-and-recommendations-of-the-scottish-civil-courts-review.pdf?sfvrsn=2, paragraph 1, 6.

15. Scottish Government (2010) at para 179–184.

16. Scottish Government loc. cit. at para 164–167.

17. Scottish Government loc. cit. at para 168–175.

18. Scottish Government loc. cit. at para 187–189.

19. Scottish Government loc. cit. at para 197.

20. Scottish Government loc. cit. at para 211.

21. Scottish Government loc. cit. at para 212.

22. Scottish Government, ibid.

23. Scottish Government, *Making Justice Work*.

24. Scottish Government Social Research, *Courts Reform (Scotland) Bill: Analysis of Consultation Responses* (Edinburgh: Scottish Government, 2013).

25. Scottish Government, *Making Justice Work*, chapter 2.

26. Scottish Government, *Making Justice Work*, chapter 4.

27. Scottish Government, *Making Justice Work*, chapter 6.

28. Scottish Government, *Making Justice Work*, chapter 1.

29. Scottish Government, *Making Justice Work*, chapter 5.

30. Administrative tribunals such as Social Security were within the jurisdiction of the British HM Courts and Tribunals Service until 2014.

31. Scottish Court Service, *Shaping Scotland's Court Services*.

32. Edinburgh (Lawnmarket), Glasgow (Saltmarket), Aberdeen.

33. Justice of the peace courts exist as separate stand-alone courts in Annan, Cumbernauld, Hamilton, Irvine, and Lochgilphead, and the others share premises with the local sheriff court in two locations—Alloa and Banff.

34. See the appendix.

35. Scottish Court Service, *Shaping Scotland's Court Services*, 5.

36. Scottish Court Service, *Shaping Scotland's Court Services*, 5.

37. Dornoch (sold and being developed as a hotel complex), Duns (for sale), Kirkcudbright (for sale), Peebles (empty), Rothesay (empty), Cupar (empty), Dingwall (empty), Arbroath (for sale), Haddington (empty), and Stonehaven (for sale). Note that over forty of the 2013 court buildings are protected by listed status (see the appendix for details), so the buildings themselves are less likely to be lost to the urban surroundings even if they are no longer used as courts.

38. Forty-three out of the fifty-six buildings in the Scottish court estate in 2013 were listed buildings; see the appendix.

39. Scottish Court Service, *Shaping Scotland's Court Services*, 7–8.

40. Scottish Court Service, *Shaping Scotland's Court Services*, 4. "At the same time, public sector funding is under severe pressure, by 2014-15 the court service running cost budget will reduce by 20% in real terms and the capital budget will reduce from £20M to £4M."

41. The Scottish Government preferred Sheriff Principal McInnes's term "Summary Sheriff" for this position over Lord Gill's "District Judge" but said it was "open to suggestions for alternatives." Scottish Government, *Making Justice Work*.

42. Judicial Office for Scotland, *Principles for Provision of Access to Justice* (2012). www.scotcourts.gov.uk/docs/default-source/scs-consultation-court-structures/statement_of_principles.pdf, section D.

43. Scottish Court Service, *Shaping Scotland's Court Services*, 9.

44. Gill, *Report of the Scottish Civil Courts Review*, 6.

CHAPTER THREE

The Development of the Modern Scottish Court System

The development of the high or central courts and the lower or local courts is marked by very different histories. The central courts that we find in Edinburgh today have had the same location around Parliament Square since their founding, and changes in these spaces of justice over the past century have been modest. The local courts, on the other hand, have undergone great changes in both their location and the kinds of work they have undertaken. The emergence and development of first the House of Lords and then the Supreme Court (since October 1, 2009) as the ultimate court of appeal on civil matters in Scots law, is not covered in this study. They have always been in London and are subject to very different pressures and forces in terms of their cultural and political background and, of course, their architectural heritage.[1]

The Court of Session and High Court

Founded in 1532 in Edinburgh, where it has always sat, the Court of Session comprised a Lord President and fourteen other Lords.[2] It was a collegiate court sitting as a group within the Inner House, with each Lord sitting for a week in the Outer House as Lord Ordinary. The Inner House comprised the Lord President and all the other judges not on circuit or sitting in the Outer House. The quorum of the Inner House was nine, and decisions were by a majority. Originally, the Outer House was not a distinct court of first instance but rather a way of preparing cases for hearing by the Inner House—taking evidence from witnesses.

The Court of Session was guaranteed by the Treaty of Union. Article 19 provided

> That the Court of Session or College of Justice do after the Union and notwithstanding thereof remain in all time coming within Scotland as it is now constituted by the Laws of that Kingdom, and with the same authority and Privileges as before the Union; subject nevertheless to such Regulations for the better Administration of Justice as shall be made by the Parliament of Great Britain. . . . And no causes in Scotland be cognoscible by the Courts of Chancery, Queen's Bench, Common Pleas or any such Court in Westminster Hall. And that the said Courts, or any other of the like nature, shall have no power to Cognosce, Review or Alter the Acts or Sentences of the Judicature within Scotland, or stop the execution of the same.

The Court of Session ceased to be a single court in terms of the Court of Session Act 1808 and was divided into two divisions. Although entitled the First Division and Second Division they had equal status, and litigants in the past had a choice of which one to use.[3] The distinction between the Outer House and Inner House emerged with the Court of Session Act 1810, which separated the Inner and Outer Houses. Five junior judges were made permanent Lords Ordinary and the number of judges in each division of the Inner House was then fixed at four.[4] Currently, the number of Court of Session judges is thirty-four with twenty-three Lords Ordinary. The facilities in the Royal Mile can accommodate the rise in numbers (see Gazetteer).

The High Court of Justiciary structure was covered by the Court Act 1672 and provided that the court should consist of a Lord Justice General, the Justice Clerk, and five other Lords of Session. They would hold commissions as Lords Commissioners of Justiciary. Hence, six of the judges in Edinburgh were both civil judges and criminal judges. The continuance of the High Court of Justiciary was guaranteed by Article 20 of the Treaty of Union, which provided it should continue with the same authority and privileges as before the Union, subject to such regulations as should be made by the Parliament of Great Britain.[5] It sat in Edinburgh with a quorum of three[6] and went on circuit twice a year to a range of Scottish towns, including Dumfries, Jedburgh, Stirling, Glasgow, Ayr, Perth, Aberdeen, and Inverness.[7] When sitting outside of Edinburgh, it occupied the local court accommodation in all locations. In the case of Glasgow separate accommodation for the High Court of Justiciary was made available in the Stark building on the Saltmarket.[8] It later sat in the former Union Bank building on Union Street from 1964 to 1997.[9] The cases in Edinburgh or on circuit were tried before a jury of fifteen with evidence led in the presence of the jury, the accused, and the accused's counsel. Cases were raised by Lord Advocates or with their concurrence by private parties injured by the crimes, and the accused parties were entitled to advocates of their choosing or those appointed by the court to act in their defense. In Edinburgh it is located currently in the former sheriff court building on Lawnmarket (see Gazetteer).

Local Courts

In the eighteenth century there was a mix of different local courts. In broad terms, in towns there were burgh courts, and the rest of the country was served by sheriff courts. The latter covered most of the country outside the towns. Although the business of the courts varied over the years with the fortunes of agriculture and local cottage industries, the pattern of courts remained constant. As we note below, this could be accommodated without undue problems owing to the prevalent practice of the sharing of facilities between town councils and the justice system. In Peebles, Haddington, and Selkirk as well as in many other locations, for instance, prior to the erection of the dedicated court building in the nineteenth century (see Gazetteer), court business was conducted in the chambers of the town council. Only in exceptional cases, like Airdrie, do we find the rise of business through the iron and coal industries unable to be in a convenient local jurisdiction (see chapter 5).

Regality and Barony Courts

Regality courts, which Walker calls "jurisdictional islands," as well as barony courts derived from feudal landholding rights, exercised criminal jurisdiction.[10] In the eighteenth century, Cairns suggests that the activity and effectiveness of these jurisdictions was unclear and probably of decreasing significance, although he notes that this view may be ill-founded.[11] Nonetheless, by the time the Commissioners on the Courts of Justice reported in 1822, they indicated that there were "few instances" of the limited criminal jurisdiction relating to "assaults batteries and smaller crimes" being used by those with rights in the barony courts.[12] There were also "stewartries," normally of small parcels of land, but which, in the cases of Kirkcudbright and Orkney and Shetland comprised counties that had defaulted back to the Crown and were administered by "stewarts" (stewards). By the 1820s it was reported that business in the burghs of barony and regality was "irregular and occasional only."[13] The situation in Falkirk was such that no one had been appointed a baillie after 1797 and the jail had fallen into ruin and shops had been built on it.[14] It seems unlikely that traces of the locations of these courts will shed much light on our concern with the nature and development of court buildings.

Burgh Courts

Within the towns and burghs the justice arrangements meant that there were local courts there as an alternative to the sheriff court. From 1124 onward there had been created by Royal Charter, royal burghs. By the time of the 1707 Treaty of Union they numbered over one hundred.[15] They reflected the major market towns and centers of trade and changes in local economies with the development of internal and international trade. Hence, in Brechin, for example, we find the local small-scale business conducted in the 1789 burgh court while more serious criminal and civil matters were dealt with eleven miles away in the county town of Forfar.[16]

Here were located the burgh courts. In larger towns with sheriff courts there was a parallel jurisdiction, and the burgh court powers were described in the early nineteenth century as "nearly the same with that vested in the Sheriffs of the shires."[17] These burgh courts were presided over by the yearly elected town magistrates appointed in accordance with the rules and regulations of the specific charter of the burgh, known as *setts*. They had both civil and criminal jurisdiction within their limits, but their right to claim jurisdiction from another court in relation to persons in their jurisdiction was abolished by statute in the Heritable Jurisdictions (Scotland) Act 1746.[18] Blackie notes how popular these courts seem to have been as late as the 1820s in relation to civil matters due to their relative speed.[19] One specialist early court whose jurisdiction did survive into modern times was the court of the dean of guild, which by the nineteenth century was restricted to an early town planning cum building regulation role controlling building within the burgh. In burghs where there was no dean of guild, this role was carried out by the burgh magistrates.[20]

By the early years of the nineteenth century in many burghs their civil court role had diminished although the number of burgh courts was still considerable. Sixty-six burgh courts were surveyed by the commissioners inquiring into the courts of justice in Scotland in 1822.[21] There was a serious inclination toward suppression of their powers[22] but no recommendation that their jurisdiction with the sheriff court be abolished as in the case of the commissary court.[23] As was pointed out, they were anomalous. There were wealthy and populous towns where there was no burgh court and "several in places which had fallen into decay."[24] There are also instances where it was reported that the role of the burgh court had almost ceased entirely. North Berwick indicated that there was "no regular court in this Burgh."[25] Tain noted that "there is little or no duty to be performed in this Burgh."[26] From both Whithorn in the south and Wick in the north, for instance, it was indicated in 1822 that "judicial proceedings seldom or ever take place."[27] As noted, there was frequently not a dedicated court building but rather sharing of civic facilities. In some instances, however, we have the extant buildings in which burgh courts took place. In Glasgow, the burgh court in 1888 was located in the remodeled city chambers on John Street and, as noted, was used for the dean of guild court in the 1970s.[28] In Brechin, the original site of the burgh court has become the location for a representational museum, which includes a jail recreation on the lines of the adaptation of the Inverary courthouse.[29] In the former independent burgh of Partick the court was located in Partick burgh hall constructed in 1871 with its frontage sporting inter alia a roundel of *Justitia* (see chapter 6).

Sheriff Courts

Justice in rural Scotland in the Scottish counties, on the other hand, had stemmed from the role of being principal local landowner. This involved administering justice through a sheriff. The office of sheriff had by the time of the Act of Union in 1707 become hereditary. The Treaty of Union provided that "all heritable offices, superiorities, heritable jurisdictions, offices for life and jurisdictions for life be reserved to the owners thereof, as rights of property in the same manner as they are now enjoyed by the laws of Scotland, notwithstanding of this Treaty."[30]

In practice, the holding of the court was undertaken by a legally qualified depute who, in turn, frequently appointed persons to do the legal work for them. These persons were known as "sheriffs-substitute" and were supported by an income from court fees and fines. [31] In 1727 twenty-two sheriffs were hereditary, three were appointed for life and only eight held office at the pleasure of the monarch.[32]

Following the 1745 Jacobite Rising and its defeat in 1746, the British government sought to control Scotland more effectively and curb sources of local power. Although many of these heritable jurisdictions were held by landowners loyal to the Hanoverian dynasty[33] it proved impossible to trace the precise origins in the records of the various heritable jurisdictions.[34] Hence the decision to abolish the heritable jurisdictions and compensate their holders where deemed appropriate by the Court of Session, although the process was by no means straightforward.[35]

These heritable jurisdictions were abolished in terms of the Heritable Jurisdictions (Scotland) Act 1746 which transferred the government of the shires back to the Crown and compensated those who had lost these "property" rights to the tune of £150, 037 12 s 2d at an average of £2,000 per claim.[36] Roderick Macleod of Cadboll asked for a total of £12,000, more than anyone else below the rank of earl.[37] They were organized on a county or shire basis. There were thirty-three counties or shires in Scotland (see the appendix). Regality courts and Barony courts, in which landowners had the right in terms of the title to their property to administer civil and criminal justice in relation to that landholding, became outdated in the wake of the Heritable Jurisdictions (Scotland) Act 1746 with its provisions for compensation operating here too.[38]

The office of sheriff principal became a ceremonial one under the Sheriffs (Scotland) Act 1747.[39] A sheriff depute was appointed to each "county, shire or stewartry."[40] In due course this process was professionalized. The deputes, drawn from the ranks of those members of the Faculty of Advocates of at least three years standing, were salaried rather than being remunerated from court fees or fines.[41] The salary was related to the population of the sheriffdom.[42] If a sheriff depute had charge of more than one county, he was aided by sheriffs-substitute.[43] There was a residence requirement for the sheriff depute as well as a prohibition on them doing other remunerated work to avoid their being subject to the influence of such employers.

Prior to the Jacobite Rising, as noted, there were some thirty-three separate sheriffdoms in Scotland each with their own Sheriff and court location.[44] The Sheriffs (Scotland) Act 1747 linked twelve of these counties in pairs reducing the number to twenty-seven.[45] The shires or counties which boasted sheriffdoms provide a guide as to what towns were of administrative significance in the mid eighteenth century. The subsequent changes and rationalizations provide some kind of indication of the ebb and flow of power and influence as locations of justice were absorbed into larger constellations. We can observe, for instance, the limited amount of business between Tain, Dornoch and Dingwall but the retention of the Tain courthouse represented an exercise of the power and influence of the long-sitting Sheriff, Donald Macleod of Geanies, whose estate was conveniently located nearby.[46]

Rationalizations took place under the Sheriffs (Scotland) Act 1853 with the merging of 16 sheriffdoms into seven units on the retiral, demise or appointment elsewhere of the relevant sitting sheriff (see the appendix) with the interim devolvement of his powers to any remaining sheriff. The Sheriff Courts (Scotland) Act 1870 continued this process (see the appendix).

The Administration of Justice (Scotland) Act 1933 made further amendments to this structure. As noted, this involved combining various smaller districts and subsuming smaller areas into larger by a process of accretion on the retiral or moving elsewhere of the relevant sitting sheriff (see the appendix). With improved communication and professionalization the number of sheriffdoms in Scotland was reduced to fifteen in 1870, ten in 1933. The Grant Committee examined the sheriff court in the 1960s and recommended that arrangements for defining the boundaries of sheriffdoms be in the hands of the Secretary of State in consultation with the Lord Advocate and the sheriffs principal.[47] In due course the current tally of six was provided for in the Sheriff Court (Scotland) Act 1971.[48] They are Glasgow and Strathkelvin; Grampian, Highland and Islands; Lothian and Borders; North Strathclyde; South Strathclyde; Dumfries and Galloway; and Tayside, Central and Fife. As noted earlier the Gill Report rejected the notion of a national sheriff court or sheriffs having all-Scotland jurisdiction and recommended that there should be a review to rationalize the boundaries of the sheriffdoms with those of other public authorities.[49]

Jurisdiction of the Lower Courts and Their Practice

Except for the "pleas of the Crown" the sheriff had jurisdiction in all breaches of the common law and old statutory law. The exceptions were murder, fire-raising, rape, and robbery unless the murder were taken "redhand."[50]

There were also other courts which exercised competing jurisdiction in civil matters. Blackie suggests that these courts were genuine alternatives to the slow and inefficient shrieval process.[51] Although they may have been swifter in their activities, those using these courts used the same lawyers and they generally operated the same scale of fees and charges as when working in the sheriff courts,[52] although there were some exceptions.[53] As noted above by the time of the Report of the Commissioners on the Courts of Justice, however, the business reported in these courts seemed to have waned significantly.[54]

The Sheriff Court's jurisdiction was gradually extended by legislation taking over the work previously carried by others. For instance, the Commissary Courts, except for Edinburgh, which had made inroads into the work of the Court of Session in relation to matters of status and testate succession up until the early nineteenth century[55] became merged in the Sheriff Courts in 1823,[56] and abolished entirely in 1876.[57] Their jurisdiction covered marriage, divorce, legitimacy, status and matters of succession to moveable property of Scots dying abroad.

The Sheriff Court (Scotland) Act 1838, also, extended the jurisdiction of Sheriff court to "all Actions or Proceedings relative to questions of nuisance or damage arising from undue exercise of the right of property, the constitution of real or praedial servitudes."[58] Clarification was also provided that the powers and jurisdictions of the High Court of Admiralty of Scotland in all maritime causes and proceedings civil or criminal were to be competent before the Sheriff, provided that the defender was amenable.[59] Additional court days were also provided for to dispose of Arrears of Business.[60] A simplified small debts action was also brought into the sheriff court in the 1838 legislation. The Sheriff Courts (Scotland) Act 1877 brought matters of heritable rights within the jurisdiction of the sheriff.[61]

The abolition of written pleadings which had grown in significance in the eighteenth century,[62] and the substitution of oral pleadings also altered the nature of the work in the sheriff court and contributed to the need for more by way of accommodation.[63] As we note in the next chapter, these changes in business complemented the perceived desirability for more adequate space for the carrying out of this expanding forensic business.

Appendix

Original Sheriffdoms and Counties Prior to 1747

Aberdeenshire; Argyll; Ayrshire; Banffshire; Berwickshire; Buteshire; Caithness; Clackmannanshire; Dumbartonshire; Dumfriesshire; Edinburgh/Midlothian; Elgin/Moray; Fife; Forfarshire/Angus; Haddingstonshire; Inverness; Kincardineshire; Kinross; Stewartry of Kirkcudbright; Lanarkshire; Linlithgow; Nairn; Orkney; Shetland/Zetland; Peebles; Perthshire; Renfrew; Ross; Cromarty; Roxburghshire; Stirling; Sutherland; Wigtownshire

Sheriffs (Scotland) Act 1747 Amendments

Clackmannanshire and Kinross united as Clackmannan & Kinross.
Elgin/Moray and Nairn become Elgin & Nairn.
Orkney & Shetland/Zetland become Orkney & Shetland.
Ross and Cromarty become Ross & Cromarty.
Caithness and Sutherland become Caithness & Sutherland (disunited in 1806).

Changes under Sheriffs (Scotland) Act 1853 (provided for when the relevant sitting sheriff ceased to occupy that office)

Banff, Elgin & Nairn united in 1854.
Dumbarton & Bute united in 1854.
Haddington & Berwick united in 1856.
Sutherland & Caithness united in 1857.
Wigton & Kirkcudbright united 1860.
Linlithgow, Clackmannanshire & Kinross united 1865.
Roxburgh & Selkirk united 1868.

Changes under the Sheriff Courts (Scotland) Act 1870

Aberdeen & Kincardine united 1870.
Caithness, Orkney & Shetland united 1870.
Ross, Cromarty & Sutherland united 1870.
Renfrew & Bute united 1871.
Stirling & Dumbarton united 1871.
Midlothian & Haddington 1872.
Roxburgh, Berwick & Selkirk united 1872.
Dumfries and Galloway united 1874.
Stirling, Dumbarton & Clackmannan united 1881.
The Lothians united 1881.
Fife & Kinross united 1881.
Inverness, Elgin & Nairn united 1882.
Aberdeen Kincardine & Banff united 1882.
The Lothians & Peebles united 1883.

Changes under the Administration of Justice (Scotland) Act 1933

Perth & Angus united 1934.
Ayr & Bute united 1946.
Renfrew & Argyll united 1946.
Caithness, Sutherland, Orkney & Zetland united 1946.
Inverness, Moray, Nairn & Ross & Cromarty united 1946.

The position under the Sheriff Court (Scotland) Act 1975

Aberdeen, Kincardine & Banff
Ayr & Bute
Caithness, Sutherland, Orkney & Zetland
Dumfries & Galloway
Fife & Kinross
Inverness, Moray, Nairn and Ross & Cromarty
Lanarkshire
The Lothians & Peebles
Perth & Angus
Renfrew and Argyll
Roxburgh, Berwick & Selkirk
Stirling, Dumbarton & Clackmannan

2012 Closures

Eleven courts within the existing Sheriffdoms were identified in plans for closure; Alloa; Arbroath; Cupar; Dingwall; Dornoch; Duns; Haddington; Kirkcudbright; Peebles; Rothesay; Stonehaven.

Notes

1. A. Paterson, *The Law Lords* (Oxford: Socio-Legal Studies, 1980); A. Paterson, *Final Judgment: The Last Law Lords and the Supreme Court* (Oxford: Hart, 2013).

2. J. Irvine Smith, "The Transition to the Modern Law 1532–1660," in *An Introduction to Scottish Legal History* (Edinburgh: Stair Society, 1958), 25.

3. Peter Robson, *Housing and Judiciary* (Glasgow: University of Strathclyde, 1979).

4. G. Paton, "The Eighteenth Century and Later," in *An Introduction to Scottish Legal History* (Edinburgh: Stair Society, 1958).

5. APS, XI, 383, 204.

6. Quorum of Justice Court Act 1681 and Justiciary and Circuit Courts (Scotland) Act 1783 (23 Geo 3, c 45).

7. Union with Scotland (Amendment) Act 1707 (6 Ann c 40) and Heritable Jurisdictions (Scotland) Act 1747 (20 Geo 2, c 43).

8. Scottish Civic Trust, *Historic Buildings at Work: A Guide to the Historic Buildings of Scotland Used by Central Government* (Edinburgh: Scottish Civic Trust, 1983). Originally in a town office, the courthouse and prison complex were designed by William Stark between 1807 and 1814; the current building on that site is a reworking of the original to a design by J. H. Craigie in 1913.

9. This building, constructed in 1841, was used as the High Court between 1964 and 1998 before becoming a bar/nightclub in 2000. The original High Court chamber is currently home to only one-armed bandits.

10. The Abolition of Ward Holdings (Scotland) Act 1747 brought an end to the requirement to attend the three head courts under the duty of suit, although this duty seems to have been little observed.

11. John Cairns, "Historical Introduction," in *A History of the Private Law in Scotland*, ed. K. Reid and R. Zimmermann, 14–184 (Oxford: Oxford University Press, 2000), 119.

12. Commissioners on the Courts of Justice, *11th Report* (London: HMSO, 1822), 5.

13. Commissioners on the Courts of Justice, *11th Report*, 147.

14. Commissioners on the Courts of Justice, *11th Report*, 149.

15. George Pryde, *The Burghs of Scotland: A Critical List* (Oxford: Oxford University Press, 1965).

16. Report of Committee on Petition of Royal Scottish Burghs regarding the Providing of Jails (1818) at p. 12.

17. Commissioners on the Courts of Justice, *11th Report*, 8.

18. 20 Geo II ch 43.

19. J. Blackie, "Judges and Parties in the Provincial Courts in the First Half of the Nineteenth Century," in *Judicial Case Management and Efficiency in Civil Litigation*, ed. C. H. Van Rhee (Antwerp: Intersentia, 2008), 141–42.

20. Commissioners on the Courts of Justice, *11th Report*, 7, although from the point of view of accommodation they never occupied separate court-type accommodation but convened in the local burgh court. This was the case, for example, in

Glasgow in the 1970s where the John Street burgh court was in use. It is currently used as the location for the licensing court of the Glasgow Council.

21. Commissioners on the Courts of Justice, *11th Report*, 5.

22. Commissioners on the Courts of Justice, *11th Report*, 14.

23. Commissioners on the Courts of Justice, *11th Report*, 13.

24. Commissioners on the Courts of Justice, *11th Report*, 13.

25. Commissioners on the Courts of Justice, *11th Report*, 132.

26. Commissioners on the Courts of Justice, *11th Report*, 145.

27. Commissioners on the Courts of Justice, *11th Report*, 146.

28. Glasgow burgh court was incorporated into the eastern extension to Glasgow city chambers built from 1914 to 1923 by Watson, Salmond, and Gray, and it is still used today for licensing board hearings by the Glasgow City Council.

29. There is now a museum of Crime and Punishment in the building constructed for the Inverary sheriff courthouse in 1813 to a design by James Gillespie Graham. It was closed as a courthouse in 1903 and its business transferred to Dunoon, thirty-nine miles away. See www.inveraryjail.co.uk.

30. Treaty of Union, Article 20.

31. C. Malcolm, "Sheriff and other Local Court Records 1386–1935," in *An Introductory Survey of the Sources and Literature of Scots Law* (Edinburgh: Stair Society, 1936), 112.

32. Ann Whetstone, *Scottish County Government in the 18th and 19th Centuries* (Edinburgh: John Donald, 1981).

33. The Duke of Argyll, one of the most prominent political figures in Scotland loyal to the Hanoverians, spoke against abolishing heritable jurisdictions in the debate on the bill in the House of Lords in 1746. Reed Browning, *Political and Constitutional Ideas of the Court Whigs* (Baton Rouge: Louisiana State University Press), 1982, 172.

34. David Walker, *A Legal History of Scotland, Volume V: The Eighteenth Century* (Edinburgh: T & T Clark, 1998), 480.

35. Cairns, "Historical Introduction," 147–151.

36. Walker, *A Legal History of Scotland, Volume V*, 481.

37. R. Munro and J. Munro, *Tain Through The Centuries* (Edinburgh: Birlinn, 2005), 84.

38. Walker, *A Legal History of Scotland, Volume V*, 489.

39. SSA 1747 s. 11.

40. SSA 1747 s 12.

41. Sheriff Court (Scotland) Act 1825 s 3.

42. Sheriff Court (Scotland) Act 1825 s 5.

43. SSA 1747 s 6.

44. Walker, *A Legal History of Scotland, Volume V*, 196.

45. Fife and Kinross; Stirling and Clackmannanshire; Argyll and Bute; Elgin and Nairn; Sutherland and Caithness; Ross and Cromarty—these 12, in effect, became 6.

46. Munro and Munro, *Tain Through The Centuries*, 94.

47. Lord Grant, *The Sheriff Court* (Edinburgh: Scottish Home and Health Department and HMSO, 1967), 249; recommendation 143 discussed at para 448.

48. SCSA s 3.

49. Lord Gill, *Report of the Scottish Civil Courts Review* (Edinburgh: Scottish Civil Courts Review, 2009), recommendation 36, 249.

50. Walker, *A Legal History of Scotland, Volume V*, 486.

51. Blackie, "Judges and Parties in the Provincial Courts."

52. Commissioners on the Courts of Justice, *11th Report*, specifically 85 (Ayr), 87 (Banff), 93 (Dingwall), 103 (Dunfermline), 108 (Dumbarton), 111 (Forfar), 112 (Forres), 113 (Haddington), 119 (Jedburgh), 121 (Kirkwall), 128 (Linlithgow), 129 (Lanark), 133 (Peebles), 140 (Rothesay), 141 (Selkirk), 143 (Stirling), 144 (St Andrews using fees for the Sheriff Court of Fife), 145 (Stranraer and Tain); 146 (Whithorn and Wick), 147 (Wigtown).

53. Commissioners on the Courts of Justice, *11th Report*, 110 (Elgin).

54. Commissioners on the Courts of Justice, *11th Report*.

55. Lord Cooper, "The Central Courts After 1532," in *An Introduction to Scottish Legal History* (Edinburgh: Stair Society, 1958), 348.

56. Commissary Courts (Scotland) Act 1823 c 97.

57. Sheriff Courts (Scotland) Act 1876 c 70 section 35.

58. Section 15. Such servitudes attached to the land and bound the landowner *qua* landowner as opposed to personal servitudes such as habitation, which ends when the person enjoying the right dies.

59. Section 21.

60. Section 17.

61. SSA (1877) section 8.

62. Cairns, "Historical Introduction," 121.

63. Sheriff Court (Scotland) Act 1853 s 12

CHAPTER FOUR

The Emergence of Modern Scottish Court Buildings

The Superior Courts—The Court of Session and the High Court of Justiciary

Edinburgh has been an important burgh and one of several royal seats in Scotland since the medieval age. It was not, however, until the seventeenth century that the city was truly developed as a modern national capital. The supreme civil court, the Court of Session, sat mainly in the city (except in times of plague[1]) from its inception in 1532, and by 1625 the Edinburgh Town Council declared that "this burgh is the principall and heid burgh of this realm."[2] It was in his struggle to assert royal supremacy over such Presbyterian authorities that in the 1630s Charles I oversaw "the first coherent programme of urban improvement in the history of Edinburgh."[3] This program entailed updating the royal palace and abbey at Holyrood, unifying the postreformation-divided St. Giles church as an Episcopalian (i.e., part of the Anglican tradition) cathedral, creating a Renaissance civic square to the latter's south side and building Parliament House there too. The accommodation in the original L-shaped plan of Parliament House consisted of a great hall and a chamber where the Court of Session sat. It was built to the design of Sir James Murray of Kilbaberton, the king's master of works. This building would replace the Old Tolbooth,[4] which until that time had performed (as had tolbooths in towns across Scotland) the function of council meeting place, court of justice,[5] town hall and place for civic events, and town jail. Parliament Hall would perform all those functions (except for jail) and would also accommodate (until the union of Parliaments in 1707) the national parliaments and conventions of estates.

As Glendinning notes, this building—Parliament Hall—is still in use today.

Although subsequently partly demolished, stripped of most of its original decoration and engulfed in nineteenth- and twentieth-century additions, much of the original structure nevertheless survives or can be reconstructed on paper.[6]

In the view of Glendinning it represents "the Scottish Parliament's most significant architectural legacy of the seventeenth century."[7] From our perspective its great significance resides in the fact that it is still the location of the principal superior court buildings in the country. Indeed, this "architectural legacy," with its permanence of location and unchanging internal aspect, represents an interesting counterpoint to the dynamism and variations in court architecture that we see across the rest of Scotland in the past three centuries. The modern-day visitor to the courtrooms is provided with a piece of high Victorian courtroom layout with tall ceilings, velvet-clad benches, and wood paneling. Combined with the original Parliament Hall, for lawyers processing up and down beneath the seventeenth-century hammerbeam ceiling and the Victorian Tudor Gothic windows, this is a unique building providing a centerpiece for the superior civil court.

The pre-eighteenth-century arrangements beyond the Parliament Hall were damaged by fire in 1700, and the current courts were constructed to the design of Robert Reid between 1805 and 1808.[8] Further accommodation was added in 1885 when the bank at the east end of the complex moved elsewhere and these premises were remodeled by W. W. Robertson.[9] Due to the location of St. Giles Cathedral it is not so easy to obtain a panoramic view of the entire court complex facade.

Its superior court counterpart in criminal matters, the High Court of Justiciary, is more grounded in the traditions of Scottish justice spaces. It occupies a site opposite the Court of Session in a conversion of the 1930s' sheriff court building. This building, completed in 1937, replaced the 1868 sheriff court by David Bryce on George IV Bridge when it was demolished to provide a space for the National Library of Scotland.[10] As a result, the current High Court of the Justiciary is not dedicated to its original purpose.

The Lower Courts: An Overview

The courts in Scotland in the twenty-first century and their emergence provide a glimpse into both the changes in the legal system and the changing political economy of Scotland in the nineteenth century and beyond. The court system we encounter at the start of the nineteenth century was the product of the local conditions in Scotland. Justice was administered in a range of ad hoc locations and places that, given Scotland's climate, were often remarkably unsuitable. Writing about the fourteenth-century royal grants of plots of ground to build or enlarge a *tolloneum* or a *praetorium* (courthouse) in places like Dundee (1325), Edinburgh (1365), Montrose (1375), and Irvine (1386), it is noted "at this period . . . it was not uncommon for burgh and sheriff courts, and council meetings, to be held in the open air or in a private house."[11]

The map of the perambulation of the burgh marches of Tain, for instance, indicates in its ten-mile circuit no less than five "court places." These perambulations, which took place thirteen times in the eighteenth century, involved the provost, magistrates, and council providing inhabitants with an opportunity to attend a formal burgh court, at least prior to the 1745 Jacobite Rising.[12] They are also recorded as taking place outdoors at the Angel Hill and the market cross in the latter part of the eighteenth century.[13]

In addition these outdoor locations could sometimes be ad hoc to allow the issue at hand to be properly seen. Such an event is recorded in Tain in 1746 where one Roderick MacLeod incurred the displeasure of the town council by encroaching on town lands with his unauthorized building of houses at St. Katherine's Cross to the southeast of Tain and "a special court (was) held at St Katherine's Cross for the leading of evidence."[14]

Prior to the 1841 improvements, accommodation was hardly palatial. Lawyer George Young describes the old sheriff's chambers in Glasgow, even by that time a town of over 200,000 inhabitants.[15]

The sheriff court business in Glasgow was conducted in an antiquated tenement building on the west side of Stockwell Street: "the premises entered from a pend close in Strang's land in Stockwell Street, and consisted of two storeys, above very shabby shops belonging to the City Chamberlain . . . (a) t the head of the entry was a dingy public-house."[16]

What we had across Scotland was a mixture of purpose-built sheriff courthouses, rooms in tolbooths and town houses, and parts of buildings designed principally for the emerging local government administration. The term "tolbooth" initially indicated the building erected for the collection of tolls in royal burghs. Such burghs were empowered to hold markets and levy tolls and customs; the word derives from the Latin for toll—"tolloneum." They were the first site of local administration where the burgh council held meetings and courts. They also were used as places of imprisonment.[17]

In the second half of the nineteenth century many town halls were built in response to the public demand for suitable venues for evangelical and other meetings and concerts, as well as civic events. In many cases they were on new sites, but at Ayr the townhouse was extended in 1878–1881 to include a large hall.[18]

Location of the Courts

The location of shrieval justice was originally at the king's local court held at the royal castle, which was the center of the sheriffdom.[19] When burghs gained in importance, the location shifted, and the sheriff court sessions were held in the head burgh of the county at the burgh tolbooth or town house.

In the case of Lanarkshire, from the middle of the seventeenth century, the county had a Lower and an Upper Ward, and there were courts in both Hamilton and Lanark In the middle of the eighteenth century a Middle Ward was added and a court held in Glasgow.[20] Courts were held in Perthshire also, in addition to Perth at Killin and Dunblane.[21] The sheriff court for the Eastern District of Ross was held at Tain and for the Western District at Dingwall.[22]

The shift from the use of the local tolbooth of head burghs for the conducting of local sheriff court business coincided with the rise of a structure of local government to administer the various tasks that had been conducted hitherto by local landowners in rural areas through the system of commissioners of supply and in burghs by the town council.[23] These expanded in the nineteenth century to encompass new issues like public health and housing along with the more traditional concerns of roads, bridges, and ferries. These functions were eventually entrusted to elected county councils under the Local Government (Scotland) Act 1889. As far as the administration of justice was concerned the decisions reflected the ad hoc and localized nature of decision making during the first part of the nineteenth century. A more structured approach developed from the 1860s onward with the passing of the Sheriff Court Houses (Scotland) Act 1860 and the role of central government in providing financial support. These changing obligations, combined with the rationalizations of the structure of the sheriffdoms, help explain the nature and timing of the building of the structures we are concerned with in this study.

From the Tolbooth to Administrative Buildings to Courthouse

It is possible to identify three stages in the development of the location of justice in Scotland. In the first instance the court, whether sheriff court or burgh court, was no more than a room attached to the local prison or tolbooth or within it. Later, when local circumstances dictated through overcrowding or inadequacy of accommodation for prisoners and court business, buildings dedicated to local government administration and court business were erected. Finally courts and civic administration separated and the courts remained in enhanced and remodeled versions of the administration/court complexes of the nineteenth century. We look at these phases now in more detail.

The Tolbooth Tradition

Traditionally, the earliest courts were situated alongside the tolbooth so the adjudication and imprisonment functions were closely allied. There are plenty of examples in Scotland of extant tolbooths since they were centrally located and of a distinct style.[24] Some of the tolbooths exist in locations where there are no longer local courts, such as Crail, Lauder, Musselburgh, and St. Andrews. In other places where we still find the tolbooth in a location with courts, such as Glasgow, Kirkcudbright, or Stirling, the later courthouse buildings were erected at some distance and the tolbooths survive as historical monuments, identifiable often by their traditional external stairs to the first floor. A specific legal obligation was laid on burghs to build and maintain sufficient jails for civil and criminal prisoners. The rationale was plain "for want of sufficient and sure prisones, Jailles, and wardehouses, sundry rebels and transgressoures of the laws, alsweill criminal as civil, escapis unpunished and justice contemned."[25]

There are also a couple of examples of an ancient tolbooth still located as part of the modern sheriff courthouse complex. For instance in Tain sheriff court, the tolbooth that exists today was built in 1708[26] and completed in 1733.[27] It adjoins the Thomas Brown sheriff court, which was built in 1848–1849. Its current state of internal repair means that it is today not safely accessible and is merely a striking link with the past. In Aberdeen the 1629 tolbooth tower was incorporated into the civic building complex erected between 1868 and 1874 by Peddie and Kinnear, which is now the sheriff court and local authority administrative headquarters. It functions as a museum at the time of writing with the emphasis on the jail conditions available to its inmates. Other tolbooths that are still extant have functions ranging from restaurants[28] to museums,[29] and in one instance operates as a church tower.[30]

Replacing the Tolbooth

It was local circumstances and initiatives that determined where the old courts were replaced. We can glean a general picture of the court setup across

Scotland from the report from the House of Commons Committee in relation to the provision of jails from 1818.[31] This committee issued a questionnaire to the burghs inquiring about the jails in their area but also asking "if the jail (was) connected with a Court House, Town Hall or other building." From the responses we can see that many courthouses had been erected in the dim and distant past. Exactly when court provision had been made was not known, for example, in Culross, Dingwall, Dumbarton, or Dunbar. They were merely described as very old premises, at least 300 years in the cases of Dunbar and Dysart. In Linlithgow the court along with town hall and jail had been built in 1660 at the expense of the burgh, in North Berwick in 1718, in Annan 1722, in Inverary between 1730 and 1740.

Some burghs had built courts in the eighteenth century, it seems to deal with their jail accommodation problems. A jail, courthouse, and town hall complex was built in Dundee in 1732 at the expense of the burgh, in Campbeltown in 1747 at the expense of assessments and voluntary contributions,[32] and in Brechin in 1789 at the expense of the burgh.[33]

Building of new courts went on throughout the eighteenth century on a sporadic basis in various locations. In 1717 in Elgin a combined jail, courthouse, and town hall was completed at a cost of £333. It had been started in 1709.[34] In Irvine the burgh erected a courthouse, council room, and jail complex in 1745.[35] Sometimes, the costs were defrayed from private sources as occurred in 1750 in Wick where the expense was borne by a local worthy.[36] In Stranraer in 1770 the courthouse and jail were replaced, and the cost of £400 was paid for by private donation.[37] The more traditional split between county and burgh funding was found in Wigtoun (sic) in 1775. Here, the complex consisted of "a hall where the sheriff and other courts and county meetings are held, with a ball-room and the prison . . . all contained within the same walls and under the same roof."[38]

These interventions were not cheap. Inverness completed a jail and court complex for sittings of the justiciary and jury courts, sheriff courts and burgh courts, as well as county meetings in the 1780s with the burgh paying but receiving a grant of £1,000 from the government from confiscated estates. Nonetheless, the revamped accommodation still brought forth complaints "in severe terms" from the justiciary judges about the "want of sufficient accommodation in the court room."[39] One of the earliest of the modern courts is found in Banff, where an entirely new courthouse, county hall, and jail were built at a cost of £3,801 0s 5d between 1797 and 1798. The cost was borne by the burgh of Banff with the landed proprietors of the county contributing £940 7s 2 1/2d.[40] In Dumfries a jail and courthouse complex was built in 1803 at the cost of £4,100. The expense was borne by the county

(£1,820), the burgh of Dumfries (£910), and voluntary subscribers (£1,370). In Selkirk, the court in which Sir Walter Scott occasionally sat had been erected in 1804 in the center of the town on the site of the old tolbooth using rubble from its demolition. It was extended in 1836 to provide space for jury deliberations and still stands operating as a museum and showing its original dual function. It was partly built as a new town house for burgh and county business and partly as a sheriff court. The principal ground floor space could be adapted for either role. The cost of £1,292 15s was shared between the county and the burgh, two-thirds and one-third.[41] In Dunfermline a similar spire-centered complex was constructed in 1809 by Archibald Elliot. The spire was added in the following year. It was initially used as the guildhall and linen exchange and then from 1816 to the late 1840s was a hotel. It was not until 1849 that it was used for sheriff court and county building purposes.[42]

In Arbroath, the decision to replace the old tolbooth premises used for administration and justice was undertaken by the town council. What emerged in 1803 was a new townhouse, containing a town hall, council chambers, offices, a courthouse, and a prison. The 2,000-guinea cost of this included the plans of the local Montrose architect, David Logan.[43]

The court in Dornoch provides an interesting variation. It was, originally, part of the ancient castle or palace of Dornoch, which it abuts today. In its original location it was fitted up and repaired in 1815 at the expense of the Marquis of Stafford at a cost of £1,363 11s 2d.[44] The subsequent insertion of a new building on Castle Street between the castle and the 1842 baronial-style jail was undertaken in 1849–1850 in an ecclesiastical style. The architect for both structures was Thomas Brown, architect to the Prison Board of Scotland.[45]

The Barony of Calton in Glasgow, which became a burgh in 1817, reported that they had obtained an Act of Parliament for paving, cleansing, and lighting the streets in 1819 as well as for "erecting a court-house, jail and bridewell, or workhouse therein."[46] As Young noted, however, writing of his practice in the middle of the nineteenth century, progress was slow.[47]

The Spirit of Voluntarism and the Court Building Boom

The process of erecting more suitable accommodation for the administration of justice then was very much dependent on local happenstance. Sometimes there were dynamic local town councils; at other times local landowners took the lead and at others private subscribers led the way. Hence, we have courts and jails being built in the eighteenth century across parts of Scotland, but in other areas prisoners confined in old dank accommodation and court rooms of varying quality. The whole process seems to have been broadly in parallel to that which Graham talks about in England with most of the building there taking place between 1790 and 1840.[48]

Decisions about court provision in the royal burghs were taken by the local council. They consisted of those elected based on a property qualification.[49] In the landward areas outside the burghs, the Commissioners of Supply were the decision makers on financial matters.[50] It is clear from the early decisions that what style to adopt and what architect to commission were solely ones for the Commissioners of Supply. Open competitions were held in a limited number of instances, as in Glasgow[51] and Dundee,[52] and closed ones elsewhere as in Aberdeen.[53] Other commissioners' committees sought tenders and decided on price and/or quality, as in Perth and Stonehaven.[54] In the case of Perth, the commissioners seemed to be ambivalent. At their first quorate meeting[55] they approved the plans submitted by Robert Reid.[56] They did, however, continue to obtain further plans. Despite apparent interest from architects in London, Edinburgh, and Aberdeen only two further sets of plans were received by April 1812.[57] Although the commissioners continued with the project, they complained that only two schemes had been submitted in addition to those of Robert Reid. They sought to advertise and attract architects from Edinburgh, Aberdeen, and London. In the end, cost seems to have been the determining factor. The story illustrates the local and particular elements at play.

To obtain a satisfactory financial basis, then, for the desired accommodation it was necessary to obtain parliamentary approval for expenditure. As noted, this was done early in the case of Perth. The question of the sheriff courthouse and county buildings in Perth was considered by the Perthshire justices of the peace and commissioners, and a local act of Parliament was procured in 1807. This was supplemented by a further act allowing the original expense of £6,000 to be increased to £10,000. This was done with the cost being shared 60/40 between the burgh and the county. The process of obtaining the ground, the finance, and the selection of acceptable plans was protracted and meant that the project was not realized in Perth until 1819. The amount raised by the land assessment meant that initially the project had to be scaled down. Despite this the preferred architect's, Robert Reid, costs escalated over the years. He was asked in 1813 to scale down his plans to a more modest budget.[58] By the following year the cost for his plans were coming to £25,000, and approval was given to approach other architects with a reduced budget of £18,000.[59] The Minute Book does not record his response. Suffice it to say that, despite his long involvement with the project and his prestige as the Court of Session architect, the commissioners had no hesitation in seeking fresh plans and estimates from other architects.[60] In the end, although the commissioners do not record this in their minutes, and although they approached Mr. Atkinson, Mr. Harrison, and Mr. Wyatt, Robert Reid was replaced by Robert Smirke, a rare Scottish in commission.[61]

In Jedburgh the old courthouse in which Sir Walter Scott had pled his first case in 1793 was replaced in 1812 by the building that stands and operates as the sheriff court into the twenty-first century. Slightly bizarre when this building was constructed, no attention seems to have been paid to the old jail adjacent to it and of whose inadequate state the burgh complained to the House of Commons investigation in 1818.[62] The construction of a new sheriff court and county buildings in Cupar took place around this time and was completed in 1817. Again, the process was for mixed use and followed a local plan by Provost John Ferguson to replace the old tolbooth and jail, known as the "Black Hole."[63]

In Inverary, the impetus to provide a new courthouse in 1814 stemmed from complaints from the judges on circuit who threatened to withdraw the spring and autumn courts entirely from Argyllshire unless conditions regarding prisoner escapes were remedied. The result was a local act authorizing an assessment of not more than £7,000 to erect a new building to provide for courts, county and burgh meetings, and a jail. This was originally to have been done to a design by Robert Reid, but in the end James Gillespie Graham received the commission.[64] In Paisley with a doubling of its population between 1781 and 1800 the local commissioners sought permission to replace the inadequate court and jail accommodation in 1815.[65]

In Forfar the matter of inadequate court facilities had been noted in 1812. It was raised again in 1821 by Mr. Sheriff Lang, who arranged for plans and estimates from an Edinburgh architect, William Burn. Another cheaper quote was obtained from a Dundee architect, Mr. David Neaves.[66] The original hope of the Commissioners of Supply had been to finance this project through voluntary assessments,[67] which was a method that Mulcahy talks of being encountered in the context of the expansion of the English courts in the nineteenth century.[68] Despite this, it was resolved to proceed by way of an act of Parliament, and the ad for the meeting mentioned that the goal was to provide the accommodation "at the lowest possible expense."[69] A bill was introduced into Parliament for erecting and maintaining a sheriff court room and other offices and passed on May 2, 1823.[70] The building was ready for inspection by May 1825.[71] It adjoined the townhouse and was later subsumed into the council buildings when the 1868 sheriff court was built, taking advantage of the changed financial arrangements of the Sheriff Court Houses (Scotland) Act 1860.

This building took place across much of Scotland. In Rothesay, parliamentary authority was given for building a "goal, court house, and offices for the burgh and county."[72] Dumbarton's replacement classical building to a design by Gillespie and Clark was completed in 1824.[73] Leith was afforded a separate sheriff courthouse under an 1827 act of Parliament, which among other things, provided for the establishment of a sheriff court at Leith and for a sheriff substitute to sit there.[74] The move from the old county hall buildings and erection of a new set of buildings comprising county buildings and a sheriff court in Haddington were completed at a cost of £5,500 by William Burn in 1833.[75] In Glasgow the matter was dealt with by Court House Commissioners established by local statute in 1836, and the first part of the civic/court complex was opened in 1841.[76]

The architect to the Prison Board of Scotland, Thomas Brown, designed both new sheriff courts in Dingwall and Peebles. The Dingwall project from 1842–1845 stemmed from his work on the prison, which was erected behind the court. The same layout can be found in Peebles, when the sheriff court moved from its location in the High Street townhouse in 1844 to the new Brown-designed complex a hundred yards away overlooking Eddleston Water on the site of the old jail.[77]

The expense and complexity of the local act of Parliament process meant, however, that the construction and improvement of local courts was a matter of local action or inaction, and many courts remained in nondedicated or shared premises. In the small settlement of Greenlaw, for instance, the then head burgh and county town of Berwickshire, a large neo-Grecian county hall by John Cunningham, was constructed in 1829–1831 next door to the old tolbooth to accommodate the court, sheriff, and rooms for county meetings.[78] With the amalgamation of Roxburgh, Berwick, and Selkirk sheriff court districts in 1872 under the Sheriff Courts (Scotland) Act 1870, this fine building lost all the judicial functions. Fast-growing areas such as the north Lanark coalfields addressed their situation with a local act of Parliament, the Airdrie Rural District Police and Airdrie District Court Houses Act 1855, which provided a combined county buildings and courthouse complex in 1858. It was burned down that year, rebuilt, and finally demolished when undermined by subsidence from mine workings.[79]

Toward a More Uniform Financial Structure

The Sheriff Court Houses (Scotland) Act 1860[80] provided that sheriff courthouses had to be provided by county councils and courthouse commissioners. The process required either three Commissioners of Supply of any county or the Sheriff Depute to make a written representation that "the Court House accommodation in such County is inadequate, it shall be lawful for the Secretary of State to remit such Representation for Investigation and report to such Persons as he may think fit, and to make such other Inquiry with respect thereto as he may think necessary."[81] If satisfied that a courthouse or addition were required, then the Clerk of Supply of the county was to be informed[82] and a meeting of the Commissioners of Supply convened within one month.[83] Burghs could also send representatives. The commissioners had the option to proceed with the erection of a courthouse or not and notify the secretary of state of their decision along with reasons if not going ahead.[84] The secretary of state was given power to override a negative decision and inform the commissioners.[85]

This procedure did not, however, constrain the local commissioners as far as choice of architect was concerned. They continued to have discretion as to whom they chose and how they made this determination. The watchword continued, however, to be maintaining control of costs throughout the process, once an architect was agreed. In Forfar, for instance, when determining that in agreement with a report from Mr. Matheson of Her Majesty's Board of Works in Scotland that the courthouse accommodation at Forfar was "inadequate" due to lack of accommodation for procurators fiscal and witness rooms, and noise and presence of only one water closet, the appointment of an architect was straightforward. The commissioners noted that "Several letters to the County Convenor in reference to the appointment of an architect were read; and on the motion of Lord Strathmore, seconded by the Lord Lieutenant, the Committee unanimously selected Maitland Wardrop of the firm of Messrs Wardrop Brown Architects, Edinburgh."[86] At his subsequent visit, he chose the site of the current court for practical reasons of good access and absence of mill and traffic noise. Plans were prepared and laid before the committee in 1868.[87] The treasury was concerned that compared with Dundee's costs of £13,000 the proposed cost of £11,000 was too high and suggested elevations of a "less ornamental character" would materially reduce the costs.[88] The commissioners responded by obtaining competitive tenders from tradesmen and forwarding them to the architect.[89] The final word recorded by the commissioners is the unwillingness of the treasury to sanction additional costs for mason work in Dunsmore stone.[90]

The method for choosing the architects of the Dundee sheriff courthouse in terms of the 1860 legislation appeared to be different. Gifford initially notes that the plans for Dundee sheriff court of George Angus from 1833 were delayed for thirty years.[91] In discussing the court he indicates simply that "the facade is taken from a design of 1833."[92] The commissioners' records make no direct mention of the earlier scheme. The impetus under the 1860 Act came from a report from the government's inspector, Robert Matheson, who in September 1860, noted that in Dundee the "accommodation is wholly inadequate . . . and another building should be erected . . . as early as possible."[93] Dundee was instructed in October 1860 to select a site and erect a suitable building as soon as possible,[94] and the committee resolved in November 1860 to seek the most suitable site.[95] Their next meeting in December 1860 was addressed by an architect, Mr. Scott, about the best location.[96] There was then a sealed bidding process between Messrs. Scott, Edwards, and Maclaren for lodging plans by February 15, 1861, with the promise that the "successful competitor shall be employed as the Architect of the Building on such terms as may be hereafter arranged."[97] Three sealed plans labeled Palladio, Stability, and Justitia were opened and carefully examined. The meeting "unanimously, generally, approved of the Plan marked Stability at the estimated cost of £9,400 subject to such practical modifications as may be arranged with the Architect. The sealed envelope marked Stability having been opened the Author was found to be Mr. William Scott, Architect Dundee and the Meeting unanimously recommended to the County that his plan be adopted" and that a meeting with the Burgh representatives be arranged.[98] In the end the modifications raised the cost to £11,938 19s 3d.[99]

The Sheriff Court Houses (Scotland) Act 1884 laid down the financial rules for such structures.[100] In Paisley, for instance, when the refurbished court was opened in 1885, it was reported that half of the £15,000 cost was met by the government and the rest by the county and the various burghs in the County of Renfrew.[101] The changes in local government introduced in 1889 meant that henceforth the role of the court commissioners was assumed by the county councils.[102]

Developments in the Twentieth Century

Although the nineteenth century represents the peak of building, one might suggest that the process of justice has always been in a state of flux. Just as new courts opened in the nineteenth century reflected the development of new and growing urban centers like Airdrie and Kilmarnock, so in the twentieth century ten courts closed. In the 1870s the growth of work prompted the demand for a new court in Dunblane.[103] The ancient town had developed with mills and a hydro based on the discovery of a spring in 1813.[104]

The developments in the twentieth century were limited. There has been the closure of several courts across the country on an ad hoc basis as their business declined. The closures occurred sporadically for local reasons rather than because of a Scotland-wide strategy. Thus, we have closures from lack of business of Tobermory (1905), Leith (1920), and Cromarty (1934).[105]

The opportunity to consider "the number and distribution of sheriff courts" arose when the Grant Committee was appointed in August 1963.[106] This was part of its terms of reference, which ranged into the function of the sheriff court, its organization, practice, and procedure as well as rights of appeal and what changes might be required to secure the speedier, more economical and satisfactory disposal of civil and criminal business.[107] Although they were tasked with reporting on the number and distribution of sheriff courts it was "with considerable reservations" that the committee made specific recommendations as to provision and closure of courts.[108] The problem as they saw it was the variations in volume of work and frequency of court sittings and how this related to the distribution of population, which was not standard across Scotland.[109] Since they acknowledged that Scotland could not be chopped into uniform sheriff court districts serving similar populations and with similar amounts of work, they approached the problem adopting a non–Procrustean viewpoint. They thought it desirable to identify "local centres to which people travel to work or to do their shopping or to do their business and then (attempt) to decide how many of these local centres need to be court towns."[110] This did not produce radical solutions since as they pointed out the courts had "grown up, over a very long period, in the places where it was most convenient to have them, and the long process of selection (had) tended to take account of distribution of population, volume of work, and communications in the various areas."[111] There were situations where the patterns were out of step with shifts of population and patterns of work, particularly postwar new town developments. New courts were confidently predicted for East Kilbride and Cumbernauld,[112] which never materialized. Their solutions involved a rationalization of the use of existing resources by extending the notion of circuits whereby sheriffs worked between several courts[113] along with some court closures. The committee was "not much in favour of closing existing sheriff courts"[114] and hence were not "prepared to recommend firmly that any court should be closed."[115] They merely listed a number of courts "where a case could perhaps be made for closure and which might be considered further by the Secretary of State to see whether their continued existence is justified."[116] The report, though, does include an appendix with the more negative views of the Law Society of Scotland recommending ten closures.[117] The Grant Committee limited the list of the courts they had in mind for possible consideration to six—Arbroath, Tain, Nairn, Stonehaven, Peebles, and Wigtown. Nairn was duly closed in 1975. Dunblane and Kinross from the Law Society list were also closed that same year.

Concerning expansion, the Grant Committee recommended new courts at Cumbernauld,[118] East Kilbride,[119] and eventually Livingston[120] as well as upgrading or replacement of the facilities in Hamilton[121] and Falkirk.[122] The new courthouse provisions, which ultimately occurred in Glasgow in 1975, were noted as being under way.[123] The suggestions by the Law Society of Scotland for new courts in Thurso and Lochgilphead did not receive a positive response and went no further than Lochgilphead having a JP court.[124]

In the twentieth century, there have also been new courts constructed. The reasons have included the need for other projects to have a home. This was the rationale for the shift from Bryce's 1868 Edinburgh courthouse on George IV Bridge to make way for the long-promised National Library for Scotland. In addition where the existing facilities could not cope with changes in demand, such as in Glasgow and again in Edinburgh, there have been major replacements.

Courthouse Design Guides

The Sheriff Courts (Scotland) Act 1971 transferred the responsibility for providing and maintaining sheriff courthouses from local authorities to the Crown effective April 1, 1973. At that point it was decided to standardize court facilities and draw up a "coherent programme"[125] for procurement of new and renovated courthouses to "plan and cost accommodation requirements of the courts on a countrywide basis."[126] To the end of standardizing courthouse design, which "varies up and down the country,"[127] the first Design Guide to give advice to architects and designers, redesigning and renovating existing courthouses and designing newly built courthouses, was published as "The Sheriff Courthouses Scotland—Joint Working Party on Design and Accommodation Standards Final Report" by the Property Services Agency in December 1973. This typescript document has proved to be the prototype in a series of distinct publications, now known as Design Guides, which have undergone a series of reiterations and developments over subsequent years. Further Design Guides were published, for example, in 1998 and 2003, and are discussed below. There have now also been Design Guides published for all types of courthouses in Scotland, such as "The

Supreme Court Design Guide" in 2005. The latest 2011 Design Guides (for sheriff courts and supreme courts) were issued in electronic format as a CD or as a web-based resource, and a new Design Guide is currently in preparation as we write.

The basic format of these documents (which will be discussed below) was established to a large extent by the original 1973 document, as a generic guide used for the purpose of briefing external consultants and designers and to interpret the aspirations of the Scottish Court Service as client, while "for every individual project a brief is developed by clients and consultants to clarify the aim of the particular project."[128] Design Guides have, however, changed over the years to reflect changes in technology, in operational delivery of justice within the courts, and in the legislative framework covering health and safety, accessibility, and related matters. There has also been a growth of supplementary documents that provide important technical specifications to be used alongside the Design Guides, such as Data Sheets, and in the most recent 2011 iteration, the Estates Technical Standards documents (such as the "ETS01 Courtrooms," and the "ETS03 Environment" documents).

The 1973 Design Guide sets out three basic types of sheriff courthouse complexes according to size—small, medium, and large. This format is repeated in later versions, with, for example, the three diagrams shown here (figures 1, 2, and 3) from the 1998 Design Guide, which set out the basic requirements and relationships between users and the space in terms of entrance to the building, accommodation needs, segregation and separation of the different users via circulation routes, and so on. The 1973 Design Guide then goes on to establish the necessary relationships and orientations that must be established in the courtroom itself between the users: "The sheriff/judge must be able to see everyone in the court room, the face of the witness must be clearly visible to the counsel, solicitors, jury and the prisoner, and relatives and public ought to have as clear a view as possible of the sheriff/judge, jury, witness, counsel and prisoner."[129] The 1973 Design Guide asserts, however, that the bench "should not unduly dominate the Court but should be just above the line of sight of all the others in the court."[130]

The 1973 Design Guide then goes on to list a series of sight lines that must be designed into the orientation of the fixtures and fittings of the court, and this is supplemented by plans and more significantly, section drawings (which show important relative heights) as shown here (figures 4 and 5). This list of sight lines is developed in all later iterations of the

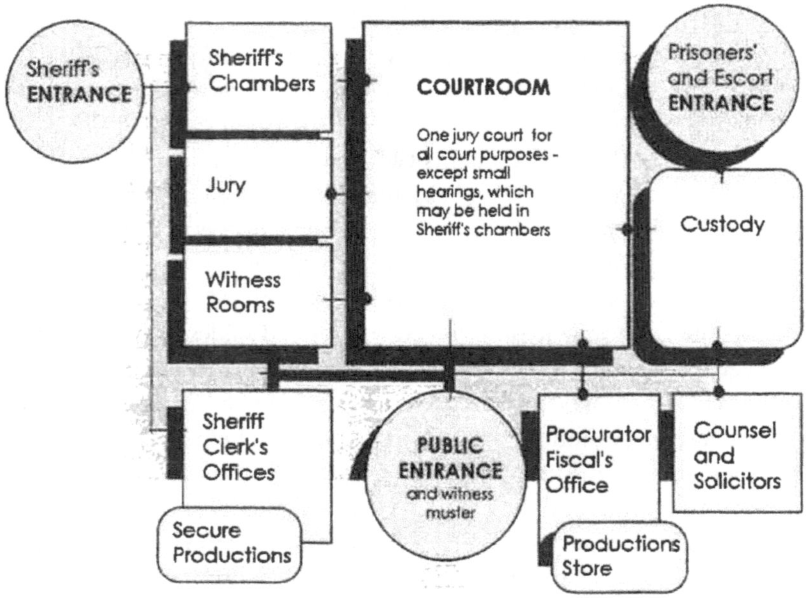

Figure 4.1. Diagram of functional relationships in a small courthouse, from Scottish Court Service, Design Guide, 1998.

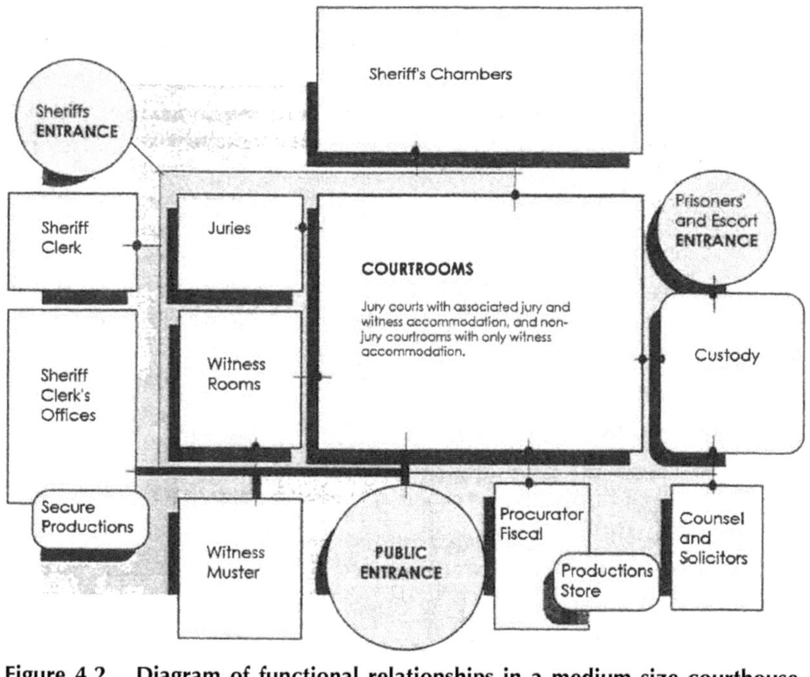

Figure 4.2. Diagram of functional relationships in a medium size courthouse, from Scottish Court Service, Design Guide, 1998.

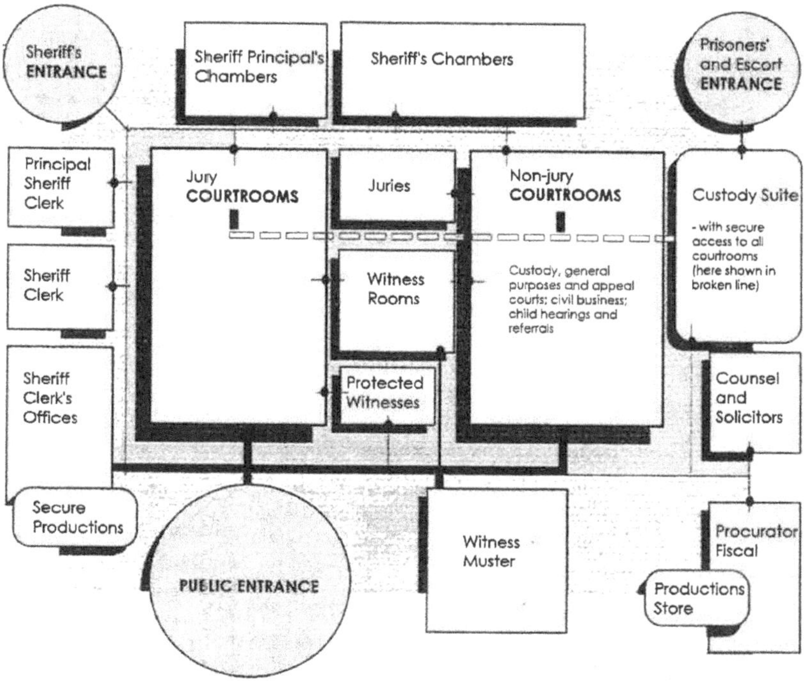

Figure 4.3. Diagram of functional relationships in a large courthouse, from Scottish Court Service, Design Guide, 1998.

Design Guide, and, for example, it appears in the 2005 Supreme Court Design Guide as

> SIGHT LINES
> In a courtroom there are essential functional relationships between the major participants; in particular, it is vital that they can see and hear each other.
>
> The following criteria apply generally to courtrooms intended for either criminal or civil use. There are exceptions; civil cases, for example, do not involve an accused person.
>
> - The judge's bench should not unduly dominate the Court but should be above the line of sight of all others in the Court.
> - The work surface of the judge's bench is 710 mm above the floor level of the judge's dais.
> - The judge must have a clear view of all parts of the courtroom.
> - The judge must have a clear and equal view of each juror and, as far as possible, be able to see what the juror is doing (e.g. reading documentary evidence, writing notes etc.).
> - Judge, jurors, counsel, witnesses and accused must be able to see each other.

- The face of the witness must be clearly visible to the judge, counsel, solicitors, the jury and the accused.
- The relative heights of the judge's bench and the clerk of court's area should be such that when the clerk stands up he is still below the judge but in a position to communicate easily with him.
- The public and relatives are to have as clear a view as possible of the judge, jury, witness, counsel and defendant, but not every seat in the public area need command a view of the dock.
- The public should have the minimum possible eye contact with the jury, in order to reduce the risk of intimidation of jurors.
- Although counsel stand to speak, sight lines between bench and dock are not required to go over the head of a standing counsel, i.e. this temporary obstruction can be ignored.
- Variations in floor levels should be kept to a minimum in the interests of disabled court users and to avoid compromising the potential for adaptability.[131]

The 1973 Design Guide also sets out a list of ancillary accommodation beyond the courtroom itself (e.g., sheriff's chambers, jury retiring room, detention accommodation, and interview rooms), and the required areas for these rooms and special facilities required are listed. In later iterations of the Design Guide the specifications for all accommodation become more refined with specialized advice on lighting levels and control, acoustic levels in decibels, types of carpeting for different areas (using the "British Carpet Performing Rating System"[132]), and finishes on the materials used (e.g., "durable, anti-vandal," "a soft floor covering"). These technical and material specifications are then developed in much more detail in the Design Data Sheets which are published to accompany the Design Guides with the recommendation that architects and designers use them together.

The Data Sheets consist of a page for each type of accommodation (e.g., "Interview Rooms"[133]) with a list of requirement category headings ("Function, Performance, Environment, Services, Equipment, Notes") and more particular aspects listed under those headings (e.g., under "Environment" are listed four separate aspects: "Design temperature, Ventilation, Acoustics, and Lighting"). For the ventilation of the interview rooms, for example, the 1998 Data Sheets list the requirement as "Natural. Air Change Rate = 6–8 per hour" and lighting requirement as "Artificial—350 Lux, Natural—Desirable." The most recent Estates Technical Standards documents to be issued supplementing the 2011 Design Guide go into great technical detail, with, for example, scientific measurement and analysis of acoustic requirements of all the individual spaces in the courthouse and

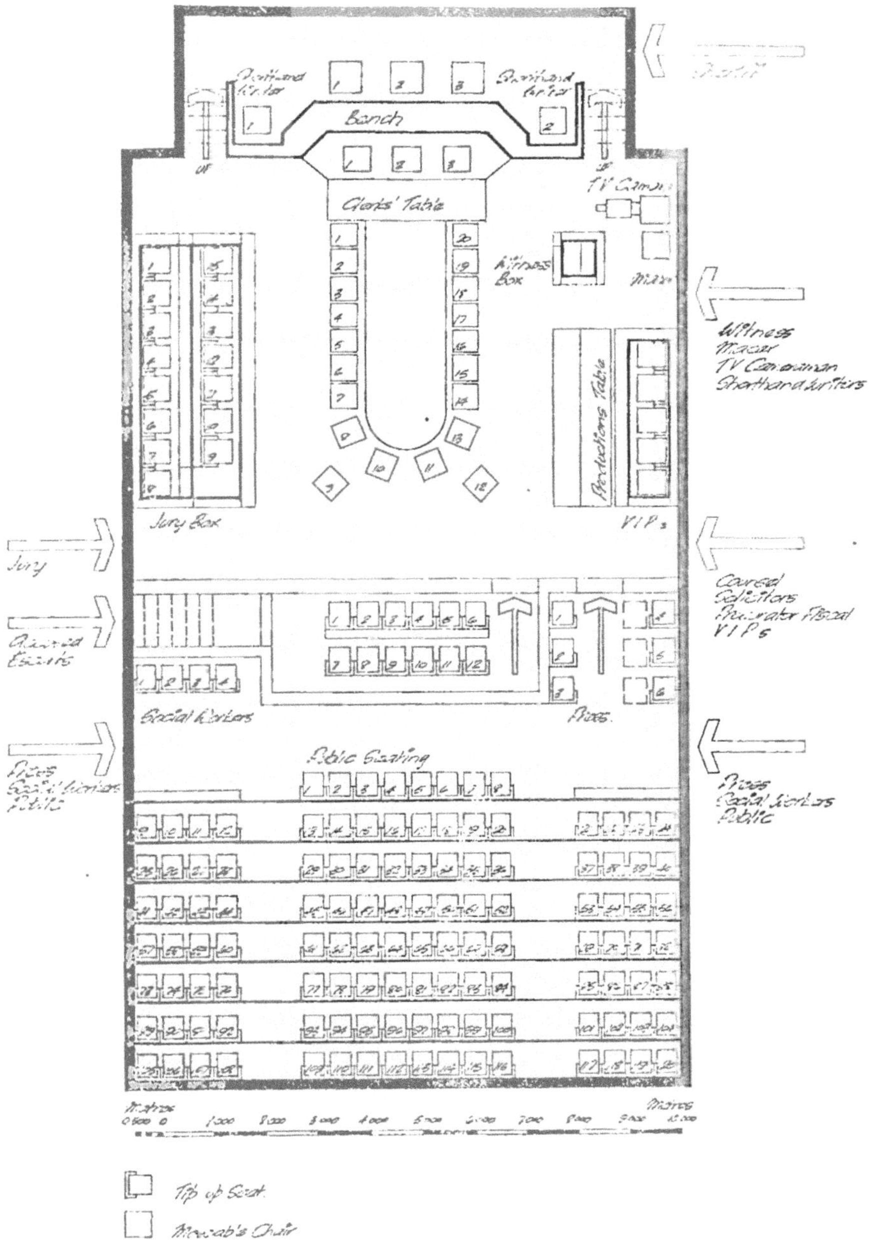

Figure 4.4. Plan of a courthouse, Property Services Agency, Design Guide, 1973. (This first Design Guide was only ever made publicly available as a typewritten manuscript.)

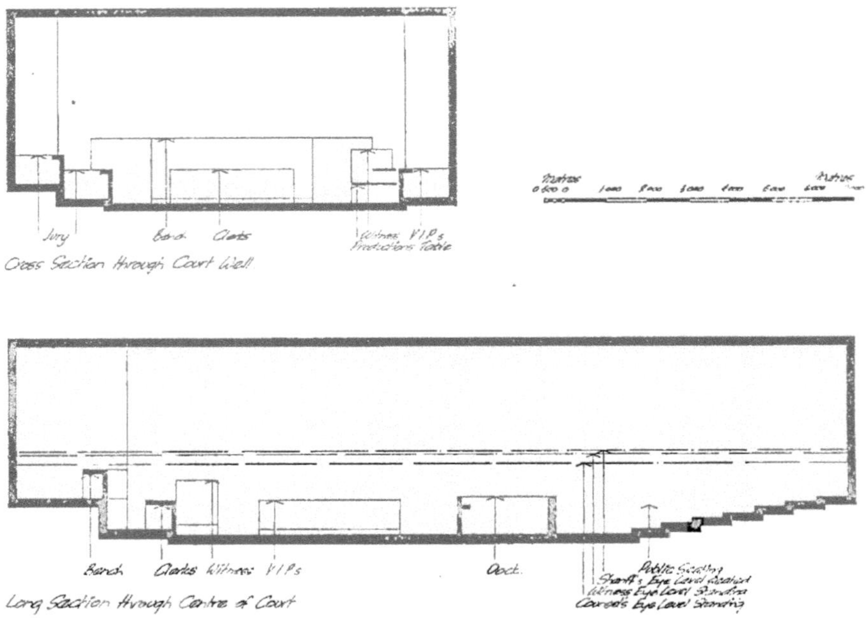

Figure 4.5. Sections of a courthouse, Property Services Agency, Design Guide, 1973.

their relationships to one another. There are also drawings with detailed ergonomic studies of accommodation and how all users, including disabled users, can occupy the space.[134] The lighting, heating, and air quality of the courthouse are also examined in rigorous scientific detail in the Environmental Performance document.[135]

At least part of the special historical importance of these documents in setting the standards necessary in the design process can be said to derive from the fact that until 2009 it was the case that "the provisions of the Building (Scotland) Act 1959 and, therefore, the Building Standards (Scotland) Regulations, which are made under the Act [did] not apply to Crown Buildings."[136] It is further set out in that same Design Guide 1998 that "because of legal and other implications" the Scottish Court Service could "not use Local Authority Building Control Departments to certify compliance."[137] Nonetheless, it was Scottish Court Service policy "to construct buildings to at least these standards," and as such they appointed "private sector consultants to certify compliance with Building Standards Regulations for all projects."[138] In practice two firms of Crown verifiers were usually used for these purposes, namely Butler and Young Associates and Cairn Property. On May 1, 2009, the law was changed[139] so that Scottish Court Service now uses the more "normal" route through the Local Authority Building Control to certify court complex design compliance with the building standards regulations. There is, however, still an anomaly in law inasmuch as the Scottish Court Service does not have to submit to the local authority for planning permission and a building warrant for custody areas within the court complex if they decide not do so.[140]

A more in-depth discussion of how a reading of these Design Guides can help us understand the development of court design over the past forty years can be found in chapter 5. In the meantime, we note that with the plan to introduce new specialist justice centers (see chapter 7), architects involved in courtroom design anticipate that there will be further great change in the specifications contained in future reiterations of the Design Guides and their supplementary documents.[141]

Architectural Style

Most of the Scottish courts that can be examined were constructed in the nineteenth century. A small number, as noted, incorporate the old tolbooth within the courthouse, but in most instances the architects started with a fresh building plot. In their Preliminary Report on Scottish Courts by Historic Scotland from October 2014, the authors suggest a development from neoclassical through Scottish Baronial to Italian Renaissance, noting a mixture of styles in the smaller courthouses. What we find interesting is, if one traces the chronology of court buildings over the century, one can find all the styles represented throughout the century. Taken together, it is possible to apply their assessment of courthouse buildings across the period and conclude that what we can observe is a "search for an appropriate national language for architecture of law and authority."[142] We discuss the shifts of style and the variations that can be observed across Scotland in the next chapter in more detail (see chapter 5).

Although the nineteenth century represents the peak of building, there have been a couple of interesting developments in the twentieth century. There has been the closure of several courts across the country on an ad hoc basis as their business declined. The closures have occurred sporadically for local reasons rather than because of a Scotland-wide strategy, as we have observed above. There have also been new courts constructed. The reasons have included the need for other projects to have a home. This was the rationale for the shift from the 1868 Edinburgh courthouse on George IV Bridge to make way for the long-promised National Library of Scotland, and also where the existing facilities could not cope with changes in demand, such as in Glasgow and again in Edinburgh. There has also been construction of new courthouses in Kilmarnock, Airdrie, Falkirk, Dunfermline, and Livingston. We assess these buildings and the nature of their construction in the next chapter.

Appendix

The impetus to provide appropriate buildings for the sheriff court was in two principal periods in the nineteenth century, the first period between 1830 and 1850 and the second phase between 1860 and 1880.

The buildings that are in use in 2013 were constructed principally in the nineteenth century (see figure 4.6). Within these general trends it is possible to provide a slightly more detailed perspective (see figure 4.7).

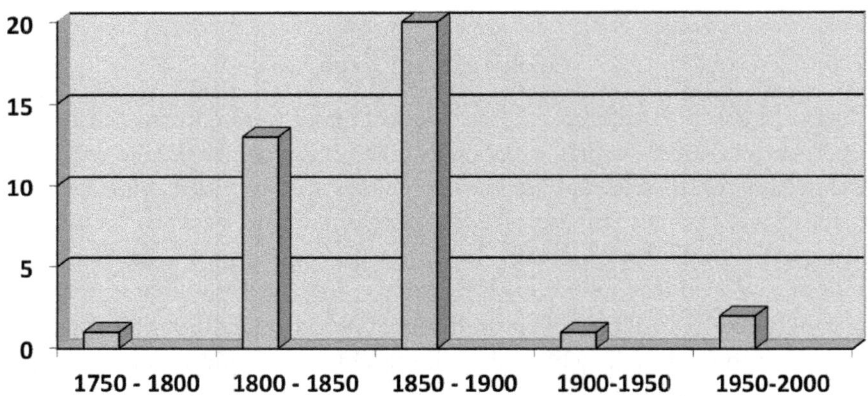

Figure 4.6. Sheriff Court Construction, 1800–2000.

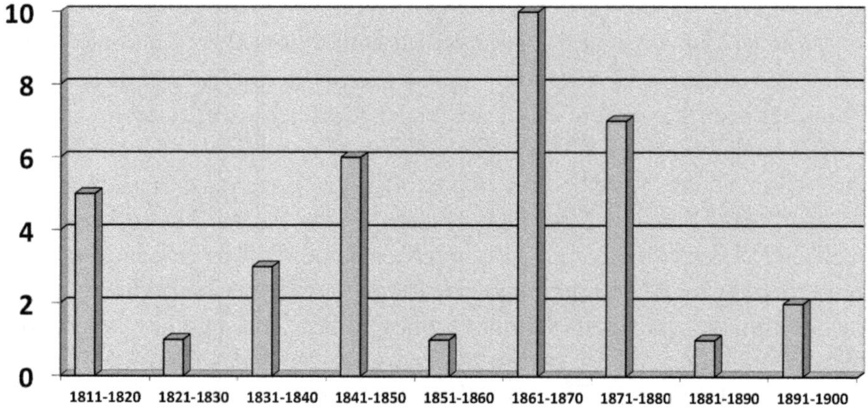

Figure 4.7. Sheriff Court construction, nineteenth century.

Notes

1. John Gifford, Colin McWilliam, and David Walker. *The Buildings of Scotland: Edinburgh* (London: Penguin, 1991), 118.

2. Miles Glendinning, *The Architecture of Scottish Government: From Kingship to Parliamentary Democracy* (Dundee: Dundee University Press, 2004), 84.

3. Glendinning, *The Architecture of Scottish Government*, 84.

4. The Old Tolbooth to the west of St. Giles was finally demolished in 1811.

5. The Court of Session had itself moved from the Old Tolbooth to be accommodated in the west end of the partitioned St. Giles church at around 1560. Gifford et al., *The Buildings of Scotland*, 119.

6. Gifford et al., *The Buildings of Scotland*, 94.

7. Gifford et al., *The Buildings of Scotland*, 94.

8. W. Douglas Cullen, *Parliament House: A Short History and Guide* (Edinburgh: Scottish Courts Administration, 1992), although the dates of 1807–1810 and 1825–1834 are given in the Scottish Civic Trust (Scottish Civic Trust, *Historic Buildings at Work: A Guide to the Historic Buildings of Scotland Used by Central Government* [Edinburgh: Scottish Civic Trust, 1983], 119). An idea of how Parliament Hall may have been used to accommodate court hearings before the specifically designed courtrooms were added to the complex in the nineteenth and twentieth centuries may be gained from a reading of Clare Graham's *Ordering Law*. Graham goes into detail in describing the Great and Guild Halls at Winchester and Chichester and how they were (like Parliament Hall) adapted and fitted out through time to stage court trials until the nineteenth century. Clare Graham, *Ordering Law: An Architectural and Social History of the English Law Court to 1914* (Farnborough: Ashgate, 2003).

9. Scottish Civic Trust, *Historic Buildings at Work*, 119.

10. Nicholson G. *The Sheriff Court at Edinburgh* (Edinburgh: Scottish Courts Administration, 1994), 16.

11. Royal Commission on the Ancient and Historical Monuments of Scotland (RCAHMS), *Tolbooths and Town-houses: Civic Architecture in Scotland to 1833* (Edinburgh: HMSO, 1996), 2.

12. R. Munro and J. Munro, *Tain Through the Centuries* (Edinburgh: Birlinn, 2005), 86.

13. Munro and Munro, *Tain Through the Centuries*, 86.

14. Munro and Munro, *Tain Through the Centuries*, 89. The matter was finally disposed of by the Court of Session in 1749, confirming the decision of the local court.

15. C. Cook and J. Stevenson, *The Longman Handbook of Modern British History 1714–1987* (London: Longman, 1883), 153–55.

16. George Young, *Reminiscences of Glasgow Sheriff Court* (Glasgow: William Hodge, 1907), 3ff.

17. RCAHMS, *Tolbooths and Town-houses*, 1.

18. Scottish Civic Trust, *Historic Buildings at Work*, 3; Ayr retained council uses until 1889.

19. Isabel Milne, "The Sheriff Court before the Sixteenth Century," in *An Introduction to Scottish Legal History* (Edinburgh: Stair Society, 1958), 352.

20. David Walker, *A Legal History of Scotland, Volume V: The Eighteenth Century* (Edinburgh: T & T Clark, 1998), 484.

21. Walker, *A Legal History of Scotland, Volume V*, 484.

22. Walker, *A Legal History of Scotland, Volume V*, 484.

23. Arbroath town council determined, for instance, in 1779 to abandon the previous seventeenth-century tolbooth/town house and resolved to build a new one in High Street (George Hay, *The History of Arbroath to the Present Time* [Arbroath: Thomas Buncie, 1876], 342).

24. Existing tolbooths can easily be found in, among others, Aberdeen, Coupar Angus, Crail, Edinburgh, Inverary, Lauder, Musselburgh, Stirling, St. Andrews, and Stonehaven; for pictures see Scottish Civic Trust, *Historic Buildings at Work.*

25. Scottish Act 1597 (ch 277).

26. Estelle Quick, *Tain Tolbooth* (Tain: Tain and District Museum Trust, 1998).

27. Although in the return to the 1818 House of Commons Committee, Tain responded that "When or at whose expense this jail was built, even tradition leaves no clue to go by."

28. Musselburgh.

29. Stonehaven and Lauder.

30. Greenlaw; see RCAHMS, *Tolbooths and Town-houses*, 102.

31. 1818 (346) Report from Committee on Petition of Royal Burghs of Scotland Respecting the Providing of Jails.

32. Cost was £750.

33. Cost was £745 11s 11d.

34. 1818 op. cit. Report at p. 36.

35. 1818 Report at p. 42.

36. 1818 Report at p. 64.

37. 1818 Report at p. 65.

38. 1818 Report at p. 65.

39. 1818 Report at p. 46.

40. 1818 Report at p. 11.

41. 1818 Report at p. 28.

42. The external plaque contains slightly different dates; it now functions as a bar/restaurant with information about its historical past prominently on display within.

43. Hay, *The History of Arbroath*, 365.

44. 1818 Report at p. 26.

45. The prison now operates as a retail complex of small shops, and the sheriff court is being adapted for commercial use at the time of writing.

46. Commissioners on the Courts of Justice, *11th Report* (London: HMSO, 1832), 74.

47. Young, *Reminiscences of Glasgow Sheriff Court*, 3.

48. Graham, *Ordering Law*, 3.

49. Ann Whetstone, *Scottish County Government in the 18th and 19th Centuries* (Edinburgh: John Donald, 1981), 62–65.

50. Whetstone, *Scottish County Government in the 18th and 19th Centuries*.

51. Scottish Civic Trust, *Historic Buildings at Work*, 179.

52. Scottish Civic Trust, *Historic Buildings at Work*, 210.

53. Scottish Civic Trust, *Historic Buildings at Work*, 44.

54. Scottish Civic Trust, *Historic Buildings at Work*, 60.

55. Strangely, given the fact that a private act of Parliament had been obtained the quorum of fifteen was not fulfilled at the first meeting on August 17, 1807, with only six people present, and further ads had to be put in the papers for a reconvened meeting in September of that year; Perthshire Commissioners Minutes (1807), August 17, 1807.

56. Perthshire Commissioners of Supply, *Perthshire Public Buildings Committee Records Minute Book* (Perth: AK Bell Library Archives, 1807–1820), September 29, 1807.

57. Perthshire Commissioners Minutes (1807), April 30, 1812.

58. Perthshire Commissioners Minutes (1813), April 30, 1813.

59. Perthshire Commissioners Minutes (1814), October 4, 1814.

60. Perthshire Commissioners Minutes (1807), October 4, 1814.

61. Most of his work was in England as architect to the Board of Works, such as the British Museum and the county courts in Carlisle; H. Colvin, *A Biographical Dictionary of British Architects 1600–1840* (New Haven, CT: Yale University Press, 1997).

62. 1818 Report at p. 48.

63. RCAHMS, *Tolbooths and Town-houses*, 68. In fact, the new jail was designed by James Gillespie Graham and ceased such operation in 1844. It is currently operating as a restaurant.

64. RCAHMS, *Tolbooths and Town-houses*, 106.

65. As is noted below, these new premises were described in very negative terms only seventy years later (*Paisley and Renfrewshire Gazette*, July 4, 1885; cutting available in Paisley Local Archive), although they appear to be at least superficially fine in illustrations in the sheriff court's folder in the archive.

66. Court Houses Committee ACC 1/16/1, Minutes of Meeting of Commissioners, April 30, 1821 (Angus Archives).

67. Houses Committee ACC 1/16/1, Minutes of Meeting of Commissioners, October 2, 1821.

68. Linda Mulcahy, *Legal Architecture: Justice, Due Process and the Place of Law* (London: Routledge, 2011), 112–18.

69. Houses Committee ACC 1/16/1, Minutes of Meeting of Commissioners, October 10, 1822.

70. Houses Committee ACC 1/16/1, Minutes of Meeting of Commissioners, May 7, 1825.

71. Houses Committee ACC 1/16/1, Minutes of Meeting of Commissioners, May 7, 1825.

72. Frank Walker, *The South Clyde Estuary* (Edinburgh: RIAS, 1992), 26.

73. RCAHMS, *Tolbooths and Town-houses*, 71.

74. Nicholson, *The Sheriff Court at Edinburgh* (1994), 12; the building on the corner of Constitution Street and Queen Charlotte Street ceased to be a sheriff court in 1920. It is pictured in Nicholson (13) and is currently a police station.

75. RCAHMS, *Tolbooths and Town-houses*, 47.

76. Commissioners for Municipal Corporations (Scotland) (1835) at 188.

77. RCAHMS, *Tolbooths and Town-houses*, 74.

78. Kitty Cruft, John Dunbar, and Richard Fawcett, *The Buildings of Scotland: Borders* (New Haven, CT: Yale University Press, 2006), 339.

79. James Knox, *Airdrie: A Historical Sketch* (Airdrie: Baird and Hamilton, 1921), 23.

80. C 79.

81. SCHAS 1860 section 3.

82. SCHAS 1860 section 4.

83. SCHAS 1860 section 5.

84. SCHAS 1860 section 7.

85. SCHAS 1860 sections 7 and 8.

86. Commissioners of Supply for Forfarshire Minutes, September 17, 1867 (ACC1/16/2) (Angus Archives).

87. Commissioners of Supply for Forfarshire Minutes, February 7, 1868.

88. Letter of April 11, 1868, reproduced in the Commissioners' Minutes, August 21, 1868.

89. Commissioners of Supply for Forfarshire Minutes, August 21, 1868.

90. Commissioners of Supply for Forfarshire Minutes, December 16, 1868.

91. John Gifford, *Dundee and Angus: The Buildings of Scotland* (New Haven, CT: Yale University Press, 2012), 59.

92. Gifford, *Dundee and Angus*, 115.

93. Commissioners of Supply for Dundee Minutes, September 28, 1860 (ACC1/1/8) (Angus Archives).

94. Commissioners of Supply for Dundee Minutes, October 30, 1860.

95. Commissioners of Supply for Dundee Minutes, November 28, 1860.

96. Commissioners of Supply for Dundee Minutes, December 19, 1860.

97. Commissioners of Supply for Dundee Minutes, February 27, 1861.

98. Commissioners of Supply for Dundee Minutes, February 27, 1861.

99. Commissioners of Supply for Dundee Minutes, September 30, 1861.

100. C 42.

101. *Paisley and Renfrewshire Gazette*, July 4, 1885 (cutting available in Paisley local archive).

102. Whetstone, *Scottish County Government in the 18th and 19th Centuries*.

103. Perth Commissioners of Supply Minutes, 1868.

104. A. Barty, *The History of Dunblane* (Stirling: Eneas Mackay, Stirling, 1944).

105. www.nrscotland.gov.uk.

106. Scottish Home and Health Department (SHHD Grant Committee), *The Sheriff Court* (Edinburgh: HMSO, 1967), Cmnd 3248.

107. SHHD Grant Committee loc. cit. at xx.

108. Loc. cit. at para 457.

109. Loc. cit. at para 443.

110. Ibid.

111. Loc. cit. at para 444.

112. Loc. cit. at para 455.

113. Loc. cit. at paras 458–67.

114. Loc. cit. at para 468.

115. Ibid.

116. Ibid.

117. SHHD Grant Committee Appendix XIII - Alloa, Arbroath, Campbeltown, Dunblane, Kinross, Nairn, Peebles, Stonehaven, Tain, and Wigtown.

118. SHHD Grant Committee, *The Sheriff Court*, para 470.

119. SHHD Grant Committee, *The Sheriff Court*, para 473.

120. SHHD Grant Committee, *The Sheriff Court*, para 479.

121. SHHD Grant Committee, *The Sheriff Court*, para 472.

122. SHHD Grant Committee, *The Sheriff Court*, para 478.

123. SHHD Grant Committee, *The Sheriff Court*, para 475.

124. Appendix XIII.

125. Property Services Agency, *The Sheriff Courthouses Scotland—Joint Working Party on Design and Accommodation Standards Final Report*, December 1973, DOE 120/12/73, 1.

126. Property Services Agency, *The Sheriff Courthouses Scotland.*

127. Property Services Agency, *The Sheriff Courthouses Scotland.*

128. Scottish Court Service, *Design Guide: Sheriff Courthouses in Scotland: Part 1*, April 1998, 1.

129. Scottish Court Service, *Design Guide: Part 1*, 3.

130. Scottish Court Service, *Design Guide: Part 1*, 3.

131. Scottish Court Service, *Supreme Court Design Guide, 2005*, 2.3.3.

132. Scottish Court Service, *Design Guide: Sheriff Courthouses in Scotland: Part 2*, 1998, 13.

133. Scottish Court Service, *Design Data Sheets 1993*, Sheet 4.

134. Scottish Court Service, *Estates Technical Standard: ETS01 Courtroom Technology and Spatial Requirements*, 2011.

135. Scottish Court Service, *Estates Technical Standard: ETS03 Environmental Performance*, 2011.

136. Scottish Court Service, *Design Guide: Part 2*, 69.

137. Scottish Court Service, *Design Guide: Part 2*, 68.

138. Scottish Court Service, *Design Guide: Part 2*, 69.

139. Building (Scotland) Act 2003, Section 53.

140. Information from correspondence with Richard Jones of Scottish Court Service, who sat on the consultation panel that examined the implications for the 2007 changes in the building regulations requirements for Crown buildings.

141. Interview with Robert Paton of McLean Architects in Glasgow on October 23, 2015.

142. Historic Scotland, *Scottish Courts: Preliminary Report* (2014), http://www.historic-scotland.gov.uk/scottish-courts-preliminary-report.pdf, 26.

CHAPTER FIVE

The Architecture of Scottish Courts

The Spaces of Justice

The spaces in which justice is enacted are examined here at three levels of significance: at the urban level, in terms of the situation of a courthouse within a town or city, such as its place on the street and its relationship to other buildings and to sets of neighbors; at the architectural level, in terms of the style in which it is built and the materials used; and at the interior level of the courtroom, with an analysis of the spatial relations between the players: the sheriff or judge(s); the clerks and administrators; the lawyers, advocates, and other legal representatives; the police, the accused, the witnesses, and the public.

Justice in the Streets: Where Are the Courthouses?

> Considerable thought has been given to the physical surroundings in which evidence has been given for centuries. Resources have been lavished on courthouses and courtrooms in order to stress that the administration of justice plays a central role in the civic landscape and imagination.[1]

The court buildings in Scotland are often found in proximity to offices and accommodation for professional and civil functions with which the justice system is associated and/or in regular intercourse. They include the procurator fiscal's office, often in the court building (as at Duns) or as an adjunct (as at Stranraer) or in the immediate vicinity (across the road at Falkirk);

the police station, next door (as at Jedburgh, Lanark, Peebles, Stonehaven, and Duns) and along the road (as in Dunfermline and Cupar); the town jail, including old or pre-nineteenth-century jails adjacent to the courts (as at Dumbarton, Inverness, Dingwall, Kirkwall, and Jedburgh), or across the road and accessed by special communicating passages/tunnels (as at Selkirk); the local burgh or council chambers, which often used to share the same complex of buildings (as at Hamilton, Ayr, and Lanark), still share the same building (as at Aberdeen), or have been recreated in a new council and court complex (as at Livingston, completed in 2007).

This agglomeration of civic buildings originally reflected the growth and consolidation of bourgeois autonomy in Scottish life in the early to mid-nineteenth century. The phenomenon of middle-class decision making and control of civil Scotland through the institutions of local government and voluntary, professional, and philanthropic associations, with little interference from a central British state with its laissez-faire ideology, has been comprehensively described as unionist nationalism, in the period 1830–1860, by the historian Graeme Morton.[2] In his study, Morton concentrates on Edinburgh society, in which the legal profession plays a prominent part, but examination of even the smallest example of a court town can demonstrate how the middle-class network was, in fact, spread seamlessly across the land. A recent history of Lochmaddy, North Uist, points out that until the establishment of the judicial infrastructure there in the nineteenth century as part of the new unified system of national justice with the spread of dedicated sheriff court buildings, there was no urban settlement on the island. The sheriff, the procurator fiscal, and the solicitor are then described as building residences that were the "finest buildings" there, and "the various Crown officials—including five policemen by 1900—provided the core of Lochmaddy's professional class."[3] Thus, we see there, in effect, what legal philosopher Andreas Philippopoulos-Mihalopoulos means when he writes that there is a "continuum between law and city" where the two are even "co-extensive and indeed tautological."[4]

Coming in the wake of the collapsed rule of feudal and aristocratic law after 1745, and before the rise of a more centralized bureaucratic state (exemplified by the establishment of the Scottish Education Department in 1872 and the Scottish Office in 1885), this local bourgeois hegemony constructed public buildings in grand historical styles that served several strategic functions. These buildings embodied civic pride and rivaled the great stone buildings of the church with courts as great "temples of justice." The newly built courts could serve as symbols of control and repression for the people flocking into the new industrial towns, for those distrusted by the middle classes as they foundered in the overcrowded, unsanitary, and poverty stricken conditions they often met there.[5] They were also monuments to the age of reform and the newly enfranchised middle-class regularization and control of business, trade, and industry so vital in the period—as witnessed in the sheriff courts' administration of employment and contract law, debt, and bankruptcy.

This original acropolis-type nineteenth-century aggregation of civil and professional functions across the towns and cities of Scotland (council libraries are often nearby too, as at Dumbarton, Duns, and Lanark) has, however, undergone more recent change and development. Just as town planning in the age of the car, the Internet, and the out-of-town shopping mall has seen the dispersal of high street functions such as post offices, utility offices (gas, electricity, etc.), hospitals, and shops to diverse locations on the edge of town, so too there has been a comparative disaggregation of the civil functions associated with the justice system.[6]

Each town no longer has its own jail. That arrangement belonged to a pre-1839 system whereby imprisonment was short term or for remand in custody and long-term punishment was meted out in the form of transportation or execution. The irony is, then, that in Scotland with the move from the punishment regime of capital punishment or transportation to one of incarceration, there was not a greater need *locally* for prison buildings, but a lesser need, as from the mid-nineteenth century, the sheer numbers meant that the prison system had to become centrally organized and administered. This change in arrangements can, however, also be understood in the context of a wider cultural shift, as so notably described and analyzed by Foucault.[7] He writes of the period from the eighteenth to the mid-nineteenth century that "It was a time when, in Europe and in the United States, the entire economy of punishment was redistributed."[8] The move to the "essentially corrective character of the penalty," entailing a long-term custodial sentence, from punishment of a more "immediately physical kind"[9] was coupled in that period, according to Foucault, with the distancing of the judicial process itself from the actual punishment to be carried out: "It is ugly to be punishable but there is no glory in punishing. . . . Those who carry out the penalty tend to become an autonomous sector: justice is relieved of responsibility for it by a bureaucratic concealment of the penalty itself."[10]

The autonomous Scottish Prison Service, as part of the new bureaucratic state mentioned above, began centralizing from the latter decades of the nineteenth century on, with the building of large prisons like Barlinnie (1882–1897) in Glasgow originally built to hold one thousand inmates. It involved the finalization of the long and gradual transfer of responsibility for prisons from county control to central government in 1926. Thus, the cells at sheriff and high courts are now merely holding cells until prisoners with custodial sentences are dispatched by van to these main national prisons by the security firm Reliance, which currently holds the Prisoner Escort and Court Custody Service contract. Those jails, which were formerly attached to or near courthouses, are now no longer used for their original function—such as can be seen in the ruin behind Dumbarton, the jail as part of the historic architectural cityscape in the Bridewell at Jedburgh, the disused jail at Lerwick, or the one behind Dingwall, now converted to housing.

The case of the historic sharing of accommodation by the court and justice system and the local council or burgh functions is, however, more complicated in its recent undoing. As mentioned above, Aberdeen sheriff court still shares accommodation with the city council in its rambling big townhouse and tolbooth building on Castle Street. Other courts, such as Hamilton and Lanark, were affected by the centralization and modernization that took place across the country with the post–World War II rebuilding program. The current Hamilton and Lanark court buildings were originally shared with both the local burgh town councils (of Hamilton and Lanark, respectively) and the Lanarkshire County council. Lanarkshire County council was formerly a peripatetic council, convening sometimes in its council chambers in Hope Street in the town of Lanark and sometimes in the council chambers in the Grecian buildings of Beckford Street of the largest town in the county, namely Hamilton. The burgh of Hamilton town council had moved out of the former county hall (now the sheriff court only) back in the nineteenth century when they built a new building (now housing the Health Board) to the north of the current sheriff court.

In 1963 the heroic modernist sixteen-story tower Lanark County building—influenced by the UN building in New York City—was completed across the road from the former council and court buildings in Hamilton, and all county council services and functions were centered there. The Beckford Street building in Hamilton was then completely taken over and converted to a sheriff court in 1964, and the former council debating chamber became sheriff court number two. Similarly the council and court building in Hope Street in Lanark became the sheriff court only. The former council debating chamber became the principal courtroom in an architectural refurbishment and conversion carried out when the Scottish Court Service finally bought out South Lanarkshire council's share in the building in 2003. This same process of council removal and building adoption and adaptation also took place in Ayr, Glasgow, and Paisley (see Gazetteer).

Architectural Styles of Scottish Courthouses

As we have noted above, Scottish courthouses from before the nineteenth century exist only in a limited number of instances in the form of the old multipurpose tolbooth, or tolbuith. Two-thirds of the structures housing Scottish justice in the early part of the twenty-first century come from the nineteenth century. These buildings and their twentieth-century counterparts encompass a range of styles and approaches to their function. The early architects were given a free hand in how they met their brief. From our examination of the commissioning of courts in the nineteenth century, the architects provided their plans with little other than a brief as to the number of courtrooms and administrative rooms required and the budget to guide them. Their choice of what kind of edifice into which to fit these functions seems to have been left to the chosen architect. As we have noted the selection of the architect was a matter for local commissioners and councilors. This localism persisted even when central government was providing part of the finance for the schemes. In the twentieth century things became more constrained and focused on function rather than form. Clear guidelines have been adopted since the shift of the responsibility for the provision of courts to a central body, the Scottish Court Service, formerly the Scottish Courts Administration.[11] We now examine what architecture was produced in these different sets of formal arrangements. We look at both the architecture of the external built structures, which is visible to the whole world, and the internal arrangements.

Nineteenth-Century Approaches

Architecture: The Buildings

There are two main architectural styles of which the nineteenth-century Scottish courthouses were built. These styles are the neoclassical, or more particularly, Greek Revival, as typified by the exemplary portico on William Stark's Glasgow High Court of the Justiciary (1814), and the neomedieval, or more particularly, the neo-Baronial or neo-Tudor/Elizabethan/Jacobean, as typified in David Rhind's 1868 Selkirk courthouse. Most of the court buildings in Scotland built from the beginning of the nineteenth century were designed in a variation of classical style (from neo-Baroque Arbroath (1801), to Greek Revival Glasgow High Court, and Roman style Ayr (1818)). In the 1830s neomedieval styles start to appear with the neo-Tudor Haddington (1833), and Castellated Norman Gothic at Inverness (1835). By the 1850s the Scottish medieval style of the neo-Baronial started to make its appearance with Dornoch (1850), Dumfries (1866), and Greenock (1869).

Out of the fifty-odd courts in this survey (still in use but for a few exceptions) twenty-four were built in one of the variations of medieval style, nineteen in variations of the classical style, and seven in post–World War II modern styles. Of the nineteenth-century courts, the tendency was for classical style to dominate in the early century with more medieval styles being built as the century progresses.

As a story of two styles, the development of courthouse architecture is very much an integral part of the growth of bourgeois industrialized and industrializing urban nineteenth-century Scotland. The institutions that under the Union had remained in Scottish control—namely education, the church, and later local government, as well as the law—manifest the same pattern of preference and development of architectural styles in their buildings over the nineteenth century. Thus, for example, in education we see William Burn's Doric Greek temple design of John Watson's school in Edinburgh 1825 (now the Scottish National Gallery of Modern Art) contrasted with David Bryce's Scots Baronial and French Gothic Fettes College in Edinburgh 1864. In local government and administration Robert Reid's Greco-Roman colonnade at Parliament Square, Edinburgh, completed by 1838, can be viewed alongside Charles Wilson's full-blown Scots Baronial Rutherglen Town Hall of 1861; and in church architecture Archibald Elliot's Greek Doric Broughton Macdonald church of 1821 in Edinburgh can be compared in its austerity with the flamboyance of McKissack's 1887 Scots Gothic Strathbungo Parish Church on the south side of Glasgow.

There is no doubt that each style carries a symbolic weight and significance of its own, which is often viewed in terms of the Romantic invocation of the native and the emotional, as against the cosmopolitan sobriety and restraint of Enlightenment Classicism. This dichotomy of neoclassical/neomedieval nineteenth-century architectural form is pushed in its most tendentious interpretations to include respectively such antagonisms as Whig cosmopolite/Tory nationalist, Presbyterian/Episcopalian, Protestant/Catholic, Bourgeois/Aristocratic, and so on. Are the messages borne by these styles in context, however, so straightforward? It is certainly in keeping with a dualistic view that the courthouse built in 1865 by David Rhind in Selkirk, where Sir Walter Scott had once been sheriff, should be a neo-Baronial castellated pile with tourelles, a circular-plan keep, and crow-stepped gables. What, then, are we to make of the fact that Scott was a great supporter of the classicist architect William Stark (who built the finely proportioned Greek Doric portico of the Glasgow High Court of the Justiciary). Scott wrote of Stark that "more genius has died than is left behind among the collected universality of Scottish architects."[12] Scott was, furthermore, among the foremost promoters of the campaign to build the ultimately unfinished, but most correctly researched Greek Revival Doric temple of the National Monument on Calton Hill. The reality is that the two styles, Greek and neomedieval and Baronial Revival, are not separate and antagonistic, but are interrelated in just such a complicated fashion as indeed are the wider concepts of Romantic and Enlightenment. It could, however, give a measured understanding of and insight into the significance of the evident stylistic dichotomy if we examine the history of how and why these styles came to prominence.

The term "Greek Revival" was not coined until the 1840s by C. R. Cockerell, who had advised Playfair on the design of the Calton Hill National Monument. An intellectual and cultural interest in ancient Greek history, art, and style had been stimulated since the mid-1700s when an easing of diplomatic relations made it possible for Westerners to travel to Greece. Since that time, scholars and critics began to examine, survey, make records, and publish on Greek culture. Among the most influential of these mid-eighteenth-century studies are Winckelmann's work on Greek art [13] and Stuart and Revett's published survey of Greek architecture.[14]

Comparisons of Edinburgh with Athens had abounded since the 1760s,[15] but it was not until the nineteenth century with the massive projects for building the Edinburgh New Town that the association with Greece became a specifically architectural one. Indeed, there is not only a comparison made between the urban form and architecture of the Scottish capital and Athens, but there is also a conscious striving—connected to the already established intellectual reputation—to build in the Greek style. There has been much speculation on why the Greek style should have an attraction for the Presbyterian Scots. It has been said that the austerity of that architecture appealed and that it allowed them to avoid the Gothic with its association with medieval Catholicism. There is, however, a more rigorous connection to the Presbyterian intellect than simple prejudice, for with the centrality of solid geometry and Euclidean mathematics to Scottish culture and specifically Scottish University teaching, the Scots could find a congeniality of spirit in the researched Greek neoclassical style as found in Stuart and Revett's work with its mathematical and symmetrical rigor in disposition and relation of solid form.[16]

Neo-Baronial was a favored Scottish version of the mid- to late-nineteenth-century Gothic Revival in architecture. Along with other medieval revivalist styles used for nineteenth-century Scottish courthouse buildings, such as the Tudor, Elizabethan, and Jacobean, it owes its impulse to seek out "authentic" "native" forms of architecture to the nationalist ideology of early Romantic writers, artists, and architects across Europe, most notably the young Goethe and Herder.[17] This Europe-wide movement had in turn been much influenced by the publication of the Ossianic poetry of James MacPherson from 1760 onward. The architectural equivalent of this Romantic literature made one of its first influential appearances in Scotland with the building of the Gothic (but not particularly Scottish) castle by English architect Roger Morris in Inveraray for the Dukes of Argyll in 1789.[18] The building by Sir Walter Scott of the grand residence for his family at Abbotsford in 1816, in a castellated Baronial style, was another important moment. This house, with its concoction of stylistic features drawn from sixteenth- and seventeenth-century Scottish feudal dwellings—corbelling, machicolations, bartizans, crow steps, etc.—was the first, albeit premature, attempt to articulate a neo-Baronial style from evidence in historic buildings for modern nineteenth-century use.

Just as Stuart and Revett's published works had provided researched models for neoclassical architects, studies, and surveys of the remaining heritage of thirteen seventeenth-century Baronial architecture were published from the mid-nineteenth century onward. These studies provided Scots architects with researched and correct Baronial models to copy, thus promoting its use in the general stylistic repertoire. R. W. Billings's *Baronial and Ecclesiastical Antiquities of Scotland* was a comprehensive four-volume study published between 1845 and 1862 with over two hundred perspective drawings of historical buildings remaining from the period. It is notable that the publishing of this influential architectural work coincided with the Sheriff Court Houses (Scotland) Act 1860 and the beginning of a decades-long program of court construction. Later, David McGibbon and Thomas Ross prepared in five volumes what is often considered the definitive survey of the style with *The Castellated and Domestic Architecture of Scotland from the 12th to the 18th Century*. First published between 1887 and 1892, McGibbon and Ross's work contains plans and detailed drawings, and is a more rigorous technical accomplishment, which, as such, influenced not only design of neo-Baronial buildings from the 1890s onward, but also the related up-and-coming proto-modern styles of the Arts and Crafts, Art Nouveau, and Glasgow styles.

In the early nineteenth century this apparent dichotomy in styles of expression—Classical/Vernacular, Enlightenment/Romantic—was not, however, one that was confined to design and the built environment. It cut across all forms of culture and political expression, and in many ways Edinburgh, the epicenter of the Scottish legal system, was also the center of an "ideological battleground."[19] Here, a repressive Tory administration in London sought, in the wake of the French Revolution and the Napoleonic Wars, to keep a firm control on any pressure for political reform. Ian Duncan writes of Edinburgh as a literary battleground between the Whig and Reformist supporters of *The Edinburgh Review* and the cultural nationalists, influenced by German romanticism, supporters of the Tory *Blackwood's Magazine*.[20] Prominent lawyers such as the Whig Francis Jeffrey (1773–1850) and the Tory Archibald Allison (1792–1867) were also heavily involved in those literary and political disputes and associated respectively with the *Review* and *Blackwood's*. It may thus appear that in the early to mid-nineteenth century, the country, and the capital city particularly, was completely riven in all forms of culture, between one faction that favored a republican ideal of civic virtue and creation of a classical built environment, and another that supported a "depoliticised regional identity"[21] and a romantic recreation of supposed vernacular models. The case of another very prominent lawyer, Walter Scott, points to a slightly more organic relation between the two standpoints. As Duncan asserts, Scott may have been a Tory in politics, but he "was educated in the moderate Whig tradition of the late Enlightenment."[22] Furthermore, Walter Scott, as mentioned above, was a central figure involved in the campaign to create the classical temple of the National Monument on Calton Hill to commemorate victory in the Napoleonic Wars. That fact reminds us that it is an oversimplification to see only ideological war such that the advocates of the two sides—classical/Baronial or Enlightenment/Romantic—are set unmoving in their ways and completely irreconcilable to the other party. Indeed, the historical novel developed by Scott (and influential in working up a fervor for all things native and romantic, including Baronial architecture) can be seen as a continuation of the Enlightenment concern for and work on history.[23] Scott's attitude, regarding the National Monument, also apparently demonstrates recognition of what Lowrey says the Greek and Baronial Revivals have in a common, namely "the contribution each made to the picturesque qualities of the city,"[24] where the former was an appropriate architectural model for Edinburgh New Town and the latter for the medieval Old Town.

Interior Space: The Courtrooms

Courtrooms, as Mulcahy points out in the context of England and Wales, are a modern development.[25] As we have noted (see chapter 4), the same is broadly true for courts in Scotland. Historically, courts could be held anywhere—including the shelter of the gable of a Highland outhouse.[26] Even in the vast space of the Great Hall of Parliament House in Edinburgh, Thomas Carlyle could describe what seemed like chaotic scenes as advocates huddled together in groups pleading before various judges:

> An immense Hall, dimly lighted from the top of the walls, and perhaps with candles burning in it here and there: All in strange chiaroscuro, and filled with what I thought (exaggeratively) a thousand or two of human creatures; all astir in boundless buzz of talk, and simmering about in every direction, some solitary; some in groups. By degrees I noticed that some were in wig and black gown, some not, but in common clothes, all well-dressed; that here and there on the sides of the Hall, were little thrones with enclosures, and steps leading up; the red-velvet figure sitting in said thrones, and the black-gowned eagerly speaking to them. Advocates pleading to Judges, as I easily understood. How they could be heard in such a grinding din was somewhat a mystery.[27]

Until the nineteenth century, as we have noted in chapter 4, there were no single-purpose built courthouses in Scotland. Across the country in pre-eighteenth-century tolbooths and in seventeenth- and eighteenth-century town houses, local courts would also be held in open rooms or halls. These buildings were used for such civic purposes as council chambers and courts; for administration of markets, trade, weights, and measures; and the town jail. The court proceedings would often be held in the same room as the council body convened, and thus there was no furniture or fixed interior design to cater to the judicial procedure. This can be seen in Peebles or Falkland townhouses.[28] In later town houses, built in the wake of the Heritable Jurisdictions Act 1747, such as Cromarty from 1773,[29] there is, though, alongside accommodation for those other functions, a fixed, fully furnished courtroom of the timber pulpit and gallery model, with bench, dock, and witness stand.

The museum of Walter Scott's Selkirk sheriff court can give us an idea of how an early court began to fix the players in a court case at certain distances, heights with respect to one another, and certain physical elements of separation. The town house at Selkirk was built between 1803 and 1805 when Sir Walter Scott, who was sheriff depute there from 1799–1832, had complained about the previous tolbooth and jail that it was "totally insufficient."[30] There was some renovation of the interior in the late twentieth century, but still the bench and chair are claimed to be those used by Scott. The basic layout of the court is such that the sheriff sits behind a bench on a platform that places him higher than any of the other pieces of furniture; the lawyers and clerks sit at a table below him inside a "pen" or a bar, which keeps the public out, and the witness stands in an isolated box to give their testimony. The atmosphere in the courtroom is one of relative openness and freedom. More of the furniture is of the movable type than of the fixed, and there are no special segregated routes in or out of the open space, outside the pen itself for witnesses, public, or accused. A couple of factors might account for this. As noted above, the room was renovated in the late twentieth century, that there is an element of speculation as to what would be the original and authentic disposition of furniture in this space.[31] It might also be said that the light load of casework processed through this court meant that there was little pressure for a stricter and more efficient spatial organization of the courtroom. Only 135 cases passed through the court in the thirty-three years of Scott's time there as sheriff.[32]

It is true nonetheless that from the early nineteenth century there was a recognition of the need to organize a uniform system of national justice. Scott's dissatisfaction with the Selkirk tolbooth would seem to be an example of this. As we have noted, there was progress in rationalizing the court system, principally by absorbing the other courts (the barony, regality, admiralty, and other courts) into the sheriff court (see chapter 3) and professionalizing the personnel. Whetstone notes that:

> The Deputy Clerk Register often complained of the difficulties caused by lack of adequate local public building in his early reports. In 1810, only ten counties had space for the sheriff clerk's records in or adjoining the sheriff court. (*The Fourth Report of the Deputy Clerk Register of Scotland* (London, 1810), App., 43-59) These ten counties were probably those in which the county had helped the head burgh build the town hall; in return for their help the county got space in the town hall. Some county court houses were built after the Napoleonic War by special parliamentary acts, but only after the passing of the Sheriff Court Houses Acts of the later nineteenth century did each county acquire a sheriff court building sufficient for the entire establishment.[33]

As we also note, salaries of sheriff deputies and substitutes were regularized (see chapter 3), and by 1839 qualifications to work at the bar and the bench were standardized (see chapter 3). Sheriff clerks also became salaried, and volumes of instruction on court procedure were published (e.g., by MacLaurin in 1836). Blackie also notes that "investment of public money was directed to the Sheriff Court which was accordingly transformed into the single cardinal provincial court."[34] Furthermore, in 1853 with the Sheriff Courts Act, oral argument was introduced into ordinary procedure, and written submissions on the law were less dominant. This created the need for courtrooms as special spaces oriented toward efficient verbal performance of justice.

Courthouse Construction

This regularization of court business was carried through into the building of new courthouses. As can be seen in our graphs in chapter 3 there were two main periods of court building, 1830–1850 and 1860–1880. At the beginning of the second period, the Sheriff Court Houses (Scotland) Act 1860 was the catalyst for a sustained program of sheriff court construction, financed 50 percent by the central government treasury and under the supervision of the local Commissioners of Supply. As already noted, the commissioners were the group of local landowners in any one county whose responsibility throughout the eighteenth and nineteenth centuries had been to collect the land tax and take care of the county's roads, bridges, and other infrastructure. After the 1865 abolition of the land tax, it was difficult to justify the continuation of the authority of the landowners, and hence the power of the Commissioners of Supply gradually fell into abeyance. Many of their functions were later undertaken by county councils after their foundation in 1889, although they remained formally in charge of the process. The commissioners had, however, often merged their different responsibilities in groups of buildings incorporating county offices and courts.[35]

Toward a Standardized-Model Courthouse

It is right from the first of the two periods of court buildings mentioned above, though, that we see the emergence of the typical nineteenth-century courtroom. In this type of courtroom, seen for example in Jedburgh, Forfar, and, still in its most original and pristine form, in Perth, there is a fixed and comprehensive parceling out of the space to the various parties present at the court proceedings. As can be seen in the plan layout in figure 5.1, the type is housed in an oblong-shaped room, the bench with the sheriff or judge seated behind is at one extreme end of the room, and somewhere around the midway point in the dock where the accused, often with seating for three or four, sits facing the judge. Between the judge and the accused, in the middle of what is often called the well of the court, is a large table where typically clerks and lawyers involved in the case will sit. Off to one side of the well is the jury box with a lateral view of proceedings between the bench and the dock, and to the other side of the well is the witness stand. Behind the dock, and usually separated from the well of the court by a low timber partition across the width of the room, is the public gallery, which typically takes up the space from there to the back wall of the courtroom.

This segmentation of the room and segregation of the various parties involved make for a clear distribution of power in the space of the courtroom. The judge is separated and sits at the stage center of all action, directly facing the accused across from and below him or her. The accused is the object of the deliberations of all who occupy the well, the judge, the clerks, the lawyers, the witnesses, and the jury. The public is excluded from participat-

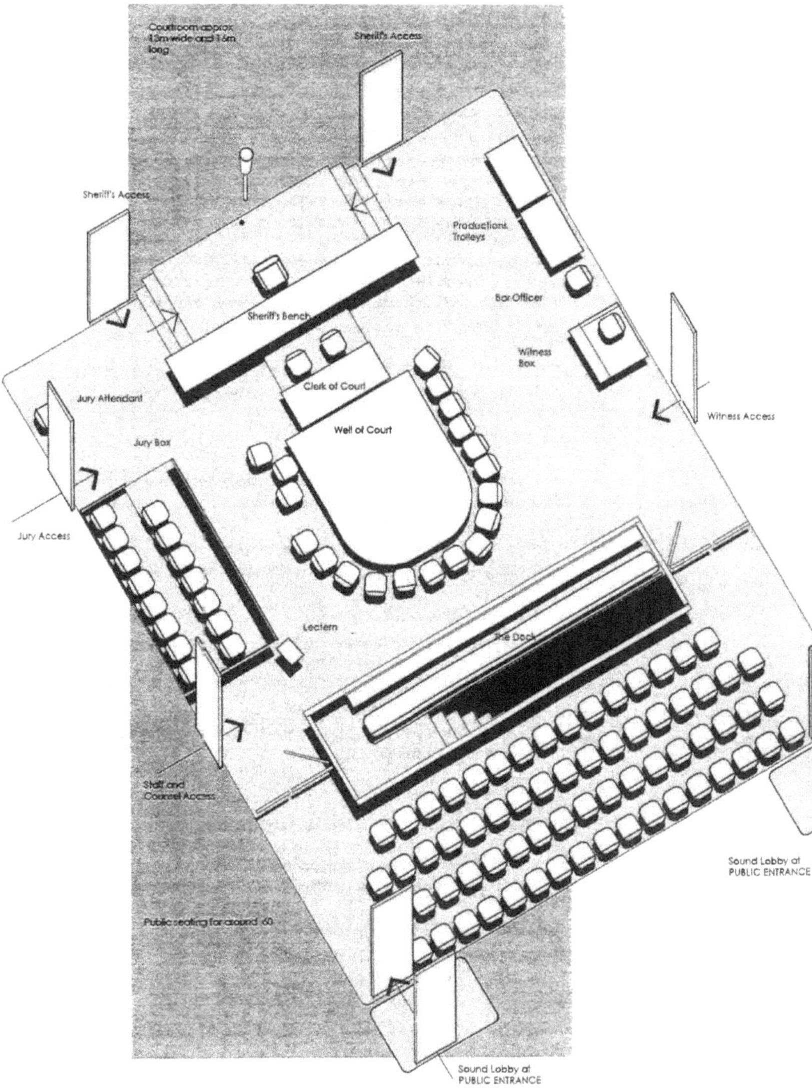

Figure 5.1. Axonometric projection of an idealized plan of a large jury courthouse, from Scottish Court Service, Design Guide, 1998.

ing in this action. The language used to articulate this spatial distribution of power—in terms of separating some parties, opening and closing sight lines, including in or excluding from the action, exposing to different degrees of attention, and allowing or disallowing certain routes of communication, verbal or otherwise—is all the clearer in some original courts like Perth, and to a lesser extent, Kirkwall, for being entirely constructed out of one material, namely timber. The sectioning out of all space with the same material makes clear the power relationships through barriers and passageways, open spaces, directional seating offering clear or obscured views, and doors communicating through exclusive circulation routes to different parts of the building (i.e., the shrieval corridor, the sheriff's chambers, the prisoners' cells).

It is important to remember, however, that the third dimension of the volume of the courtroom, not shown on the plan, also plays a vital role in the articulation of this space. Not only is the judge separated from the rest of the court and marked out as a special individual by the bench, the coat of arms above his head, and often a canopy, as at Stirling and Perth, above his seat, but the timber bench is the highest feature made from that material within the well of the court. The height of the judge's seat is most immediately contrasted with the bench in the dock, where the accused sits, the center of attention, at the lowest point in the courtroom. Between them the witness box is also relatively high. It is not usually as high as the bench, but has a vertical orientation, denoting that the witness's participation, while being of utmost significance, is however, an ephemeral center of attention. This contrasts with that of the judge, sitting permanently at the high, broad bench in charge of the proceedings. These relative heights are now set as specifically recommended in the Design Guides, and sectional drawings detail them in Appendix 2 of the original 1973 Design Guide (see figure 4.5).

When it comes to the public seating area in the typical nineteenth-century courtroom the question of height seems to admit of more ambiguity. The area at the back of the court is usually raked, often very steeply as in the case of Stirling or Alloa. Where there is a shallower rake, this is often supplemented by a further public gallery on a first-floor balcony, as seen at Jedburgh, Perth (court number one), Dundee, Aberdeen, Dornoch, Glasgow High Court, and Greenock. This upper-floor gallery or steep rake often means that members of the public take their seats at a higher level than the judge. The question of the symbolic importance accorded to the public by building them to this superior position is, however, mitigated by the fact that the accused, as object of the discourse played out before the on-gazing public, sits with his or her back to them, and fleeting glimpses of his or her face could be seen only on his or her entry or departure from the court.

It is to be stressed that the plans in figure 4.4 and figure 5.1 are abstracted "typical" models of the nineteenth-century courtroom. Each courthouse from that era presents its own variations on that model. Some of the variations are indeed more extreme and noteworthy than others—such as the lateral public gallery at Stornoway with the dock against the back wall, and the semicircular plan at Inverness and at the former courthouse at Inveraray. What is consistent, however, is that a rigorous spatial planning was used to help shape a formal set of social interactions and etiquette for the court process. It designates the relative status of the various parties in attendance and allows for set degrees and modes of participation. It is again clear here that the interior design of the courtroom, in its rigid observation of certain physical rules of appropriate space, had an important symbolic role to play. In many ways, again, we can see how this typical model of the nineteenth-century court conforms to Foucault's critique of architectural forms as an important part of the apparatus of the "disciplinary society."[36] The changing and densely urbanizing society of nineteenth-century Scotland evolved to provide a more spatially ubiquitous and effective form of control of its populace than had been possible in the society preceding, which had more specifically made a spectacle out of physically punishing aberrance and disorder. Equally, the more casual courtroom experience as entertainment, which Cockburn talked about in relation to Parliament Hall and the Outer House,[37] and which Graham[38] and Mulcahy[39] describe in relation to England, has been designed away. Thus, the fixed partitions, calculated distances, heights, and sight lines between a hierarchically ordered range of participants provided codes of usage and allotted space to each person or group in the space. Thus, the nineteenth-century courthouse, no less than the prison, the hospital, the factory, the school, and the asylum, can be seen as an exemplary mechanism of Foucault's three techniques of disciplinary control, namely, hierarchical observation, normalizing judgment, and the examination.[40]

Twentieth Century

Buildings

The twentieth century, as we noted elsewhere, saw a limited number of new court buildings. Indeed, only one court was built in the first seventy years, the former sherriff court in Edinburgh's Lawnmarket (1937). That court was removed from its former position on George IV Bridge to accommodate the siting of the National Library of Scotland.

The later designs of more recent Scottish courts fall somewhere between the two poles of the more ideal "justice without walls"[41] approach to staging the judicial process, as advocated by Mulcahy, and the pragmatic display of the symbolic power of justice, as practiced by architect Jean Nouvel (see discussion of Nouvel later in this chapter). In fact the new courts, while obviously a part of the national justice system, seem in their powerful civic status—the heavy presence of Glasgow sheriff court on the banks of the Clyde and Livingston in the massive civic center there—to owe much more to the anchoring and continuation of a long Scottish civic and municipal tradition in the administration of justice. It could of course be argued that the long-term plan to reduce the number of sheriff courts to sixteen mainland justice centers over ten years represents a loosening of attachments to local traditions and loyalties. Nonetheless, as the Scottish Court Service points out, the distribution of population across the country is such that "around 86% of current sheriff and jury business is already held across planned specialist jury centres."[42] So the civic presence and accessibility of the justice system remains very strong. This anchoring of the courthouse in the civic realm has undoubtedly been regularized and strengthened recently by the obligation placed on court buildings since 2009 to seek certification of compliance with building regulation standards from local authority building control departments (see chapter 4). The 1973 Design Guide noted, and this has been repeated in later iterations[43] of the Design Guides, that "New court buildings should be located as close as possible to communication and urban centres and, in particular, they should be easily accessible by public transport."[44]

Furthermore, and as noted in chapter 2, even though Lord Gill appeared in his report to be removing local connections by the recommendation to shut down many courts and move to the justice center model, he still rejected the notion of a national sheriff court or of sheriffs having all-Scotland jurisdiction, and recommended that the boundaries of sheriffdoms be rationalized with those of other public authorities.[45]

Interior Space

Many of the nineteenth-century courthouse interiors were revamped in a program carried out by the Scottish Court Service in the 1990s. Some notable and consistent changes were made to the interiors of those buildings, including Tain, Haddington, Duns, and Arbroath. It is useful to examine these renovations alongside the newly built courts and new extensions to existing courts that have also been constructed over the past forty years—Livingston, Kilmarnock, Kirkcaldy, Dunfermline, Glasgow sheriff, and Airdrie. In her study of English courts, Mulcahy identifies several tendencies in courtroom design that have had long-term effects on the power dynamics of the proceedings. Both the new courts in Scotland and the nineteenth-century courtrooms renovated in the 1980s and 1990s have public accommodation either laid out completely horizontal to the rest of the court in front of the bar or have an exceptionally shallow rake, creating an almost imperceptible height differential for those who sit there. This recent removal of a third spatial dimension from the public's experience of and engagement with the court proceedings is also underlined by the complete closure of all public first-floor galleries, where they still exist—such as at Glasgow high court, Dundee, Greenock, and Jedburgh.[46] Mulcahy writes in this regard that it "has become common in modern times for court architecture to represent law as increasingly democratic."[47] The initial rationale for closure and removal of these galleries seems to have been based on cost. The 1973 Design Guide declares that the galleries "add considerably to the cost of the courthouse." It does, however, expand upon this, adding "more flexible use of the courtroom seating strongly indicates that the Gallery should be omitted with consequential savings in cost."[48] Nonetheless, there is no doubt that the more horizontal modern court has improved accessibility for the public especially for disabled, elderly, and infirm persons. There is indeed a specific requirement in the Design Guides that "Variations in floor levels should be kept to a minimum in the interests of disabled court users and to avoid compromising the potential for adaptability."[49] In considering the question of designing for accessibility and democracy, however, those of design for sight lines and audibility also arise. The overall public view of the well of the court, where all the action takes place, seems to have diminished because of this new horizontality. The new Estates Technical Standards documents, which supplement Design Guide 2011, provide, as noted in chapter 4, thorough analyses of acoustic requirements of all the individual spaces in the courthouse and their relationships to one another. They also provide drawings with detailed ergonomic studies of accommodation showing how all users, including disabled users, can occupy the space. Other acoustic experts seem to be of the view that raked seating is an advantage in an auditorium. McMullan, dealing under the heading "Hall Shapes" in his chapter on "Room Acoustics," writes: "*Raked seating* prevents absorption of direct sound paths as well as reducing blocked views. Provision of good vision usually ensures a good sound path."[50]

Mulcahy considers this lowering of the public vantage point and consequent further separation from the action as symptomatic of a "tendency to treat the public as irritants who lacked legitimate purpose."[51] In tandem with the new post-9/11 security-conscious safety measures—the public is subject to electronic surveillance, frisking, and checking of bags at the entrance to several of the busier courts, including all Edinburgh, Glasgow, Aberdeen, Airdrie, and Hamilton courts—a court visit can feel like a very disempowering experience. Mulcahy goes on to point out that new positioning of the public in English courts is prescribed in the *Court Standards and Design Guide*[52] to minimize direct eye contact with and intimidation of jurors by the public. This is also stressed in the Design Guides for Scottish courtrooms: "The public should also have the minimum possible eye contact with the jury, in order to reduce the risk of intimidation of jurors."[53] A further public disadvantage has been encountered with the placing of plasma video screens for evidence purposes, which cannot necessarily be seen from the lower galleries.[54]

Mulcahy also writes of the increasing isolation of defendants in the English courtroom design, so much so, that the dictum "innocent until proved guilty" is comprised, not to say belied, by the spatial exposure and/or exclusion of the defendant. Elsewhere,[55] and along with the group JUSTICE, Mulcahy has called for the abolition of the dock in criminal trials in England and Wales. Regarding this point, the question of "concerns in relation to the protections afforded by Article 6 of the European Convention on Human Rights"[56] has been raised. The 2005 Design Guide is, nonetheless, peculiarly explicit on the aims of designing for such "safe containment and production of prisoners in court":

> Attendance at Court for most in custody is stressful, and this is exacerbated by confinement; natural frustration and anxiety are compounded by these circumstances. Violent or irrational behaviour may be directed at other prisoners, the custody staff or the fabric of the building. Prisoners may resort to noise, soiling or attempting suicide. The ingenuity of prisoners with time at their disposal should be allowed for in the detailed design of the fabric and fittings.
>
> The planning and detailed design should help to: frustrate the opportunist; delay the escapist (and those who may try to assist); ensure physical safety; and deny the public direct view or contact with prisoners while they are within the custody area except during authorised visits.[57]

This isolation has been achieved not only by segregated entrances and corridors, but also by the raising of the height of partitions and placing glass screens around the dock. In the typical nineteenth-century Scottish court, until recently, the accused, as discussed above, sat in the dock with their back to the bar and the public gallery. With only one or two exceptions like Stornoway and, to a lesser extent, Inverness, the public does not get to look the defendant in the face while the court procedure is ongoing. With more recent built courthouses and extensions, there is a notable shift toward an English model, in which the dock is against the back wall of the courtroom, where from the gallery, the public can indeed see the face of the accused.[58] In Kirkcaldy, for example, the diagonal orientation of the courtroom across the square plan space (in court 3 in the extension built in 1979) means that with the sheriff in one corner and the gallery spread across two walls opposite, some members of the public have a clear view of the accused's face. At Livingston, the most recently completed courthouse in Scotland (2007), there was an explicit attempt to create secure docks by isolating them.[59] Accordingly, in two out of the six courtrooms (3 and 4) there is a lateral public gallery so that, ranged along one side, the public can see the full proceedings, with the sheriff back against one short side and the dock and witness stand against the wall opposite. This simultaneous exclusion and exposure of the accused is effected further by the glass paneling (to the height of 1.6 meters), which in many courts runs around the back of the dock or indeed, all the way along the bar (see Arbroath, Kirkcaldy, and some courtrooms in Glasgow and Edinburgh sheriff courts for this feature). Mulcahy tells us that the English 2010 *Court Standards Guide* "emphasises the dangers posed by the defendant in the trial rather than protection of their presumption of innocence,"[60] which explains that this glass partition protects the public from attack by the defendant and vice versa. The 1998 Design Guide Part 2 suggests that in Scottish courtrooms

> Clear glazed screens to a height of 1.6m may be required to the back and sides of the dock to ensure that no contact is possible between the accused and
> -Witnesses when they are approaching or leaving the witness box, and
> -Anyone sitting in the public seating area.[61]

There can be no doubt that the use of such glass partitions also heightens the sense of exclusion of both parties—the public from the proceedings in the well of the court and the accused from society at large (see chapter 1).

There has been much discussion by both theorists and designers of the modern courthouse as to how desirable it is to have a closed, discrete, symbolic building for the administration of justice where the various parties are separated and obscured from one another. This seems to be especially important in the age where the physical boundaries of the "traditional" court have been broken down by evidence given on video screens, by remote trials in Camp Zeist and Guantanamo Bay, and by the terrorist laws. On the one hand, justice is essential to good government, a fact substantiated in the solid stone buildings of nineteenth-century Scotland, which contained both sheriff courts and regional administration. On the other hand, the state's violence in handing down a judgment surely has obvious consequences for peace and security, and any obscurity there must be damaging to democracy. As Resnik and Curtis note, "Every act of judgement results in a state imposition of force, reallocating property from one civil claimant to another or depriving criminal defendants of their liberty and (in some eras or places) of their lives."[62]

Mulcahy writes of how new court design can improve environmental conditions specifically to do with space and light in a courtroom. As noted above, there is much discussion in scientific terms of lighting, heating, and acoustic standards in the courtroom, how to attain and maintain them, and so on in the Estates Technical Standards documents, which since 2011 have supplemented the published Design Guides. It is not clear, however, what the relationship is, other than a metaphorical one, between light and space and material in the courtroom, and transparency and democracy in the court process. Resnik and Curtis criticize the rhetoric of transparent material often employed in new courthouses while inside there is strict segregation of routes and spaces allocated to various parties involved in the court.[63] Meanwhile, architectural critic Hal Foster takes a more fundamental stance in his questioning of the relationship between material transparency and procedural transparency, between architectural and political openness:

> Is it out of a sentimental attachment to the old virtues of transparency, and the wistful hope that appearing so will make it so? In any case such transparency is subject to different interpretations: open office spaces might appear non-hierarchical and democratic to the architect or even to the boss, but panoptical and oppressive to the employees. Then, too, as suggested, what once seemed transparent can now appear spectacular, whereby light and glass no longer signify civic accountability so much as mass attraction.[64]

Hal Foster criticizes the English architects Richard Rogers and Norman Foster, who have both been involved in building recent new court buildings around the world. Hal Foster notes that Norman Foster Architects claim on their website that the new supreme court they completed in 2005 in Singapore was designed with the principles of "dignity, transparency and openness."[65] There is much use of glass walling across the facades of the massive Singapore building, and it is surmounted by a disc-type rotunda feature (which echoes the stone dome of the nearby old colonial supreme court), which has 360-degree fenestration, giving a panoramic view of the city. We might question, with Hal Foster, on confrontation with this building, whether the impressive monumental scale of its transparent materials is not aimed at the spectacular rather than at openness and "civic accountability." The actual "civic" location of this court in fact leads Hal Foster to deeper skepticism over the question of architectural transparency and its functions. He points out, of the "touted" openness and transparency of a Singapore governmental edifice, that "it seems absurd given the track record of that government in general."[66]

By contrast, in the Scottish courts there has been a recent move—at least in some sense—to less open and transparent courts. The Scottish nineteenth-century courts were usually built as particularly open and well-lit spaces with lots of natural light. It is common for those courthouses to be on the first floor of the building with either several long windows along the lateral side (as at Stirling, Arbroath, Dornoch, and Cupar), or with windows in the wall behind both the bench and the public space (as at Dingwall, Tain, Dumbarton, and Fort William), or with some combination of those two arrangements of fenestration (as at Alloa, Dunoon, and Kirkcaldy). In the newer court designs, however, there is much less reliance on natural light and more use of design features—shadow gaps, uplighting, and so forth—to avoid glare and give an even distribution of artificial light. Thus, in Glasgow sheriff court and Glasgow high court extension; in Livingston; and in the main courts in Kilmarnock, Kirkcaldy extension, Peterhead main criminal courtroom, and Dunfermline, there are no windows whatsoever in the courtrooms, whereas in Edinburgh sheriff court some courtrooms have small windows behind the bench, and in Airdrie and Falkirk there is some natural light from clerestory windows. This attempt to control the quality of light by excluding natural light is, however, not only found in modern Scottish designs. Indeed the assignment of either a pragmatic or a political importance to the question of light in the court building and the courtroom has been a fundamental issue at the heart of new court design across the globe.

In the 1990s the French Ministry of Justice initiated an "audacious and novel"[67] program to rebuild much of its estate. They engaged many well-established architects—including Henri Ciriani, Jean Nouvel, and Richard Rogers—and tasked them to build courts not to a template, but to designs that "capture the government's ambitions."[68] By the end of 2004, forty-two courts had been either renovated, rebuilt, or designed and built as new. Such a massive undertaking, interpreted and carried out by numerous individual architects, allowed for a range of responses and differing levels of success. We can see there a dialogue emerging on various questions, including, particularly, that of light and transparency. On that question we could examine the design responses of two completed courts that seem to occupy opposite ends of the "light use spectrum." At one end, we could place the Bordeaux *Palais de Justice* completed in 1998 by Richard Rogers, and at the other the Nantes *Palais de Justice* completed just two years later by Jean Nouvel.

The Bordeaux building (figure 5.2) employs local cultural symbols to create a striking iconic image in the city: seven courtrooms, modeled in the form of vast cedar-clad wine flasks, are set visibly to the public realm surrounded by an open, glass-walled shed. The building, which also features a huge sculpted bronze bell on its floor (by Pascal Couvert) invoking a call of civic weight and value, is supposed, by the architects, to suggest "the accessibility of the French judicial system."[69]

In Jean Nouvel's prize-winning courthouse at Nantes, the themes for the building were announced as "visibility and monumentality." Yet in the very somber courtrooms of that building there is next to no natural light whatsoever. The contrast with Richard Rogers's supposed "accessible" building could not be starker. The Nantes courthouse (figure 5.3) with its dark, classical temple profile, industrial scale, and use of materials, its bars and grills, dim spaces, and undecorated dark red wood-paneled courtrooms, has come under criticism for a "jailhouse aesthetic, its sinister color and its heavy symbolism."[70] The architect, however, defends the building because of its monumentality. His defense may contain an implicit criticism of the Rogers's design: "Justice must express its power. Nothing is more mean than to make out justice for something kind, and anodyne. A courthouse presented as a cultural center is dishonest about itself. It's also very dubious on a democratic level."[71]

While the debate on the relationships between lighting, transparency, and accessibility in all its political and civil ramifications has thus had a full and frank airing in the redesign of French courts and in the critical literature thereon as noted above, it is not at all clear that in recent Scottish courthouse design there has been any debate on how changes in transparency of materials, viewpoints, and lighting of courts affect equality of the access to

Figure 5.2. Palais de Justice, Bordeaux. Photograph by Niamh Thomson.

Figure 5.3. Palais de Justice, Nantes.

justice, or the quality of justice itself. It appears that with the predominant dependence on artificial light, often with comprehensive use of systems of uplighting, shadow gaps, and so forth, and to the exclusion of any natural light, that the design has aimed at utilitarian environmental control and consistency rather than any theoretical or symbolic explorations of power relationships in public space.

Notes

1. Linda Mulcahy, *Legal Architecture: Justice, Due Process and the Place of Law* (London: Routledge, 2011), 169.

2. Graeme Morton, *Unionist Nationalism: Governing Urban Scotland 1830–1860* (East Linton: Tuckwell Press, 1999).

3. M. MacGregor, *Between Two Worlds, Lochmaddy 1600–1995* (North Uist: Taigh Chearsabhaigh, 1996), 23.

4. Andreas Philippopoulos-Mihalopoulos, ed., *Law and the City* (London, Routledge, 2007), 7.

5. For example, Glasgow's population in 1801 is estimated at 77,000 and in 1901 at 762,000; Reports of General Medical Officer of Health for Glasgow. http://www.understandingglasgow.com/indicators/population/trends/historic_population_trend.

6. This dispersal of high street functions has become sufficiently prominent a phenomenon in recent times to engage government policymakers in an initiative to rally behind and support reinvestment in town centers. Thus, the Scottish government and COSLA's *Town Centre First Principle* states that "*We must take collective*

responsibility to help town centres thrive sustainably, reinvent their function, and meet the needs of residents, businesses, and visitors for the 21st century." http://www.gov.scot/Topics/Built-Environment/regeneration/town-centres/TheTownCentreFirst-Principle.

7. Michel Foucault, *Discipline and Punish: The Birth of the Prison*, trans. A. M. Sheridan Smith (Harmondsworth: Penguin, 1991).

8. Foucault, *Discipline and Punish*, 7.

9. Foucault, *Discipline and Punish*, 8.

10. Foucault, *Discipline and Punish*, 10.

11. The Scottish Court Service (originally called the Scottish Courts Administration) was created in 1995 by the Scottish Office as an executive agency. This autonomous status was to prevent direct ministerial involvement in the administration of justice. On April 1, 2010, it was established by section 60 of the Judiciary and Courts (Scotland) Act 2008 as an independent body, governed by a corporate board and chaired by the Lord President, the most senior judge in Scotland.

12. W. Scott, *Sir Walter Scott's Journal*, ed. D. Douglas (Edinburgh: Douglas, 1891), 290.

13. Winckelmann had never actually been in Greece.

14. James Stuart and Nicholas Revett, *The Antiquities of Athens and Other Monuments of Greece* (London, 1762).

15. J. Lowrey, "From Caesarea to Athens: Greek Revival Edinburgh and the Question of Scottish Identity in the Unionist State," *Journal of the Society of Architectural Historians* 60, no. 2 (2001): 136–57, 136–37.

16. G. Davie, *The Democratic Intellect* (Edinburgh: Edinburgh University Press, 1961), 112.

17. W. Douglas-Robinson, *The Younger Goethe and the Visual Arts* (Cambridge: Cambridge University Press, 1981), 38.

18. Some parts of the building were designed by William Adam.

19. I. Duncan, "Urban Space and Enlightened Romanticism," in *The Edinburgh Companion to Scottish Romanticism*, ed. Murray Pittock (Edinburgh: Edinburgh University Press, 2012), 73.

20. Duncan, "Urban Space and Enlightened Romanticism."

21. Duncan, "Urban Space and Enlightened Romanticism."

22. Duncan, "Urban Space and Enlightened Romanticism," 74.

23. A concern typified by David Hume's much cited opinion "I believe this is the historical Age and this the historical Nation"; J. Greig, *The Letters of David Hume*, 2 vols. (Oxford: Clarendon Press, 1932), vol. 2, 230.

24. Lowrey, "From Caesarea to Athens," 136–57, 143.

25. Mulcahy, *Legal Architecture*, 6.

26. David Walker, *A Legal History of Scotland, Volume V: The Eighteenth Century*. (Edinburgh: T & T Clark, 1998), 188.

27. W. Douglas Cullen, *Parliament House: A Short History and Guide* (Edinburgh: Scottish Courts Administration, 1992), 16.

28. Royal Commission on the Ancient and Historical Monuments of Scotland (RCAHMS), *Tolbooths and Town-houses: Civic Architecture in Scotland to 1833* (Edinburgh: HMSO, 1996), 164, 90.

29. RCAHMS, *Tolbooths and Town-houses*, 59–61.

30. RCAHMS, *Tolbooths and Town-houses*, 182.

31. It is interesting to note in this context that the Justice Group Report "What Is a Court" (2016, see paras 3.17 7 3.18) proposes the use of modular furniture in the courts of England and Wales to facilitate "intelligent configuration" and flexibility, and it also draws attention to extensive use of modular courtroom furniture in the United States since 2000.

32. J. Blackie, "Judges and Parties in the Provincial Courts in the First Half of the Nineteenth Century," in *Judicial Case Management and Efficiency in Civil Litigation*, ed. C. H. Van Rhee (Antwerp: Intersentia, 2008), 135.

33. Whetstone, *Scottish County Government in the 18th and 19th Centuries*, 127.

34. Blackie, "Judges and Parties," 142.

35. D. Moody, *Scottish Towns: Sources for Local Historians* (London: Batsford, 1992), 104.

36. Foucault, *Discipline and Punish.*

37. Cockburn, cited in Cullen, *Parliament House*, 9.

38. Clare Graham, *Ordering Law: An Architectural and Social History of the English Law Court to 1914* (Farnborough: Ashgate, 2003), 121ff.

39. Mulcahy, *Legal Architecture*, 43–48.

40. Foucault, *Discipline and Punish*, 170–94.

41. Mulcahy, *Legal Architecture*, 6.

42. Scottish Court Service, *Shaping Scotland's Court Services* (2013). http://www.scotcourts.gov.uk/docs/default-source/scs-consultation-court-structures/response_to_the_consultation_and_recommendationspdf.pdf, 5–6.

43. See, for example, Scottish Court Service, *Design Guide* 2005 at p. 8.

44. Scottish Court Service, *Design Guide* 1973 p. 6.

45. Lord Gill, *Report of the Scottish Civil Courts Review* (Edinburgh: Scottish Civil Courts Review, 2009), recommendation 39, 249.

46. Prior to the closure of the court, the Dornoch gallery had also been closed.

47. Mulcahy, *Legal Architecture*, 95.

48. Scottish Court Service, *Design Guide* 1973 6.1.2.

49. Scottish Court Service, *Design Guide* 2005 2.3.3.

50. R. McMullan, *Environmental Science in Building* (London: Macmillan, 1983), 186.

51. Mulcahy, *Legal Architecture*, 88.

52. HMCS, *Court Standards and Design Guide* (2010).

53. Scottish Court Service, *Design Guide* 1998 Part 1, p. 19.

54. High Court of Justiciary, Edinburgh; Court 2 is an exception.

55. Linda Mulcahy, "Putting the Defendant in Their Place: Why Do We Still Use the Dock in Criminal Proceedings?" *British Journal of Criminology* 53, no. 6 (2013): 1139–56.

56. A. Marks, *What Is a Court?* (London: JUSTICE, 2016) at para 5.29.

57. Scottish Court Service, *Design Guide* 2005, 2.12.2.

58. Mulcahy, *Legal Architecture*, 47.

59. In an interview, Richard Jones of the Scottish Court Service stated that courts 3 and 4 at Livingston have this layout because they were originally intended to contain secure docks.

60. Mulcahy, *Legal Architecture*, 71.

61. Scottish Court Service, *Design Guide* 1998 Part 1, 2.3.6, p. 18.

62. Judith Resnik and Dennis Curtis, *Representing Justice: Invention, Controversy, and Rights in City-States and Democratic Courtrooms* (New Haven, CT: Yale University Press, 2011), 13.

63. Resnik and Curtis, *Representing Justice*, 340–44.

64. Hal Foster, *The Art-Architecture Complex* (London: Verso, 2011), 48–49.

65. www.fosterandpartners.com/projects/supreme-court-singapore/ last viewed 23/02/16.

66. Foster, *The Art-Architecture Complex*, 48.

67. Resnik and Curtis, *Representing Justice*, 197.

68. Resnik and Curtis, *Representing Justice*, 197.

69. Foster, *The Art-Architecture Complex*, 29.

70. N. de la Casiniere, "A Nantes, le style du palais sévèrement jugé," *La Liberation*, July 10, 2000. http://www.liberation.fr/societe/2000/07/10/a-nantes-le-style-du-palais-severement-juge_332632.

71. de La Casiniere, "A Nantes."

CHAPTER SIX

The Iconography of Scottish Justice

This chapter examines the iconography of the Scottish justice system. What are the symbols that are currently used and have been used historically to mark and signpost the places where justice is enacted? In addition to a discussion of the materials, forms, and disposition of these symbols around the physical estate of the justice system, we contrast the Scottish use of such symbolism with that of other jurisdictions around the globe. It appears that compared to the ubiquitous use of specific symbols (e.g., Lady Justice/Themis) to adorn courthouses around the world, the employment of such standard visual language by Scottish courthouses is scant. In seeking to understand such an evident cultural anomaly, recourse to Scottish history, particularly Scottish religious history, would appear to furnish us, in the story of the sixteenth-century Scottish Reformation and its strong iconoclastic tradition, with an explanation. Yet we ask, did this iconoclastic tradition with roots in the sixteenth century hold just as strongly for the nineteenth-century Scottish society that built the clear majority of courthouses still in use? On a more extensive examination of the built environment in nineteenth-century Scottish towns and cities, we find that iconography flourishes there, and on financial, commercial, and municipal buildings there appears to be a proliferation of carvings of Lady Justice. The use of symbols on or around Scottish courthouses, as analyzed here, admits of a very particular and complex history.

Symbolizing Justice

In terms of overt use of the iconography of justice, the physical precincts of the Scottish justice system have a thin history. Symbols regularly found painted or sculpted on or around the *Palais de Justices*, tribunals, and courthouses of other countries, such as Justice with her scales and sword, Solon the Greek lawmaker, or representations of the Judgement of Solomon, are rarely, if ever, encountered here. There is, of course, a definite symbolism in the use of architecture and interior design in the height of the judge's seat compared to that of the accused, for example. Regarding the iconography in terms of plastic or visual symbols, however, every courthouse must display the Crown Coat of Arms, which itself validates the judicial proceedings. There are indeed several material versions of that design, as is noted in the descriptions below. There is also the display of the ceremonial mace when the High Court is in session. Beyond those official and ceremonial seals, however, the traditional nineteenth-century courthouse displays little except the occasional academic portrait of patrons, such as the full-length portraits of the Duke and Duchess of Buccleuch at Selkirk sheriff court; or portraits of former sheriffs or provosts, such as Alexander Graham Speirs of Culcreoch at Stirling sheriff court; or a portrait or bust of Queen Victoria, as at Hamilton sheriff court. This section examines both symbols that are present and those that are conspicuously absent from the courthouse and court process.

The Courthouse Interior

The Crown Coat of Arms

Any judgment of a sheriff is validated by being handed down under the aegis of the Crown Coat of Arms, which is the royal coat of arms of the Kingdom of Scotland. In theory a sheriff court could take place anywhere as long as the coat of arms is set up there in view of everyone in attendance at the proceedings. The coat of arms consists of a rampant lion and a unicorn bearing between them a shield that has quartered designs, two bearing arms of the Kingdom of Scotland, one of England, and one of Ireland. Surmounting the shield is a lion seated on a crown bearing a mace and a sword. "In Defens," the shortened form of the motto of the royal coat of arms of Scotland and the United Kingdom, *In My Defens God Me Defend*, appears above that. The motto of the royal Stewart dynasty, "Nemo Me Impune Lacessit," appears on the ground below the feet of the unicorn and the lion.[1]

The coat of arms appears in every Scottish court and in some tribunals, such as employment tribunals. It is usually attached to or painted on the wall behind the judicial bench. It is a very colorful relief sculpture in bright gold, red, blue, and green and visible throughout the courtroom. There are, however, variations in its material and placement. In Glasgow sheriff court, the arms are a wall relief in plain white plaster enclosed in a large plaster circle; in Fort William the arms are etched on the glass in the window behind the sheriff; in Kilmarnock the arms are made of a bronze-colored metal; in Kirkwall the large-sized arms are carved in wood against a painted large navy-blue oblong panel; in Stirling and the Court of Session in Parliament House and in some other courts, the coat of arms is perched atop the wooden canopy over the judge's chair. At Livingston the lion and "In Defens" motto is etched in black into the glass wall that separates the court accommodation from the rest of the building. In a couple of instances, however, on the exterior of court buildings, the mottoes of the British monarch for use outside Scotland are found. These mottoes are either *Dieu et Mon Droit* and/or *Honi soit Qui Mal y Pense*.[2] We found this symbol outside the former doorway of No. 1 Parliament Square and carved in relief on the exterior wall at Alloa sheriff court.

The Mace

The mace, or scepter, is a staff bearing a seal, usually decorated in precious metals, which is borne into an assembly to symbolize civil authority and power. It has its origin in a weapon of war, and its presence in court is thus a legacy and a physical reminder of the violent origins of the law in the fundamental role of the judge as the one who hands down punishments fit for crimes, and of the pain and suffering that could be inflicted by the judge's sentence.[3] Until very recently such physical violence, be it torture or punishment, still played an important role in the courts' business. In Tain for instance, Donald Pender, "a common notorious theife" who had broken into a house and stolen eighty merks (old Scottish money) was sentenced to be "conveyed to the meikle tree standing at the gavill of the schoolhouse . . . and yor ear to be nailt with one double plenission nail."[4] Foucault points out that hanging as a form of death sentence (the last judicial hanging in Scotland took place in 1963), which entails endurance and suffering rather than immediate death, is a form of torture.[5] Judicial torture was used in Scotland, as part of the trial and punishment process, as it was in most countries in Europe, until forbidden in 1708.[6] Physical punishment of offenders continued to be available as an option for Scottish courts, however, until the 1948 Criminal Justice Bill abolished corporal punishment (actually birching) of boys under sixteen.[7] Yet even now, after physical punishment and torture have been abolished, it is evident that there are still forms of violence at the heart of the judicial process, as Resnik and Curtis put it:

> Every act of judgement results in a state imposition of force, reallocating property from one civil claimant to another or depriving criminal defendants of their liberty and (in some eras and places) of their lives. Every government seeks to demonstrate its ability to provide peace and security by employing such violence, and every government needs to legitimate its own use of force against the disobedient by demonstrating that those who have breached the rulers' law are identified and sanctioned after being found responsible.[8]

It is therefore significant that the mace is required to be present only for the ritual of the High Court, where the most serious and often violent crimes are tried, and where the most violent constraints on the body of the guilty party are imposed by the judge in terms of long custodial sentences.

Maces are employed now in their various manifestations to denote that a civil assembly is in session. Thus, a mace specially made in 1999 is installed between the speaker and the members when the Scottish Parliament is sitting. The mace for the Scottish High Courts is similarly used symbolically to denote the court is in session and to validate its judgment. Where the coat of arms is usually placed above or to the side of the judge/sheriff, when the High Court is in session the mace is brought in ceremony into the court in front of the judge by the mace bearer and inserted into a bracket on the wall.

Besides the Court of Session in Edinburgh and the High Court of Justiciary in Edinburgh, Glasgow, and Aberdeen, there are several sheriff courts that also serve as a circuit for the High Court. These courts were, at the time of writing, Dunfermline, Dumbarton, Inverness, Kilmarnock, Livingston, Paisley, and Perth, and regular sittings at Edinburgh sheriff court. At other sheriff courts that formerly served as part of the High Court circuit, such as Dundee, the bracket to hold the mace can still be seen against the wall behind the bench. The use of the mace is meant to add symbolic weight to the High Court process. Even so, Oliver Cromwell famously expressed his contempt for the political deliberations of the Rump Parliament at Westminster by referring to its mace as a "fools' bauble."[9] Nonetheless, Cromwell might have agreed with King Seleucus, whose advice, cited by Montaigne, was "that he who foreknew the weight of the sceptre would not deign to pick it up." Montaigne goes on to explain that "This he said by reason of the weighty, irksome and painful charges that are incident unto a good king."[10] Its association with strength and power seems clear from these citations, but nonetheless the mace used in the High Courts of Scotland is very slender and diminutive in comparison with the bulk of the typical parliamentary or royal versions.

The Courthouse Exterior

The architecture of the Scottish courthouses is discussed in chapter 5, but it is noted that those exteriors give minimal indication that the function of the building is in any literal way related to law or justice. The buildings are also described in chapter 5 in their location near the centers of the communities they serve. Formal recognition of their function usually consists in a simple plaque to the left of the main entrance. The wording is modest. Outside the busiest court complex in Europe, a blue and white notice reads "Glasgow Sheriff Court" and incorporates a symbol indicating the location of disabled access. The sign measures fifteen inches by twelve inches and can only be read from close to it.[11]

Thus where, for instance, many (especially older) courthouses in Australia bear the words *Court House* and the date of their construction prominently for all to see in the pediment on the frontage (see, for example, Northam Courthouse, Seymour Victoria Old Courthouse and Armidale Courthouse), in Scotland where the building has a pediment there is no such signage displayed. Nor usually are there any accompanying carved or fixed adornments such as a statue of Justice or roundels or friezes displaying justice themes.

Iconography

Resnik and Curtis discuss the gradual replacement in the iconography of European justice of the Christian symbol of St. Michael with the Roman God "Justice" or her Greek versions in Themis (human justice) or her mother, Dike (divine justice). They question why there was a need to retain only one of the symbolic virtues as an operative principle for a secular pantheon: "Over time states gained monopolies over legal jurisdiction and, through this display of judicial authority, rulers sought to bond individuals to them and to legitimate their powers."[12] Thus, the court was a rival to church power. Resnik and Curtis also note that Justice was once part of a foursome known as the Cardinal Virtues.[13] They were derived from Plato's list of four qualities, "wise, brave, moderate and just,"[14] found in *The Republic*, and included Prudence, Temperance, and Fortitude along with Justice.

By way of emphasizing the universal nature of the recognition of the iconography of Justice, Resnik and Curtis suggest that even readers of *The Economist* on viewing the image of a blindfolded woman, draped in

Grecian robes and holding the scales and a sword, "would connect the picture to justice."[15] Indeed, they assert that the use of the symbol is found everywhere, and they point to instances in Australia, Azerbaijan, Zambia, Canada, and Japan.[16] Perhaps the most well-known statue of Lady Justice is the one by F. Pomeroy at the Old Bailey, or Central Criminal Court, in London, but she also appears at the Supreme Court of Brazil by Alfredo Ceschiatti, the high courts in Teheran, the county court in Los Angeles, and the Gerichtkeitsbrunnen in Frankfurt. There are, however, only two notable statues of Justice at Scottish courts. One is the Justice statue now kept in the corridor at Parliament Hall, the Court of Session. It was originally part of a pair, "Justice and Mercy," carved in 1637, by Robert Mylne for the door to the Parliament Hall, which was taken down in the early nineteenth century. The other is the low relief art deco type of statue of Justice in the tympanum of the former sheriff court and now High Court of the Justiciary on High Street (the Lawnmarket) in Edinburgh. It was carved and finished three hundred years after Mylne's work by Alexander Carrick in 1937 for the then new Edinburgh sheriff court.[17]

The interesting point about the otherwise total lack of representations of Justice on the other fifty-odd Scottish courts is that neither of these sculptures were created during the nineteenth-century heyday of Scottish court construction. None of the nineteenth-century courts has an authentic and original statue of Justice on its frontage or in the interior. Thus, while Sir Walter Scott, sheriff of Selkirk, could verbally invoke Justice (by her Greek name Themis) about the prominent position of the law and the legal position in early nineteenth-century Scottish society—"The Scots seem to conceive Themis the most powerful of goddesses"[18]—it is significant that there is no statue of Justice on the sheriff courthouse where he practiced in Selkirk (see Gazetteer).

In considering this lack of iconography, however, and in attempting to assess its historical significance, the obvious, or even automatic, response would be to see it as part of the Presbyterian tradition of iconoclasm and the long-time emphasis in the Scottish polity and in Presbyterian culture on the word and the rejection of perceived forms of idolatry. The case of Scott's verbal invocation and the lack of iconic physical manifestations of Justice on his own courthouse would seem to confirm this explanation. Such a "tradition" of iconoclasm was initiated in the sixteenth-century Scottish Reformation, when, for example, in 1599 the thousands of followers of Knox's Reform moved across the country, and "as they passed, where they found in their way any churches or chapels, immediately they purged them, breaking down the altars and idols in all places where they came."[19]

The text that would be the *locus classicus* for the propagation of iconoclasm in Scottish religion and civil life in general is a passage from John Knox's *First Blast of the Trumpet against the Monstrous Regiment of Women*: "that much that the form and appearance but lacketh the virtue and strength which name and proportion do resemble and promise. As images have face, nose, eyes, mouth, hands and feet painted but the use of the same cannot the craft and art of man give them."[20] This text, in turn, would take its inspiration from the words of Psalm 115: "they have mouths but they speak not, eyes have they, but they see not."

Is this understanding of Scottish history, however, sustainable? And is it solely Scottish courthouses that eschew the deployment of iconography on their exteriors? We noted above that many Australian courthouses bear the word "courthouse" on their frontage; they often do this instead of bearing any of the internationally recognized symbols of justice. Equally as many Australian courthouses, however, have no such lettering or symbols, or they bear only the Crown Coat of Arms in their pediment (see, for example, the supreme courthouses of South Australia and New South Wales and Young, Darlinghurst, and Yass courthouses). There is a similar lack of external iconography on many of the courthouses in Canada. Resnik and Curtis point to the even more widespread phenomenon (especially in the United States) of courthouses built throughout the twentieth century where artworks were not employed as a mode of recognition, decoration, or symbolism. Their comment on this phenomenon hints at an austerity inherent to the taste and judgment of the legal and judicial professions of that era: "Some of that lack of interest can be attributed to intellectual disdain for the didacticism of allegory, to dislike of ornamentation, and to aesthetic affection for line and form, as well as to the absence of institutional structures pressing for art production."[21]

These several factors cited may have played out in various ways across the countries considered here. Is it not plausible, for example, that in their historical relative remoteness from cosmopolitan centers, Scotland, Australia, and Canada may well have had weaker institutional structures representing the interests of art and artists? As former colonies and part of the British Commonwealth, there was a strong Scottish influence on both Australian and Canadian culture, and it is also conceivable that the Presbyterian iconoclastic tradition had as strong an influence there as it did in Scotland. Yet we must ask then of both the Scottish and the putative Australian and Canadian cases whether the iconoclastic tradition was still strong at the period when the courthouses were being built as it was in sixteenth-century Scotland.

Most of the building of courthouses in Scotland took place in the nineteenth century: Can we say that the beliefs and practices in nineteenth-century society regarding iconography were unchanged from those of three hundred years previously? It appears not, for both buildings and public spaces of the nineteenth-century town are liberally adorned with a wealth of public statuary, both the representational type, such as Sir Walter Scott, Queen Victoria, Robert Burns, and many others in George Square in Glasgow, and the allegorical statues on buildings. It cannot be that the architects and builders of these nineteenth-century courts did not utilize such iconography simply because nineteenth-century Scots were unaware of the symbol of Justice (again see Scott's invocation), nor that they had some theoretical or theological objection to her representation in the public or civic realm. In fact she appears at that very same period sculpted on the facades of numerous other types of buildings, including financial, commercial, and municipal. She appears, for example, on banks, such as the carving by John Rhind on the 1806 headquarters of the Bank of Scotland on the Mound in Edinburgh. She is also found on other commercial buildings, such as the 1894 North British Rubber company building at 60-2 Buchanan Street in Glasgow (by an anonymous sculptor),[22] as well as on municipal buildings, such as William Mossman Jr.'s carving of 1872 on Partick burgh halls.[23]

Ray McKenzie comments that "the use of a figure symbolizing Justice on a building erected as 'business premises' is difficult to account for."[24] Could we speculate that in the nineteenth century with the rapid urbanization and industrialization of that era, and with the gathering of capital and riches into so few hands, that bankers felt a need to appeal to their dealings with riches as "just"? In the Bank of Scotland's coat of arms, flanking *Justice* with her scales *appears as a twin figure* with Plenty with her cornucopia of money.[25] The Latin motto "*Tanto Uberior*" means "*so much the more plentiful.*" In their comprehensively international survey of the different ways Justice is represented, Resnik and Curtis note that public authorities once put forth a much richer pictorial array than the lone virtue, Justice, as an icon for good governance.[26] This broader perspective is seen in the way in which some of the buildings that had public functions, such as town halls and police offices, have a recognition of other Virtues. This we can see, for instance, in the context of Glasgow city chambers and the county buildings in Paisley.

There are, however, some interesting exceptions to the general rule of the absence of carved iconography on the exteriors of nineteenth-century built Scottish courthouses. One such type is the case of buildings that display statues or carvings of Justice on their exteriors, but were not originally built as courthouses and were adapted to that function for only a certain period. There are two such buildings in Glasgow. One is the former high court building on Ingram Street. Originally completed by David Hamilton in 1842 as the headquarters of the Union Bank of Scotland, this Italianate building had eight standing allegorical figures by John Mossman, one of which was Justice with her sword and scales.[27] It was acquired by the Lanarkshire County council and used between 1929 and 1994 as the High Court. The other Glasgow building is the former Glasgow district court on Turnbull Street, which was originally completed as the central police office in 1906 by A. B. McDonald. This building displays figures of Law and Justice by Richard Ferris on either side of the central gable.[28] Another example is found at Arbroath sheriff court, where there is a sculpted panel portraying Justice high on the middle bay of the Guildry building. Again, however, and as noted in the Gazetteer, the Guildry building was not an original part of the sheriff courthouse and was brought into use as an extension to the original courthouse in 2000. Paisley also has a Justice statue that adorns its recently renovated court complex. Again, however, like the Union Bank/High Court building in Glasgow, this was originally constructed for other purposes. In this case, however, it was for municipal local authority functions. Pomeroy, before creating his iconic 1902 Old Bailey Justice, provided a statue to the county for the Renfrewshire County building in 1890. This representation was flanked by Justice, Charity, and Law and Order.[29] This same building also had six relief sculptures of seventy classical figures that represent inter alia agriculture, the thread industry, mining, and boat building. They were sculpted in Ayrshire blue stone by the sculptor John Rhind (1828–1892).

The final exception to the absence of exterior iconography is perhaps the most highly visible and prominent in the public realm. It is to be found at a low level on a busy street in the country's largest city, on the building that formerly housed the sheriff court. The former Greek temple–style Glasgow city and county building was completed in 1842 by Clark and Bell. It had a council function combined with housing the Merchants' House and the sheriff court, though the Merchants' House function moved out in the 1870s and the local government functions shifted later to the nearby city chambers. The Ingram Street building then operated solely as the Glasgow sheriff court until 1975. There is a stone frieze of 1844 by Walter Buchan, carved on the Wilson Street stylobate. According to McKenzie it depicts a trial by jury[30] with the participants cloaked in classical togas. While it is thus a stylized representation of the legal process, it is not actually an allegorical work as are Justice statues.[31] Once that building was used solely as a courthouse, the carving found itself not over the public entrance to the courthouse on

Ingram Street, but by the entrance for lawyers on Wilson Street, at the rear of the building.[32]

Use of Art and Iconography on More Recently Renovated or New Court Buildings

The main thrust of the argument about the relative paucity of iconography in Scottish courthouses is focused on the nineteenth-century buildings that make up the bulk of the estate. When it comes to more recent additions or adaptations to that built estate, however, it is not clear whether there has been a change in attitude to the use of iconography and/or art in, on, or around the courthouse, or if indeed, there is any consistent attitude to the issue. Examination of the Gazetteer of courthouses across the country (below) will show that among the most recent additions and adaptations—namely Glasgow High Court of the Justiciary Extension (1997), Aberdeen High Court and Sheriff Court Extension (2004), Livingston Sheriff Court (2009), and Edinburgh High Court of the Justiciary (adaptation) (2011)—there is quite a variance in evidence of their commissioning, display, or employment of art and iconography.

The walls of the atrium in the 2011 adaptation of the Edinburgh High Court of the Justiciary are hung with four panels of a tapestry ("In Camera") by Alice Kettle. These textiles were completed for the original conversion of the building (1992–1994) in 1997. They appear in their bright tones and simple abstracted forms of scenes from the courtrooms—judges in their scarlet robes and folks in their "Sunday best" for their day in court—to be decorative and ornamental supplements to the institution rather than fully engaged or critical works. In Glasgow High Court Extension by contrast, the carvings by Gary Breeze are engaged not only as an integrated fixture on the structure of the building, but as a provocative and critical comment on the process of the law. Excerpts from three different texts are carved in three different respective styles, forming a frieze on the Portuguese limestone balcony in the entrance atrium above the reception.[33] The texts displayed prominently there are from David Hume's *Enquiry Concerning the Principles of Morals* (1777), Baron Hume's *Commentary on the Law of Scotland* (1797), and the biblical Book of Solomon. The cultural resonance of these texts in this place, where the process of Scots law is effected, is striking: one is from Scotland's greatest moral philosopher; one from his nephew, an advocate and a recognized institutional writer[34]; and one from the Old Testament. Texts, and particularly the Old Testament, have played a central role in Scottish culture and history—especially religious history. Yet if this sort of display of text in the courthouse is thus felt as appropriate, then it still has no precedent in the Scottish courthouse. There is, however, a historical precedent for this type of work in the traditional displaying of texts on the walls of some English courts,[35] and there is also a modern parallel in the work of artist Jenny Holzer, among whose works are the flowing LED texts on law that run across screens in Jean Nouvel's court at Nantes (see above).

Meanwhile, in the 2004 conversion of a nineteenth-century building that serves as both a high and sheriff court in Aberdeen, there appears to be no displaying or use of artworks whatsoever, and in the most up-to-date new courthouse in Scotland, in Livingston, completed in 2009, there are no artworks whatsoever. The only iconographical innovation is a small polished steel roundel at the entrance with a black etching of the lion emblem and the "In Defens" motto adopted by the Crown Office and Procurator Fiscal Service.

If it is disappointing that there is currently no evidence of a nationally coherent approach to the commissioning of art in courthouse buildings across Scotland, then it is also worrying, given that the Scottish Court Service has already launched a massive program for change in the use of its built estate. Resnik and Curtis discuss how with the great late-twentieth-century upheavals across many court systems around the world—the change in use of courtrooms, numbers and types of people using them, and the role of the court toward more experimental and conciliatory forms of hearing—art can play a vital role in its deployment in court design.

> One can use both buildings and art to bring lessons about law's history and its failures into courthouses and invite lessons about how courts can become vibrant centres of democratic debate. Courts could remain important sites within the public sphere(s) to provide opportunities to practice democracy by acknowledging rather than ignoring justice's shortfalls.[36]

They then go on to discuss how in some jurisdictions, such as in the United States and France, a more engaging use of art is integrated within a comprehensive program for modernizing and rebuilding the estate of the justice system (see chapter 7). In the United States the long-standing Art in Architecture Program for commissioning artworks for federal buildings has been adapted by the General Services Administration's Design Excellence Program with regulations establishing in 2008 that artworks must be incorporated into federal buildings and must emphasize the work of living American artists.[37] As such American artists have become involved as significant players in the design of new court buildings, which feature a range of work from well-known contemporary artists, such as Jenny Holzer and Tim Otterness.

In France, alongside their comprehensive program for rebuilding courts (see chapter 7), there is also a law known as "le 1% decorative," which ensures that 1 percent of the budget of all public buildings is spent on art, and that an integrated plan for the use of art must be developed early in the building design work. Again, as in the United States, this has not only ensured a proliferation of art in court buildings but also an innovation in the role of art in engaging the public in new understandings of the work of the courts, of their access to these buildings, and of meanings and approaches to the law. This can be seen in the work of Jenny Holzer's LED screens at Nantes and Pascal Couvert's sculpted bell at Bordeaux. This program has seen some projects that were more successful than others, and while it is symptomatic of their comprehensive approach that in 2000 the French Ministry of Justice should instigate a survey of all art commissioned since 1993, the lawyer in charge, Laurence Depambour Tarride, reported that "A great variety of imagery and materials, perhaps evocative of law's new diversification of modalities—or denoting the lack of clarity of vision about contemporary aspirations to do justice."[38]

Meanwhile, the Scottish court system has not had the opportunity to have such a mixed bag of art successes and failures, simply because it has had no consistent engagement with art. The odd one-off success like the carvings at Glasgow High Court Extension is a notable exception. There is no full government program, or even a law, to ensure a percentage for art in public buildings in Scotland, but neither has there been any comprehensive engagement with the public, the design community, or the architectural profession to ensure the design of much needed new court buildings. As seen in France and the United States the question of artworks for court buildings cannot be separated from the overall design and procurement question, and this latter question is discussed further in chapter 7.

Conclusion

Law and Justice have their symbols within the Scottish justice system. They are found in the coats of arms, maces, and other ceremonial aspects of the courts. The external architecture and internal courtroom layout, as we have seen, contribute to creating a special aura around the processing of crimes and civil disputes. There has, however, been a reticence in linking the notions of justice with the daily locations where law operates. Other than noting, as with the example of Walter Scott's comment cited above, that there has been a long historical emphasis on the importance of the word over that of the image in Scottish culture in general, it is difficult to determine exactly why there should be such a paucity of imagery and symbolism used on the exterior of Scottish courthouses, which were mostly built in the nineteenth century. The allegorical portrayal of Justice, as we have noted, *is* encountered in Scotland, but not where one might expect to see it. This does not, however, seem to be part of a rejection of statues as such. While historically the reformed national church may have had views rejecting the use of iconography in general, and particularly the use of statues in churches,[39] nineteenth- and twentieth-century civil Scotland has had no problem with representations of both actual persons and allegorical figures in certain areas of the public realm, including, of course, the looming figure of Knox himself in Glasgow's Necropolis. The evidence from more recently built courts, indeed, suggests that there has been little change in the attitude to art and iconography around the Scottish court estate in the twenty-first century. Might we not, then, be more likely to find explanation for that persistence in the territory of intellectual disdain, aesthetic taste and judgment, and bureaucratic and governmental inertia, as proposed by Resnik and Curtis, rather than through the dubious influence of a mostly outdated and much weakened set of religious beliefs?

Notes

1. This translates as "no one provokes me with impunity."

2. The first motto translates as "God and my right" and was adopted as the motto of England and placed on the royal arms of the Kingdom of England by Henry V (1386–1422); the other motto is translated as "Shame on him who thinks evil of it" or "shame on him who evil thinks."

3. Judith Resnik and Dennis Curtis, *Representing Justice: Invention, Controversy, and Rights in City-States and Democratic Courtrooms* (New Haven, CT: Yale University Press, 2011), discuss the way in which modern views of justice tend to offer few clues to the pain of justice both to its recipients and those applying it; see chapter 3, 38–61; Michel Foucault, *Discipline and Punish: The Birth of the Prison*, trans. A. M. Sheridan Smith (Harmondsworth: Penguin, 1991).

4. Estelle Quick, *Tain Tolbooth* (Tain: Tain and District Museum Trust, 1998), 23.

5. Foucault, *Discipline and Punish*, 33.

6. R. D. Melville, "The Use and Forms of Judicial Torture in England and Scotland," *Scottish Historical Review* 2, no. 7 (1905): 225–48, 226.

7. L. Mahood, "'Give Him a Doing': The Birching of Young Offenders in Scotland," *Canadian Journal of History* 37, no. 3 (2002): 439–57. It remained an option in the classroom for teachers until abolished by a decision of the European Court of Human Rights in 1982. It was inflicted through the medium of a leather strap, or "tawse," to the hands.

8. Resnik and Curtis, *Representing Justice*, 13.

9. Andrew Bissett, *History of the Commonwealth of England* (London: John Murray, 1867), 463.

10. de Montaigne, Michel. *Shakespeare's Montaigne: The Florio Translations of The Essays*. Translated by John Florio. New York: New York Review of Books, 2014, 78.

11. There is a relief representation on the right side of the court entrance that is much larger but is so discreet that it was noticed by one of the authors only after having used the building for thirty years.

12. Resnik and Curtis, *Representing Justice*, 25.

13. Resnik and Curtis, *Representing Justice*, 344.

14. Resnik and Curtis, *Representing Justice*, 344.

15. Resnik and Curtis, *Representing Justice*, 1.

16. Resnik and Curtis, *Representing Justice*, figures 2–12.

17. Although Nicholson mentions it in his study of the evolution of the sheriff court at Edinburgh, he does not comment on the rarity of such an icon as a phenomenon; G. Nicholson, *The Sheriff Court at Edinburgh* (Edinburgh: Scottish Courts Administration, 1994), 18.

18. W. Scott, *Sir Walter Scott's Journal*, ed. D. Douglas (Edinburgh: Douglas, 1891), 36.

19. Alex Ryrie, *The Origins of the Scottish Reformation* (Manchester: Manchester University Press, 2006), 186.

20. J. Knox, *The Works of John Knox*, ed. David Lang (Edinburgh: Wodrow Society, 1855), 391.

21. Resnik and Curtis, *Representing Justice*, 182.

22. Ray McKenzie, *Public Sculpture of Glasgow* (Liverpool: Liverpool University Press, 2002), 37–38.

23. McKenzie, *Public Sculpture of Glasgow*, 47.

24. McKenzie, *Public Sculpture of Glasgow*, 373.

25. Versions of the Bank of Scotland arms, which incorporates Justice holding her scales, are found on the major branches of the Bank of Scotland throughout Scotland.

26. Resnik and Curtis, *Representing Justice*.

27. The other statues represent Navigation and Commerce (globe and sexton), Britannia (trident), Wealth (cornucopia), Peace (olive branch), Industry (bobbin), Glasgow (key and coat of arms), and Mechanics and Agriculture (sheaf of corn, sickle, and wheel).

28. McKenzie, *Public Sculpture of Glasgow*, 384.

29. Refrewshire Council Department of Planning and Transport, *Paisley's Public Sculptures* (Paisley: Refrewshire Council Department of Planning and Transport, 2001).

30. McKenzie, *Public Sculpture of Glasgow*, 427–29.

31. A full-size copy of this frieze was installed in the justiciary court in the Saltmarket but was lost in the modifications of 1911. A plaster replica was made at that time and is in the courthouse today; McKenzie, *Public Sculpture of Glasgow*, 429.

32. Its most recent public showing was in an article publicizing the autobiography of celebrated Glasgow lawyer Ross Harper where he is photographed in a suitably "legal" setting standing directly in front of the back of the old Glasgow sheriff court. In the background the frieze shows up clearly along with the restaurant that now occupies the ground floor, aptly named *Citation-Sunday Mail*, September 11, 2016.

33. Johnny Rodger, *Contemporary Glasgow: The Architecture of the 1990s* (Edinburgh: Rutland Press, 1999), 25–26.

34. Scots law, with its civilian tradition, has among its sources the writings of a few commentators ranging from Stair, Erskine, and Bell to Hume and Rankine. In the absence of any other statute or case law, their works are regarded as authoritative.

35. Linda Mulcahy, *Legal Architecture: Justice, Due Process and the Place of Law* (London: Routledge, 2011), 89–90.

36. Resnik and Curtis, *Representing Justice*, 192.

37. Resnik and Curtis, *Representing Justice*, 184.

38. Resnik and Curtis, *Representing Justice*, 200–201.

39. Knox, *The Works of John Knox*, 391.

CHAPTER SEVEN

Scottish Courts Going Forward into the Future

The votes of the September 2014 referendum on Scottish independence, the May 2015 British general election, and the June 2016 United Kingdom "Brexit" from the European Union, together with all their political repercussions, have interesting implications for the Scottish justice system and the courts in which it operates. Resnik and Curtis assert that "during the second half of the twentieth century courthouses came to be icons of government" throughout the world.[1] In Scotland, a country with its own quasi-autonomous judicial system, but no full state, the complex nexus of legislative, executive, and judicial bodies might make the relationship between government and public buildings less obvious. Although it might seem at first that we have, in Edinburgh, a Scottish administration committed to public service and, in London, a "small State privatising" government, the contrast is, on deeper analysis, much less marked. Reductions of expenditures on those public services within the remit of the Scottish government were signposted in 2015 with the courts suffering an expenditure cut of £11m.[2] Saving money on those items of public expenditure that lack demonstrable immediate public benefit, such as libraries and infrastructure maintenance, is always attractive. The lack of obvious constituents to fight for expenditure on the justice system leaves it unlike, for instance, education, with few sympathetic cheerleaders. The legal profession, those with the closest perspective on the impact of cuts, have a limited level of public sympathy[3] and seem currently committed to a "value for money" agenda with its inherent dangers.[4] The future for the justice system, and for our particular interest, the buildings in which its work is carried on, does not look promising at the time of writing.

The Late-Twentieth-Century Context of Justice Service Provision

The changes in the volume of business in the courts and the concentration of this has altered since the last sustained examination of this some fifty years ago in the Grant Report. At the time of their deliberations in the early 1960s the population of Scotland was 5,157,482.[5] It was served by fifty-four sheriff courts[6] divided into twelve sheriffdoms[7] each with its own sheriff principal and a further fifty-eight sheriff substitutes.[8] In the years between 1950 and 1965 criminal trials in the courts had increased. Summary trials had gone from 2,975 to 7,957[9] and solemn from 191 to 356.[10] Civil business also saw small debt cases almost triple from 47,379 to 138,266. For ordinary actions the rise was more modest from 12,395 to 21,943.[11] The business of the Court of Session also saw modest rises through the 1950s into the 1960s, both civil[12] and criminal.[13]

The local authority structure consisted of more than four hundred local authorities: thirty-three county councils (four of which were paired as "joint county councils" for most purposes), four county or city corporations, 197 town councils (administering twenty-one large burghs and 176 small burghs), and 196 district councils.[14] As Grant noted, this too was under scrutiny by the Royal Commission on Local Government in Scotland under Lord Wheatley. This had been set up in February 1966 and duly reported in September 1969.[15] Its principal recommendation of a two-tier local government administration was duly enacted in the Local Government (Scotland) Act 1973. This set up eight regional councils and thirty-three district councils with responsibility divided. Regions were to have power over major planning, social work, police, and education, and district councils were to have power over local planning, planning applications, building control, libraries, licensing, and housing.[16] Its principal impact on the operation of the justice system was the introduction of district courts based on the new post-1975 districts under the District Courts (Scotland) Act 1975. These replaced the existing burgh and justice of the peace courts and were themselves superseded by justice of the peace courts under the Criminal Proceedings etc (Reform) (Scotland) Act 2007 after a review by the Summary Justice Review Committee.[17] They were outside the remit of the Gill Report, whose recommendations left their jurisdiction intact. Their work and role are discussed in the McInnes Report.[18]

The concerns of the Conservative administration, which set up the Grant Committee, had remarkable parallels with those of their twenty-first-century successors. The terms of reference were in a context that required them to address the function of the sheriff court and the changes that were required "in order to secure the more speedy, economical and satisfactory dispatch of civil and criminal business."[19] There was no nostalgic commitment to maintaining the status quo, and in fact their remit specifically included a term of reference to "consider the number and distribution of sheriff courts."[20]

The future that Grant expected was one in which "the work-load, in general (would) continue to increase"[21] and "the number of criminal cases coming before the sheriff court (would) go on increasing"[22] with criminal business "to a greater extent than at present, (dominating) the work of the courts."[23] Concern was expressed at the delays in the courts in the time the courts were taking to dispose of business[24] and, in particular, summary criminal cases.[25] As they noted only about 30 percent of trials took place within two months of the pleading diet when the case first appears in court, and there were busy courts where the interval was as much as six or nine months.[26] Given its restriction to the sheriff court as opposed to the whole justice system, then perhaps it is not surprising that the Grant Committee adopted a relatively narrow focus. They made no mention of the impact of changes in technology, and the world they operate in envisages gradual changes rather than anything seismic. It was written at a time when the whirr of an electric typewriter was an unusual sound in a legal office and when dry copiers were a rarity. The tone of their successors is different in the wake of the emergence of computers, FAX machines, and myriad mobile devices. There is no mention of changes in the organization of the profession. Although the other criminal courts in the system then, burgh and justice of the peace courts, dealt with a significant percentage of minor criminal matters (see table 7.1), their role was referred to only briefly in the context of sheriff court jurisdiction as dealing with "trivial offences."[27]

Table 7.1. Criminal Justice in Scotland: Persons Called to Court, 1974–2004

Court Procedure	*1974*	*1984*	*1994*	*2004*
Solemn and summary	235,004	209,280	183,674	129,733
Solemn	2,979	4,067	5,250	4,644
Summary	232,025	205,213	172,542	125,087
Sheriff courts	142,679	106,710	93,466	77,196
Lower courts	89,346	98,503	79,076	47,891

Source: Scottish Criminal Justice Annual Reports

The 2009 Review of Civil Justice in Context

By the end of the first decade of the twenty-first century much had been altered in Scottish society in the fifty years from the work of the Grant Committee. The population of Scotland had risen to 5.3 million.[28] The country was served by forty-nine sheriff court districts divided into six sheriffdoms[29] each with a sheriff principal and 146 sheriffs.[30] The Court of Session's complement of judges had reached almost thirty.[31] The local authority structure consisted of thirty-two multipurpose unitary authorities[32] ranging in size from Glasgow with 600,000 inhabitants to Orkney with twenty thousand.

In the twenty-first century the number of civil cases coming before the courts had reached a plateau. The caseload of the Court of Session was around six thousand cases, of which half were personal injury actions.[33] In the sheriff courts the number of total civil actions had risen steadily and then leveled off at around 130,000 actions annually after hitting a peak of 192,545 in 1991.[34] The crude figures disguised major shifts in such areas as a major decrease in small claims actions,[35] while ordinary causes were steady[36] and administrative work rose significantly.[37] As noted above, the justice of the peace court structure was introduced in the Criminal Proceedings etc (Reform) (Scotland) Act 2007 and was completed in 2010.[38]

The Changes in the Legal Profession

There has been a major expansion in the number of those working within the justice system. In place of the part-time law degree studies taught around breakfast and tea time, full-time law degrees were introduced in the early 1960s.[39] This increase continued with the Faculty of Advocates growing from 276 members in 1990 to 456 in 2008. The number of solicitors rose from 3,450 in 1960[40] to a 1990 figure of 7,087, to 9,873 in 2008[41] and to the current 2014 figure of eleven thousand.[42]

The Changing Nature of Litigation

Although the Grant Report had a wide remit, its terms assumed that how disputes were resolved was a matter for individuals with the state providing the mechanism to determine their resolution. In twenty-first-century Scotland, the Scottish Civil Courts Review Consultation Paper asked whether "as a matter of public policy, the courts should be regarded as the last resort for the resolution of disputes after all other suitable methods of dispute resolution have been proved ineffective."[43] There were, it was suggested, "choices to be made about priorities for investing in the civil justice system, and about where the balance should lie as between on the one hand, investing in formal structures such as the courts, and on the other, supporting the provision of advice and other methods of dispute resolution which aim to prevent disputes ending up in court."[44]

The Role of Mediation and Alternative Dispute Resolution

We find no mention of any alternatives to litigation within the pages of the Grant Report. By the time of Gill, as far as mediation and its impact were concerned, the Consultation Paper was outlining the factors that had led to an increase in mediation and alternative dispute resolution (ADR)—increase of conflict and disempowerment of the less articulate and financially well off, as well as noting that litigation limits the outcomes that include a party simply wanting "an apology or an undertaking to behave differently in future."[45] The provision of the services of Family Mediation Scotland (FMS), where children were involved[46] as well as other pilot schemes, were noted,[47] and the implications of extending its role.[48] The Gill Report, while noting the support for mediation types of procedure, and being happy for courts to encourage ADR in any type of case and at any stage of a case,[49] did not consider that the court should have the power to compel parties to enter into ADR.[50] The Scottish government noted this position, but believed that mediation offered "significant opportunities to reach an acceptable settlement of disputes, potentially at less cost to the public purse, and often with less distress and inconvenience to the parties."[51]

The Gill Reforms and the Size and Nature of the Court Service

The Scottish government broadly welcomed the recommendations within Gill.[52] Regarding the closure of courts, or as the response blandly expressed it, "service configuration," this was a matter "for the Scottish Court Service, in consultation with the judiciary, court users and the Scottish Government."[53] Unlike the Grant Committee[54] the remit of the Gill Committee did not explicitly cover court closures although any review looking at civil justice with a view to providing "best use of resources" might infer that this was implied. Nevertheless, Gill's many recommendations regarding the structure of the civil court system, covering such matters as the sheriff appeal court, the office of district judge, and enhanced case management, made no direct mention of the implications for accommodation. All that we find is the recommendation that "(b)oth district judges and sheriffs would be accommodated in the existing sheriff court and JP court estate."[55]

The follow-up to the overarching civil court recommendations was a consultation paper *Shaping Scotland's Court Services* in September 2012.[56] This was guided by the *Principles for Provision of Access to Justice* agreed with the Lord President, Lord Justice Clerk, and sheriff principals in February 2012. A report of the result of the ensuing discussions and response to the consultation document was published in April 2013. It contained far-ranging proposals as far as the location of Scottish justice was concerned.[57]

The High Court would sit as a court of first instance primarily in dedicated High Court centers in Edinburgh, Glasgow, and Aberdeen.[58] These reflected the original proposals in the Consultation Paper and were not swayed by notions of justice being seen to be done in the local community or arguments about the additional travel costs. A fourth location might also be used when the Lord Justice General or Lord Advocate deemed it to be in the interests of justice.[59]

As far as the lower courts were concerned, this process was more complex. The SCS Report proposed to limit mainland sheriff court business to sixteen locations, where all civil and criminal business would take place. As in the proposal to limit the locations of the High Court, the consultees argued that this would affect local access to justice and community cohesion adversely. The visibility of local justice, its delivery, and reporting would suffer.[60] These comments were rejected on the basis that those affected already had to travel for their specialist services and amenities.[61]

This was all to take place via a two-stage process. First, there was to be some rationalization of the existing structure.[62] Thereafter, a radical alteration in the way in which justice has been conducted in Scotland was to be introduced. In place of the notion of courts being physically accessible in the places where people lived and worked, the plan for the future envisaged a small number of specialized sheriff-centered locations.[63] These sixteen "justice centers" were to be located across Scotland in place of the existing forty-nine sheriff courts,[64] five separate justice of the peace courts, and eight High Court locations.[65] As the SCS explains the locations were selected with the notion of proximity based on projections that "in the majority of cases will be at a distance of less than 20 miles."[66]

Of course, these changes to the spaces of justice and how it operates was in the context of major changes in the system. The context and assumptions behind the changes to the court structure were

> (a) a new salaried judicial office of summary sheriff, below the rank of sheriff, dealing with summary criminal cases, summary cause and small claims litigation and some other civil matters, including family cases;

(b) a new sheriff appeal court dealing with both civil and criminal appeals from the sheriff courts and justice of the peace courts;
(c) a sheriff personal injury special court, probably in Edinburgh, with other judicial specialisation managed within sheriffdoms;
(d) the redistribution of civil cases from the Court of Session to sheriff courts, and at the lower level from sheriffs to summary sheriffs;
(e) more active management of sheriff and jury cases, in particular a sheriffdoms-wide approach to matching cases to court capacity;
(f) increased use of video-conferencing and other arrangements to support vulnerable witnesses and victims of crime[67]

The Justice Centers

The notion of flexible working arrangements between the different arms of the state dealing with crime is not a new thing. For pragmatic reasons related to the size and nature of traditional Scottish justice arrangements, the juxtaposition of police and social work is not a new feature. In places like Dunfermline, Duns, Jedburgh, and Stonehaven these buildings used to adjoin the police and social work offices. Such proximity was both planned and accidental. In the modern construction of, for instance, Livingston, the court meets the ideal goal of the Scottish Court Service in the twenty-first century: "In Livingston we have achieved the arrangement to which we aspire. There the court facility forms part of the civic center which houses local authority, police, procurator fiscal, children's reporter and the West Lothian Community Health Partnership."[68]

These changes are, of course, dictated by financial and professional imperatives. As the SCS pointed out the cuts to the justice budget appears to be significant both in terms of operation and capital expenditure: "Our operating budget will reduce by 20% in real terms by 2014/15 compared with 2010/11. Our capital budget, which we use to provide buildings and technology, will reduce from £20.3 million in 2011/12 to £4.0 million in 2014/15."[69]

The English Experience

In broader terms the perceived problems of having a collection of nineteenth-century buildings in which to operate a modern changing justice system is one that is shared in England and Wales and is worth noting, although there is no compelling evidence that the two systems draw on the experience of the other, other than by way of courtesy references. The themes of cost cutting, demystification of the legal process, and the impact of digitization are made more explicit in the English context and are instructive. There are, of course caveats. Although the language of the near future envisages a world of justice centers, the meaning that this has been given, hitherto, in England is a little different from what Gill envisages. For instance, the Manchester justice center has a different remit with the complex containing Manchester's county court and the Manchester District Registry of the High Court, the city's family proceedings court, the district probate registry, and the regional and area Offices of the Court Service.[70]

Following closure of 140 courts in 2010 in England and Wales,[71] in July 2015, further consultation documents were published indicating that there should be a further reduction of the spaces available for the administration of justice.[72] The speed of implementation of the changes to the physical location of justice is also linked to the changes proposed in relation to the Civil Court Structure Review undertaken by Lord Justice Briggs and published in July 2016.[73]

The closure of eighty-seven courts is envisaged. The thinking behind the changes stems from the same perceived need to reduce expenditure and to consider alternatives: "The estate is made up of a complex picture of freehold, leasehold and casual hire arrangements occupying 460 courts and tribunal buildings. . . . This is an opportunity to stand back and reconsider the existing arrangements and to rationalize the estate so that best value for money is provided for users and taxpayers."[74] The underuse of assets is seen as a major issue linked with changes in digital technology to a future where physical court attendance can be reduced and the spare capacity of the redundant buildings can be put to other uses: "Disposal of surplus estate would provide potential opportunities for development of residential and commercial space benefiting local communities."[75] The approach to the proposed use of buildings is, however, slightly different. It represents a very definite shift away from the notion that purpose-built buildings are required for hearings.[76] This is only one option, and the consultation was keen to hear on alternative provision through civic or other buildings:[77]

> To ensure that access to justice is maintained, even in more rural locations, we are committed to providing alternative ways for users to access our services. That can mean using civic, and other public buildings, such as town halls, for hearings instead of underused, poorly-maintained permanent courts.[78]

The notion of appropriate distance is measured in terms of time rather than distance and assumes car use: "It will still be the case that, after these changes, over 95% of citizens will be able to reach their equipped court within an hour by car."[79]

The same notion of a limited number of dedicated hearing centers is envisaged with economies of scale with shared back office functions adding to efficiency. [80] This reverts, one might note, to the multipurpose spaces shared between civic authorities and the justice system in such places as the 1804 Selkirk building, over which Sir Walter Scott presided over two centuries ago,[81] in the 1829 Greenlaw County building,[82] and in the 1822 Ayr County building.[83]

Interestingly, there has been a closer relationship between the courts and tribunals in England than has been the case in Scotland. It has been commonplace for tribunal sittings to be held in magistrates courts in England and Wales. This matter has been complicated by the fact that not all the tribunals that sit in Scotland do so under devolved powers and so traditionally came under the control of the Courts and Tribunals Service for England and Wales. The Court Reform (Scotland) Act 2014 addresses this issue administratively.

The closest example of interchange of venues to be found in Scotland has occurred in the use of rooms for employment tribunals in Glasgow. Some of those rooms used for employment support allowance appeals at the Eagle chambers on Pitt Street have a different configuration.[84] As noted in chapter 5, there are a modest number of tribunal venues currently in Scotland,[85] and these sit in buildings that have been adapted from the standard office function that they previously had to allow seating for the parties, the clerk, and the tribunals of one to three members. All the furniture is moveable, and the parties sit at the same level with a distance from six to ten feet separating the appellants and respondents from the decision makers. The buildings are also indistinguishable externally from other offices.

Many of these proposals have not been challenged in their general thrust, and it is reasonable to suppose that the court services of the digital age have the potential to be very different. A comprehensive analysis of the England and Wales proposals and a set of recommendations and advice to the legal authorities has been published in a report by a Working Party from the group JUSTICE. This London-based group is an all-party law reform and human rights organization working to strengthen the justice system. It is a membership organization, primarily of the legal profession, comprising barristers, solicitors, legal executives, academic lawyers, law students, and interested nonlawyers. It seeks to inform debate, frame issues, and influence decision makers from across the political spectrum by providing evidence-based analysis. The response of the JUSTICE organization to the proposals embraces the shift away from a focus on dedicated court buildings for much low-level routine business and is based on efficiency in the use of resources/saving of money, adaptability for unforeseen future changes, and faith in technology.

The JUSTICE Report of May 2016 cuts to the core of the problem, and its radical approach is demonstrated in its title "What Is a Court?"[86] The Working Party locate their report in the world where digitization transforms the whole notion of court business. They "explore ways of improving upon the existing estate, re-using rooms and buildings freed up once digital documentation becomes the norm."[87]

Centering on a system that is "fair and accessible; open and transparent; effective and efficient; independent and impartial and delivered at a proportionate cost to the taxpayer"[88] the Working Party look back to the flexibility of the multifunctional early spaces for justice. They opt for this as a way of facilitating the provision of justice by allowing for responses to changing circumstances.

For England and Wales, the Working Party envisages three categories of "justice space"—simple, standard, and formal. They reflect different needs including the level of security risk, the need for formality and/or solemnity, the degree of public participation, the degree of segregation of the parties required, and the extent to which the participants accede to the judicial process.[89]

The "simple justice space" would be less formal and highly flexible such as we already find in the tribunals of the Social Entitlement Chamber.[90] All that is needed is sets of tables and chairs in a room. By contrast, the "standard justice space" would involve some formality or solemnity and might be appropriate for such matters as applications for child arrangements orders[91] where a balance between the need for solemnity and security and avoiding alienation and intimidation of vulnerable parties is required.[92] These types of dispute do not, it was suggested, need much more than a raised bench for the judge and could use the kind of flexible furniture used in the "simple justice spaces." The only adaptations would be a need for "escape routes" as well as room for advocates, social workers, and others to work effectively and with a degree of confidentiality.[93] The "formal justice space" would be required for high security, a high degree of formality, a considerable amount of public interest, and high levels of segregation such as serious crime and serious family matters. Even here, though, the Working Party does not envisage fixed furniture as long as it is lockable.[94] Nonetheless, due to the need for segregation of the parties they expected that the formal space would "need to be located in a purpose-built building."[95]

Within this broad framework, the Working Party envisaged different kinds of locations for dispensing justice ranging from "Flagship Justice Centres, Local Justice Centres, 'Pop-up' courts, remote access justice facilities and digital justice spaces."[96]

Flagship justice centers would be present in all major urban centers and would represent the full majesty of the justice system with both simple and formal justice spaces accommodating formal criminal trials, as well as less formal low-level civil and tribunal proceedings.[97] Local justice centers would be in every major town center and would comprise simple and standard justice spaces with the potential for formal justice spaces.[98] The notion of "pop-up" courts is a response to the closure of court and tribunal buildings and would be necessary in only the most rural areas. They would include peripatetic tribunals and courts appearing on a weekly or monthly basis as well as ad hoc courts for such matters as inquiries.[99] They would be in local council buildings, libraries, community centers, schools, or universities.[100] Finally, remote participation in justice would be provided through accredited spaces in such places as schools and community centers.[101]

The central driving force for the changes is the promise of "the elimination of paper case files, their storage and transportation."[102] The interesting key phrase that the Working Party employs is "technology-driven working methods" citing the proposed trialing of a "digital online portal case management system" that will lead to a "considerable reduction in face-to-face hearings."[103] This seems to us a strange way to organize a justice system where the possibility of saving time and money outflanks whether this is the best method of obtaining credible evidence. It might be appropriate for covering the parking offenses of the Traffic Penalty Tribunal, which the Working Party cites as an exemplar of the new digital justice, but it is of doubtful value when dealing with, for instance, appellants claiming sickness and disability benefits or with claims of unfair dismissal.

Nonetheless, the commitment to a future driven by the "revolution in technology" has been made by the government with an online system for starting and managing cases across the criminal, civil, family, and tribunal jurisdictions.[104] Over time, then, the courts in England and Wales will use online, virtual, and traditional hearings, and the government anticipates that more and more cases will be carried out virtually or online. This will require fewer buildings, using the existing ones more efficiently and with courtrooms that are more adaptable.[105]

In Scotland, the most recent assessment of the way forward from the progenitor of the reforms of the Scottish justice system, Lord Gill, suggests a similar trajectory. In a post–Brexit Scotland, he noted that the "current system was not an attractive form for litigation" and that there was a need for "an evidential regime appropriate to the digital age."[106] This points the way to the virtual court, and to courts and tribunals reverting to a justice system based on written evidence wherever possible without the need for expensive, if attractive, buildings. Sadly, however, the debate about the changes in Scotland has taken place between the institutions involved in the legal and judicial systems (e.g., the Scottish Court Service and the Judiciary) and the powerful representatives of those institutions, like Lord Gill. There has been very little input from wider Scottish civil society, and there has been no major published and disinterested critique by any laybody, such as JUSTICE with the report on English changes, cited above, from its membership of independent but qualified, engaged, and professional citizens.[107] Given the connections, stressed above by Resnik and Curtis, between the legislative body, judicial system, and democratic processes, this top-down, elitist, and undisturbed in-house procedure cannot reflect well on the health of Scottish participatory democracy.

The Future of the Legal Profession

During the twentieth century the legal profession was professionalized, with standards, skills, and values being altered as lawyers retreated to more technical and advisory roles in stable and protected markets and shifted toward a logic of social trusteeship. The lawyer became counselor and adviser, not market maker, except to mediate between different sectors of the market, for example, companies and banks.[108]

This description of the nature of the law firm in England and Wales could equally apply to Scotland. When the Grant Committee examined the sheriff court in the 1960s, the maximum permitted size for a legal partnership in Scotland was twelve members. The big two Edinburgh law firms, Shepherd & Wedderburn and Dundas & Wilson had twelve and ten partners, respectively. Most of the law firms in Scotland had four partners or fewer. The business of many law firms was dominated by private client work, with many firms secure in their ability to generate profits from the fees payable for conveyancing work. Fixed pro-rata fees and the absence of estate agents in Scotland provided a comfortable degree of financial security. The changes wrought by a range of factors altered this from the 1970s onward. The changes included the arrival of estate agents in Scotland, changes to conveyancing fee calculation, and occasional property slumps.

The changes that have occurred in the provision of legal services in England have also been reflected in Scottish experience. Specialization within urban centers has gone on apace. To this, one would add a rapid expansion in the size of solicitors' firms. The twentieth-century progress of lawyers has been described as one in which the legal profession became professionalized.

Besides this professionalization there has also been the arrival of the mega-law firm. Law firms, it has been suggested, "although national in origin, now depict themselves as global, international or regional."[109] Just as the rise of mega-accounting allowed there to be talk of the Big Four in the world[110] so the legal profession in the business world has become a transnational enterprise. These firms "globalise at an accelerated rate,"[111] and in the context of the Legal Services Act 2007, their ownership is not restricted to lawyers; along with the opening up of the English market for legal services to alternative business structures, the potential for a change of culture is immense.[112] In terms of Scotland, too, these changes in the nature of the legal profession have possible implications for the spaces of justice.[113] With the emergence of mega-law firms it is suggested that a new type of transnational lawyering has emerged as a result of globalization that alters the relationship between lawyers and their clients, which too has implications for the nature and volume of business in the Scottish justice system.[114] There would seem to a bifurcation of the business of providing legal services between the expanding corporate world and the small firm with limited resources.

In terms of the way in which justice to operate in Scotland in the future, these changes do not appear on the face of it to have a major impact. For instance, as we have seen, most of the work of the courts is concerned with minor crimes.[115] In other matters, however, large firms with the potential to bear the cost of litigation may be able to intimidate opponents and bulldoze their clients to success.

The Impact of Technology on Litigation in the Future

Just as the phenomenon of global change is difficult for national governments to alter radically, so too technological changes seem to have a momentum of their own. Richard Susskind suggests a very different future for legal practice and litigation as a result. This time the changes are driven by changes in technology. In a series of books and articles Susskind indicates that the kind of law experience that will be commonplace in the future consists of seismic changes for both individual clients and commercial enterprises.

In the first place, as he pointed out twenty years ago, "information technology will eventually enable and encourage legal service to change from being a form of advisory service to a type of information service."[116] By the turn of the millennium he explained how these changes represented not simply a smoothing out of inefficiencies but a "a complete shift in legal paradigm."[117] These were centered around the changing nature of legal knowledge as something shared rather than the preserve of the expert, through online legal services rather than "expert systems."[118] A more radical outcome has emerged in his more recent work with its provocative title, *The End of Lawyers?*,[119] emphasizing the potential of technology to address the questions of how clients can obtain "more for less." The solution to the search for cheaper expertise, he suggested, was the sharing of the costs of legal services for in-house layers and using a standardized or computerized service in place of bespoke work.[120] Support from paralegals, legal executives, and outsourced legal service providers will replace areas where legal experience is not required. The future tasks of lawyers, though, which Susskind envisaged ranging from project managing, strategy and management consultancy, market expertise, and deal brokering would be very different from the traditional purveyor of bespoke advice.[121]

Again the implications are profound,[122] and like the empirical observations of Flood and others do not bode well for the small, nonspecialized firm or specialized court practitioners.[123] As we have noted above, Gill, in his recommendations on case management, embraced the opportunities that technology offers to cut down on the time lawyers spend in face-to-face discussion within the courtroom.[124] Whether the changed nature of the proactive legal enterprise, seeking out new markets and aggressively selling their services, will alter the throughput of the justice system links us with the related question of seeking alternatives to litigation to save both time and money.

The Future of Alternative Dispute Resolution (ADR)

The reforms in England and Wales in the context of civil litigation were aimed to reduce the cost of litigation and the complexity of their rules. The conclusions of Lord Woolf's Report, *Access to Justice*, in July 1996,[125] suggested that civil litigation should be avoided wherever possible and become less adversarial and more cooperative. The subsequent white paper, *Modernising Justice*, has produced a boost for the cause of ADR. Fewer cases are being pursued in the courts than hitherto both in England and Wales as well as Scotland.

Alternative dispute resolution has been slow to have an impact in Scotland,[126] partly through the defensive posture of the legal profession,[127] as well as the legal culture engendered by legal education limitations.[128] Various areas have experimented with alternatives to taking cases to court including commercial issues[129] and construction disputes.[130] Any expansion of either commercial or domestic mediation, one would infer, will have an impact on the formal justice system. This, of course, poses problems for citizens' rights since the central point of mediation is the securing of a settlement rather than vindication of legal rights. In areas like family law, recent research in family disputes suggests that this trend to mediation may well deny people the rights they are entitled to since mediation undercuts securing those rights.[131] The Court Reform (Scotland) Act 2014, however, makes no direct reference to ADR. It will be interesting to see whether the early confidence that the growth in mediation will not impact on the crucial question of lawyers' income is borne out eventually.[132]

Design Issues in the Future

One advantage of a radical overhaul of the locations in which the justice of the future can operate is the possibility of considering design issues and other factors that did not feature 150 years ago when so many of the courts in the current system were built. The changes in technology with the recording of sound and televising of proceedings did not exist. Nor were security concerns a prominent factor. These are issues that Mulcahy discusses in her examination of the English court system.[133] In chapter 5, we also mount a discussion of the effect of recent design changes regarding horizontality, the closure of galleries, and so on; use of glass barriers; and the effect of these changes on the acoustics and sight lines in the courtroom. We then take that discussion further to the deeper issues of democracy, inclusivity, trial before one's peers, and public acknowledgment of and participation in the judicial process. The awaited publication of new Design Guides may offer substantial clues as to how the Scottish Courts and Tribunal Service and judiciary envisage the physical organization of spaces in the new justice centers to come.

These current and projected changes in the estate of the justice system and its design can best be critiqued in terms of their significance and scope in a comparative exercise with other judicial systems across the globe. Resnik and Curtis point out that by the end of the twentieth century "many court systems focussed on 'long range planning'" and that there was a "'quiet crisis' of aging facilities in poor condition, and growth in caseloads and prison populations."[134] We have already noted in chapter 5 the massive and ambitious program commenced in the 1990s by the French Ministry of Justice to rebuild much of its estate, and among the similar programs instituted by many other jurisdictions; the long-standing example of the US Design Excellence Program could be an instructive example.

In comparison with the French process of commissioning modern court buildings, which has made for open public dialogue and debate on the relationship of architectural and design forms to the culture and processes of justice, the design of recent Scottish courts has hitherto been bound by convention and uniformity. Again, as noted above, this is due to a procurement policy in Scotland that has directed design via the templates to be found in the Design Guides produced by the Scottish Court Service. In their "What Is a Court" report, the JUSTICE working party make a claim for a similar "overstandardization" of design in the courts of England and Wales. The report asserts that "As the *Court Standards and Design Guide* has developed, spatial requirements have become more rigid, and furniture more fixed, in ways that make the flexibility we suggest impossible."[135] They go on to say in conclusion that use of centralized design via Design Guides "represents a technocratic rather than a 'performative' brief."[136] As such, it appears that debate may have been stifled by bureaucratic control, and there has been little expression of any design "ambition" on the part of court authorities. In the French case, however, architects were left a great deal of freedom to use their own professional expertise to examine and explore the issues that here are regulated by the Scottish Design Guides. In France that "ambition" of the government also led to the commissioning of some of the top architects to design new buildings (see Richard Rogers, Jean Nouvel, and Henri Ciriani as described in chapter 5); the spending of six billion francs on projects from 1995–1999 and the public profile gained by their designs ensured that debate on the relationship between design and architecture and justice was given an open public airing (see chapter 5). In Scotland, meanwhile, the tendering, commissioning, and design processes have tended—with one or two exceptions, like Glasgow sheriff court—to be very low profile, with few architects of well-established national or global public profile taking part, and little public awareness or debate about the processes or outcomes. It could not be said in general, however, that keeping the design and building of new public buildings low profile is currently a dominant governmental or cultural trait in Scotland. There have been numerous notable instances of high-profile well-established architects, of both national and global provenance, who have been commissioned and completed public buildings over the past couple of decades, including Enric Miralles's Scottish Parliament, Zaha Hadid's Transport Museum, and Steven Holl's new Glasgow School of Art building. That high profile has also ensured that there has been much public discussion and debate over the success or otherwise of those buildings. It remains to be seen whether the project to create sixteen new justice centers in Scotland will aim at or encourage a similar open and public process of procurement and debate on the design of new buildings. It would take a great change from the current culture both of tendering and commissioning, and of vision and ambition, to achieve such transparency. It appears, for the moment, that despite the fact we are on the cusp of making great changes in the physical extent and form of the Scottish court system, neither the client, the Scottish justice system, nor the architectural profession has the appetite to make the design and production of great public buildings a matter of public urgency.

It is, however, just such a culture of vision and ambition that characterizes recent expansion of the estate of the court system in the United States through the Design Excellence Program. The ambition is expressed there not only in the conscious effort to create important buildings but to involve the legal, architectural, and governmental professionals together as well as the public. Between 1996 and 2006 forty-six courthouses or annexes were built at a cost of $3.4 billion. A diverse range of world-class architects have been involved in the projects, including the American Richard Meier, the Argentinian Cesar Pelli, and the deconstructivist avant garde group Morphosis. This has come about in several ways that can be examined by looking at the roots of the Design Excellence Program and its engagement across society.

The Design Excellence Program (DEP) was set up in 1994 by the body that procures public buildings in the United States, namely the General Services Administration (GSA). On its website the DEP declares that its roots are in the Guiding Principles for Federal Architecture, which were published in 1962 in an initiative by President John F Kennedy:

> These principles stated that the government should (1) produce facilities that reflect the dignity, enterprise, vigor, and stability of the federal government, emphasizing designs that embody the finest contemporary architectural thought; (2) avoid an official style; and (3) incorporate the work of living American artists in public buildings.[137]

To achieve these aims the DEP instigated a rigorous, engaging, and transparent program to enlist the best architects for the job. In their recruitment program they organize charrettes to debate workshop issues like security and art and architecture commissioning with architects, landscape designers, and urbanists. Then, during the design process the work is continually peer reviewed for excellence by panels of experts in architecture, sustainability, construction contracts, landscape, and so on. To a certain extent, however, the ground for this open, collaborative approach had already been tentatively prepared by the American architectural profession itself. In the 1970s the American Institute of Architects (the equivalent of the Royal Incorporation of Architects in Scotland or the Royal Institute of British Architects) sponsored an "Academy of Architecture for Justice" group. Since that time this group has convened meetings; held international conferences (e.g., the

2007 New York City "Sixth International Conference on Courthouse Design"); made awards for best buildings and designs; and published a journal, the *Justice Facilities Review*, since the early 1990s.[138]

The result of the program has been to provide prominent, successful public buildings, like the Boston courthouse (1998) by Pei, Cobb, and Freed Architects and the Sandra O'Connor US courthouse in Phoenix, Arizona by Richard Meier, whose "siting, form, layout and materials express the fundamental democratic principles of equality, fairness, openness and accessibility."[139] The success of the program seems to be appreciated as much by architects as it is by the clients, as is evidenced in citations by architects involved such as Richard Meier, "This is a program that clearly looked to architects to achieve excellence in design," and Kieran Timberlake, "There is an insistence in fairly equal terms that the architecture for the government of the US both perform and that it be beautiful and be moving."[140] But such successes are surely possible only because of the vibrant, transparent, and broadly accessible and participatory culture of courthouse design, building public engagement that has been undertaken by all the professions involved and coordinated largely by the Design Excellence Program. This public culture of understanding, appreciating, and participating in the design and building of the justice estate is sustained and encouraged by the DEP through their very public-facing activities, their website, their initiatives like making films, and in publishing glossy color monographs showcasing the individual buildings completed by architects as works of significance.[141]

It is thus that as far as Scotland is concerned, while the program of current court closures and the project to move to a more concentrated system of sixteen justice centers from the more even geographic spread of sheriff courts constitute a plan for great administrative and organizational changes (along lines common to "many court systems since the late twentieth century" as described above by Resnik and Curtis), there seems to have been no corresponding shift in the conception of the design and procurement of the physical estate of the judicial system. Unlike the United States, in Scotland there has been no nurturing of a public culture of the courthouse as an important civic institution, no outreach (films for public consumption, user-friendly websites, etc.), no publication program (disciplinary journals and glossy monographs on new buildings), no engagement in debate and discussion through a program of charrettes, workshops, and conferences, nor any lobbying of government for specific funding whether by the judiciary, the courts, administration, or the architectural profession.

In his October 2014 budget speech the then Scottish Finance Secretary John Swinney announced that three sites had been identified for the building of the first new justice centers.[142] The project was to cost £60M overall, and the sites were in Inverness, Airdrie, and Kirkcaldy. Nine months later the press revealed that the projects were being delayed because the Scottish Courts and Tribunal Service was "unable to raise the capital it needs to have a stake in the projects."[143] The new plan was that the justice center "schemes could be delivered over a longer period of time as capitally funded schemes, as and when money becomes available."[144] In the light of such disappointing news, the more recent announcement (in August 2016)[145] that the commissioning of the first new justice center for Inverness is going ahead seems to signal an upturn in the situation. Unfortunately, the details of the project do little to allay the fears, as outlined above, of a relative lack of vision for the building of new courts in Scotland. The £23 million building will be completed in 2018 and will house a "unique centre of community justice and support services for witnesses, victims, accused and those convicted in courts situated on a former bus depot near the city's Burnett Road Police Station. The most disappointing factor in the commission is that the project will not be architect-led."[146] There has been none of the decades-long wooing and nurturing of architects as seen in the American and French cases, no attempt to illustrate and debate exemplary design through various formats—publication, conferences, and so on. Instead, a construction company was first appointed, Robertson Construction, and they in turn appointed the Edinburgh-based architects Reiach and Hall on a design and build contract.[147]

Conclusion

The architect Stephen Quinlan expressed the view that the new Manchester civil justice center was not recognizable as a courthouse. Mulcahy paraphrased Quinlan's concern: "Devoid of the form, signs and symbols associated with this established building type, Quinlan's critique claimed that England's most important new court building rendered the notion of 'courthouse' meaningless."[148]

This challenge to what Graham claimed to be the certainty of external recognition[149] is one that stems from the very temporary nature of the split between political and judicial power. With the absorption of a broader range of legal, civic, and social facilities and functions in the planned development of justice centers, the movement seems to be away from self-standing, sole-function courthouse buildings and back to the mid-nineteenth-century model of a shared, multiuse facility under one roof, as seen in Scotland's most recent courthouse and council offices development in Livingston. As both Graham and Mulcahy demonstrate throughout their 2003 and 2011 works, in the context of England, and we have noted in relation to Scotland, the notion of "court architecture" is a heuristic device, albeit with different specific histories. Its demise, *pace* Quinlan, is something about which we do not feel much regret needs to be expressed, other than for the loss of some handsome buildings available for public functions. When considering the issue of the heritage and civic identity that courts might represent, the SCS was impassive:

> We recognise that, some communities regard the presence of a court, even one that sits infrequently, as an important element of each community's heritage and civic identity. However, this needs to be balanced against the fact that many other or similar communities function without a dedicated local court and both transport and media information services are vastly different from the Victorian period when many of the current courts were built.[150]

We are not too concerned at one aspect of these changes. We posed the question at the start of this study whether, in the twenty-first century, we should worry about the correspondence between the reality of actual experience of litigants, accused, witnesses, or jurors and its representations in popular culture. As we suggested, maintenance of a physically impressive setting, which is, in effect, an exercise of power, may be something that should be resisted. Gill in pursuit of saving money, certainly adds to the process of stripping away some of these decorative auxiliaries to power. Perhaps the artificial lighting and functional seating of the modern court are to be preferred to rooms that seek to evoke the majesty of the law with impressive ceilings and decorative courtroom furniture. It depends on what perspective one takes on the Resnik and Curtis suggestion that the courts are for the most part the settings for the exercise of power, cloaked in the language of legality. Whatever one's view of the procedure in the courtrooms of twenty-first-century Scotland, losing handsome buildings of historic pedigree and ornate internal settings might be regarded as a price worth paying for improvement in the legal process and a more efficient, humane, transparent, and democratic production of justice, even if it comes at the end of a computer screen linkup in a "pop-up" justice center.

Notes

1. Judith Resnik and Dennis Curtis, *Representing Justice: Invention, Controversy, and Rights in City-States and Democratic Courtrooms* (New Haven, CT: Yale University Press, 2011), 193.
2. Scottish Budget Draft Budget 2015–16, Table 9.01, www.gov.scot/Resource/0046/00462296.pdf.

3. M. Asimow, S. Greenfield, G. Jorge, S. Machura, G. Osborn, P. Robson, C. Sharp, and R. Sockloskie, "Perceptions of Lawyers: A Transnational Study of Student Views on the Image of Law and Lawyers," *International Journal of the Legal Profession* 12 (2005): 407–36.

4. Lord Gill, *Report of the Scottish Civil Courts Review* (Edinburgh: Scottish Civil Courts Review, 2009), Introduction per Lord Gill at i.

5. http://www.scotlandscensus.gov.uk/timeline-years/1961.

6. Lord Grant, *The Sheriff Court* (Edinburgh: Scottish Home and Health Department and HMSO, 1967), para 18 and appendix II

7. Grant, *The Sheriff Court*, para 18 and appendix II—Lanark; Lothian and Peebles; Aberdeen, Kincardine, and Banff; Ayr and Bute; Caithness, Sutherland, Orkney, and Zetland; Dumfries and Galloway; Fife and Kinross; Inverary, Moray, Nairn, Ross, and Cromarty; Perth and Angus; Renfrew and Argyll; Roxburgh, Berwick, and Selkirk; Stirling, Dunbarton, and Clackmannan.

8. Grant, *The Sheriff Court*, para 19.

9. Grant, *The Sheriff Court*, appendix VI, table III—prosecutions on summary charges rose from 45,437 in 1954 to 94,456 in 1965.

10. Grant, *The Sheriff Court*, appendix VI, table II—persons charged on indictment went from 1,347 in 1954 to 2,062 in 1965.

11. Grant, *The Sheriff Court*, appendix III.

12. Grant, *The Sheriff Court*, appendix IV, table I—994 petitions in 1954 and 1,368 in 1965; table II—General actions rising from 3,538 in 1954 to 4,138 in 1965.

13. Grant, *The Sheriff Court*, appendix VI, table I—persons charged on indictment rose from 178 to 258 between 1954 and 1965.

14. David *Turnock, The Wheatley Report: Local Government in Scotland (Oxford: Blackwell, 1970)*.

15. 1968/9, Cmnd 4150.

16. Local Government (Scotland) Act 1973.

17. Set up in 2001 and chaired by Sheriff Principal John McInnes; http://www.gov.scot/Publications/2004/03/19042/34181.

18. John McInnes, *The Summary Justice Review Committee: Report to Ministers* (Edinburgh: Scottish Executive, 2004), http://www.gov.scot/Publications/2004/03/19042/34181, chapter 4.

19. Grant, *The Sheriff Court*, para 1.

20. Grant, *The Sheriff Court*, para 1.

21. Grant, *The Sheriff Court*, para 31.

22. Grant, *The Sheriff Court*, para 32.

23. Grant, *The Sheriff Court*, para 32.

24. Grant, *The Sheriff Court*, para 32.

25. Grant, *The Sheriff Court*, para 39.

26. Grant, *The Sheriff Court*, para 39.

27. Grant, *The Sheriff Court*, para 39; on the issue of "trivial offences," see Z. Bankowski, N. Hutton, and J. McManus, *Lay Justice* (Edinburgh: Edinburgh University Press, 1987), 176–79.

28. www.scotlandscensus.gov.uk/; from 5 million in 2001—www.scotlandscensus.gov.uk/key-facts-2001-census.

29. Lord Gill, *Scottish Civil Courts Review: A Consultation Paper* (2007), www.scotcourts.gov.uk/docs/default-source/civil-courts-reform/scccompleter-(2)7CDD54ABAE89.pdf?sfvrsn=2, para 29.

30. Gill, *Scottish Civil Courts Review: A Consultation Paper*, iv.

31. www.scotland-judiciary.org.uk/34/0/Senators-of-the-College-of-Justice, by 2016, 32.

32. Local Government (Scotland) Act 1994 s 2.

33. Gill, *Scottish Civil Courts Review: A Consultation Paper*, 97, table 1.

34. Gill, *Scottish Civil Courts Review: A Consultation Paper*, 117, table 22.

35. Gill, *Scottish Civil Courts Review: A Consultation Paper*, 118, para 6.4.

36. Gill, *Scottish Civil Courts Review: A Consultation Paper*, 119, table 24.

37. Gill, *Scottish Civil Courts Review: A Consultation Paper*, 120, table 25.

38. The Justice of the Peace Courts (Sheriffdom of South Strathclyde, Dumfries and Galloway) etc. Order 2009 SSI 2009/332.

39. Peter Robson, *Housing and Judiciary* (Glasgow: University of Strathclyde, 1979), 45–60. This move to full-time degree study as an integral part of professional qualification is paralleled across the professions in Scotland at that time, for example, with the move to full-time degrees in architecture from the previous system of part-time study plus apprenticeship, and the Mackintosh School of Architecture at Glasgow School of Art offering a full-time course of study in architecture from 1968.

40. www.theyworkforyou.com/debates/?id=1960-07-13a.1531.1.

41. Gill, *Report of the Scottish Civil Courts Review*, x.

42. www.lawscot.org.uk/news/2014/11/number-of-scottish-solicitors-reaches-all-time-high/.

43. Gill, *Scottish Civil Courts Review: A Consultation Paper*, para 1.10.

44. Gill, *Scottish Civil Courts Review: A Consultation Paper*, para 1.10.

45. Gill, *Scottish Civil Courts Review: A Consultation Paper*, para 5.18; the need for changed attitudes including apology rather than simply money is a feature in real-life litigation, which Jan Schlichtmann fails to fully appreciate, with disastrous consequences, in A *Civil Action* (1999).

46. Gill, *Scottish Civil Courts Review: A Consultation Paper*, 49, para 5.21.

47. Gill, *Scottish Civil Courts Review: A Consultation Paper*, 50, para 5.24.

48. Gill, *Scottish Civil Courts Review: A Consultation Paper*, 51, para 5.28.

49. Gill, *Report of the Scottish Civil Courts Review*, 171, para 23.

50. Gill, *Report of the Scottish Civil Courts Review*, para 24.

51. Scottish Government, *Scottish Government Response to the Report and Recommendations of the Scottish Civil Courts Review* (Edinburgh: Scottish Government, 2010), www.scotcourts.gov.uk/docs/default-source/civil-courts-reform/scottish-government-response-to-the-report-and-recommendations-of-the-scottish-civil-courts-review.pdf?sfvrsn=2, 44, para 217.

52. Scottish Government, *Scottish Government Response*, 5.

53. Scottish Government, *Scottish Government Response*, para 102.

54. Lord Grant, *The Sheriff Court* (Edinburgh: Scottish Home and Health Department and HMSO, 1967), para 1; Term of Reference 2 covered "the number and distribution of sheriff courts"—see chapter 4.

55. Gill, *Report of the Scottish Civil Courts Review*, 249, recommendation 43.

56. www.scotcourts.gov.uk/consultations/docs/CourtStructures/ShapingScotland-sCourtServices.pdf.

57. Scottish Court Service (SCS), *Shaping Scotland's Court Services* (2013), www.scotcourts.gov.uk/docs/default-source/scs-consultation-court-structures/response_to_the_consultation_and_recommendationspdf.pdf, 10–13, para 1.31.

58. SCS, *Shaping Scotland's Court Services*, 16, para. 2.8 (a).

59. SCS, *Shaping Scotland's Court Services*, 16, para. 2.8 (c)

60. SCS, *Shaping Scotland's Court Services*, 18, para. 3.3

61. SCS, *Shaping Scotland's Court Services*, 18, para. 3.5

62. SCS, *Shaping Scotland's Court Services*, recommendations 4, 5, and 12.

63. SCS, *Shaping Scotland's Court Services*, recommendation 2, para 3.11.

64. SCS (2013) at para 1.2.

65. SCS, *Shaping Scotland's Court Services*, recommendation 1, para 2.8.

66. SCS, *Shaping Scotland's Court Services*, para 1.21.

67. SCS, *Shaping Scotland's Court Services*, para 1.19.

68. SCS (2013) para 1.5.

69. SCS (2013) loc. cit. at para 1.12.

70. Manchester justice center details available at https://www.gov.uk/government/organisations/hm-courts-and-tribunals-service.

71. Ministry of Justice, *Proposal on the Provision of Court and Tribunal Estate in England and Wales* (2015), https://consult.justice.gov.uk/digital-communications/proposal-on-the-provision-of-court-and-tribunal-es/user_uploads/reform-estates-national-consultation_official-sensitive_final.pdf, 11.

72. Ministry of Justice, *Proposal*; see also Max Chambers, Charlotte McLeod, and Ruth Davis, *Future Courts: A New Vision for Summary Justice* (London: Policy Exchange, 2014), http://www.policyexchange.org.uk/images/publications/future%20courts.pdf.

73. Although the Briggs Report, *Civil Court Structure Review: Final Report*, looks principally at the structure of English civil justice, its terms of reference include making "recommendations for the deployment of judges," which includes where this will take place—https://www.judiciary.gov.uk/civil-courts-structure-review/.

74. Ministry of Justice, *Proposal*, 9.

75. Ministry of Justice, *Proposal*, 9.

76. Ministry of Justice, *Proposal*, foreword.

77. Ministry of Justice, *Proposal*, 8.

78. Ministry of Justice, *Proposal*, foreword.

79. Ministry of Justice, *Proposal*, foreword.

80. Ministry of Justice, *Proposal*, 11.

81. See Selkirk in appendix, Court Gazetteer.

82. Kitty Cruft, John Dunbar, and Richard Fawcett, *The Buildings of Scotland: Borders* (New Haven, CT: Yale University Press, 2006), 339.

83. See Ayr in Gazetteer.

84. The tables and chairs at which the tribunal and the appellants are seated are in the body of the room at 90 degrees to the bench to lessen the perceived intimidation impact of the raised judicial seating.

85. Tribunals sit in Glasgow, Edinburgh, Stirling, Hamilton, Ayr, Campbeltown, Oban, Dundee, Aberdeen, Kirkcaldy, and Inverness.

86. Alexandra Marks, committee chair, *What Is a Court?* (London: JUSTICE, 2016), https://justice.org.uk/what-is-a-court/.

87. Marks, *What Is a Court?* i.

88. Marks op. cit. at para 2.5.

89. Op. cit. at para 3.12.

90. Op. cit. at para 3.15.

91. Known in Scotland as "contact orders."

92. Op. cit. at para 3.21.

93. Ibid.

94. Op. cit. at para 3.25.

95. Op. cit. at para 3.26.

96. Op. cit. at para 4.3.

97. Op. cit. at para 4.5.

98. Op. cit. at para 4.7.

99. Op. cit. at para 4.12.

100. Op. cit. at para 4.13.

101. Op. cit. at para 4.28.

102. Op. cit. at para 2.23.

103. Op. cit. at para 2.22.

104. Ministry of Justice, *Transforming Our Justice System* (London: HMSO, 2016), 6.

105. Ministry of Justice, *Transforming Our Justice System*, 6.

106. *The Scottish Legal System—What Next?* Parliament House, July 14, 2016.

107. There is a JUSTICE Scotland organization that exists in relation to the larger "UK" body. When last viewed its website consisted of seven pages with the London address and phone number given. There are brief discussions of various hot topics of the legal system there, but there is no addressing of the major changes to the court estate in the offing. https://justice.org.uk/justice-scotland/, last viewed 10/8/2016.

108. Daniel Muzio and John Flood, "Entrepreneurship, Managerialism and Professionalism in Action: The Case of the Legal Profession in England and Wales," in *Handbook of Research on Entrepreneurship in Professional Services*, ed. M. Reihlen and A. Werr, 369–86 (Cheltenham: Edward Elgar, 2012), 381.

109. John Flood and Peter Lederer, "Becoming a Cosmopolitan Lawyer," *Fordham Law Review* 80 (2012): 2513–39, 2513.

110. Touche Ross, Ernst and Ernst, KPMG, Arthur Anderson—Flood and Lederer, "Becoming a Cosmopolitan Lawyer," 2530.

111. John Flood, "Institutional Bridging: How Large Law Firms Engage in Globalisation," *Boston College Law Review* 54, no. 1 (2013): 1–35, 1.

112. Flood, "Institutional Bridging," 33.

113. http://www.heraldscotland.com/business/13071757.Six_Scots_legal_firms_included_in_UK_top_100/ and http://www.legal500.com/c/scotland/regional-review.

114. Flood, "Institutional Bridging."

115. See chapter 2 in this volume and SCS, *Shaping Scotland's Court Services*, para 130, and appendices to this chapter.

116. Richard Susskind, *The Future of Law: Facing the Challenges of Information Technology* (Oxford: Clarendon Press, 1996), 286.

117. Richard Susskind, *Transforming the Law* (Oxford: Oxford University Press, 2000), ix.

118. Susskind, *Transforming the Law*, x.

119. Richard Susskind, *The End of Lawyers?* (Oxford: Oxford University Press, 2008).

120. Susskind, *The End of Lawyers?* 271.

121. Susskind, *The End of Lawyers?* 273.

122. Susskind, *The End of Lawyers?* 278–284.

123. Susskind, *The End of Lawyers?* 279.

124. Gill, *Report of the Scottish Civil Courts Review*.

125. Woolf, Lord. *Access to Justice*, 1996.

126. R. Mays and B. Clark, *Alternative Dispute Resolution in Scotland* (Edinburgh: Scottish Office Central Research Unit, 1996).

127. B. Clark, *Lawyers and Mediation* (Edinburgh: Edinburgh University Press, 2012), 11.

128. Clark, *Lawyers and Mediation*, 51.

129. B. Clark and C. Dawson, "Scottish Commercial Litigators and ADR: A Study of Attitudes and Experience," *Civil Justice Quarterly* 26 (2007): 228–49, 234.

130. Clark, *Lawyers and Mediation*, 77.

131. R. Hunter, *Impact of Mediation on Divorce* (RCSL Conference, Andorra, 2016); T. Contioso, *Mediation and Divorce in Spain* (RCSL Conference, Andorra, 2016).

132. Clark and Dawson, "Scottish Commercial Litigators and ADR," 239.

133. Linda Mulcahy, *Legal Architecture: Justice, Due Process and the Place of Law* (London: Routledge, 2011); Linda Mulcahy, "Back to the Future? The Challenge of the Past for the Courthouses of Tomorrow," in *Architecture and Justice*, ed. N. Temple, J. Simon, and R. Tobe (Farnborough: Ashgate, 2013), 80–81.

134. Resnik and Curtis, *Representing Justice*, 193.

135. Marks, loc. cit. at para 3.8.

136. Marks, loc. cit. at para 5.17.

137. From Design Excellence Policies and Procedures, section 2.2 5, published 2016 by GSA, http://www.gsa.gov/portal/mediaId/219495/fileName/Chapter_2.action.

138. Resnik and Curtis, *Representing Justice*, 194.

139. Resnik and Curtis, *Representing Justice*, 161.

140. Both architects cited on the Design Excellence website, www.gsa.gov/portal/content/104455.

141. There are thirty monographs of courthouse buildings that can be viewed on the DEP website, and the film *Designing for Democracy: 20 Years of Design Excellence* can also be seen there: http://www.gsa.gov/portal/content/104455.

142. *Partnership Bulletin*, October 9, 2014, http://www.partnershipsbulletin.com/news/view/83271, last viewed 13/8/2016.

143. *Partnership Bulletin*, August 28, 2015, http://www.partnershipsbulletin.com/news/view/91059, last viewed 13/8/2016.

144. *Partnership Bulletin*, August 28, 2015.

145. Building Design, August 3, 2016, http://www.bdonline.co.uk/reiach-and-hall-wins-%C2%A323-million-scottish-justice-centre/5083000.article, last viewed 3/8/16.

146. Building Design, August 3, 2016.

147. Design and build contracts put a contractor in charge of the design of a project (for which they then appoint an architect) rather than the client appointing both an architect (to come up with an original design) and a contractor. In that sense there may be less design freedom with this type of procedure.

148. Mulcahy, "Back to the Future?" 71.

149. Clare Graham, *Ordering Law: An Architectural and Social History of the English Law Court to 1914* (Farnborough: Ashgate, 2003), 328–33.

150. SCS, *Shaping Scotland's Court Services*, para 1.24.

APPENDIX

Courthouse Gazetteer—Sheriff Courts Followed by High Courts

Aberdeen

Urban Situation

A successful trading port and the metropolis of the northeast, Aberdeen was made a royal burgh in the seventeenth century. It traded cloth and tea and was exporting granite by the eighteenth century. It grew rapidly in the nineteenth century with the fishing industry and since the late twentieth century, has boomed with the discovery and extraction of oil from the North Sea.

The sheriff court is housed in the town and county buildings on the Castlegate in the heart of Old Aberdeen. The building abuts the tolbooth, with a belfry, clock, and spire, and parts of which date from the seventeenth century. The sheriff courthouse shares its current facilities with the city council. The Castlegate was the original marketplace in the medieval city, first used as such in the twelfth century.

Architecture: Historic Scotland Listed Building, Category A

The town and county building is a five-story granite Flemish baronial building with a lofty tower of its own at the west end with four corbelled bartizans, clocks on each façade, and a spire. The building was completed in 1874 by Peddie and Kinnear. There are two conical roofed tourelles on the main façade, the ground floor has a full arcade, and there is also a dwarf arcade on the first floor.

Interior

In the interior the accommodation to the street façade, consisting of council chambers and reception rooms, is accessed by the grand stairway. The six

sheriff courtrooms sit in a jumble of extensions reaching out into the rear of the building, and a glass-ceilinged waiting hall joins the two sets of accommodation. The main courtroom, court one, sits parallel to the Castlegate frontage and is entered from the hall via a few short steps up to the rear of the public gallery on its west side. It is a full original timber courtroom, as in Perth, with a double height space and pilasters against the walls. There is a disused balcony over the low-raked public gallery and a timber canopy over the seat at the bench. Court six, further out the back, along an onyx columned corridor with archways, has some interesting features. It is on a completely horizontal level, has modern furniture, pilasters on the walls to a certain height, and Greek-patterned wallpaper above. The color Crown Coat of Arms is mounted on a mirrored panel, with a violet baize/felt panel below and a purple felt-covered canopy above.

Airdrie

Urban Situation

Airdrie was a small town with a weekly market and four fairs a year. It developed originally as a center of handloom weaving and had a population of 2,500 by the end of the eighteenth century. In the nineteenth century it boomed as local coal and iron ore deposits were dug out and worked in the town. In 1821, by a private Act of Parliament, it became a free and independent burgh of barony with all the powers of a royal burgh. The 1822 town house in Bank Street, designed by Alexander Baird, originally housed courtroom proceedings and is still in use. A separate sheriff court was constructed under private legislation in 1855. It was replaced after subsidence damage proved irreparable in 1874. This building was demolished and the site became a supermarket. The town has a current population around 36,000.

Architecture

The sheriff courthouse is in Graham Street, a principal road in the commercial and administrative center of town. It was originally built in the nineteenth century and still has many stone-fronted Victorian buildings, including banks, shops, and offices.

The sheriff courthouse is a low, flat-roofed series of blocks completed in 1974 by Lanark County Council Architects. The court originally was of white aggregate panels with a green slate-clad entrance tower bearing the Crown Coat of Arms. Renovation has spoiled the clean-cut cubist aesthetic of the building by cladding the whole in buff stone and render panels, and running a roof ridge across the front of the tower, defacing its verticality. Its characterless profile now resembles a supermarket or garden center in a retail park. A glass and steel porch is now added to the front entrance. The entrance area sits lower than the street and is obscured further by surrounding shrubbery. Given that this is a place where a chance but hidden meeting of legal and perhaps dangerous antagonists could take place, this is a highly questionable design, offering no defensible space via casual public surveillance (see also Dunfermline for poor design decisions).

Interior

The entrance hall to the court is, however, open and light, with a double-height, fully glazed elevation on the south side of the tower. There are five courtrooms in the building. The main and largest courtrooms are disposed respectively on north-south and east-west axes, and fortunately renovation did not despoil them of their fine original materials. They are both horizontal-floored oblong spaces with high-strip clerestory windows. The spaces have a somber and modern feel to them with black onyx walls behind the bench and the Crown Coat of Arms set against an oblong timber paneling that is topped by a broken pediment. The side and back walls of the court are also timber paneled.

Alloa

Urban Situation

Alloa, with a current population around nineteen thousand, grew as an eighteenth-century town with its own harbor and ferry port. It is the administrative center of Clackmananshire. Main industries included coal mining, brewing, and glassmaking; the oldest glassworks in Europe still on its original site is in the town. The port was closed in 1970.

Architecture: Historic Scotland Listed Building, Category B

The sheriff courthouse, built as the county and police buildings, stands on the gushet between Mar and Drysdale Streets. It stands opposite the mid-eighteenth-century Ochill House, a villa that was converted into the court and council buildings for use between 1844 and 1863. The town hall by Marshall in 1888 stands across the way.

With its eighty-foot pyramid-roofed clock tower, and its crow-stepped and string-coursed gable on the corner, the sheriff court forms an impressive ceremonial gateway to the town center. An eclectic mixture of Flemish-French Gothic and Scots Baronial style, this two-story building was completed in 1865 by Brown and Wardrop at a cost of £6,500. The disused broad basket arched entrance on Mar Street stands in the center of seven bays under an ornamental carved balcony with stone lions at each end. There are three crow-stepped gablets above the first-floor windows to the main courtroom. Each gablet has a finial, and the largest central gablet has a carving of the "Royal" Arms—that is, and strangely, not the Crown Coat of Arms, which validate the proceedings of a sheriff court with its motto "Nemo Me Impune Lacessit," but with the English motto "Dieu et Mon Droit."

Interior

Today, the entrance is by a door in the passage between the tower, with its multiple corbellings, and the extension in Drysdale Street, built in 1910 by John Melvin and Son. This extension, formerly the police station, is now an office of the Citizens' Advice Bureau.

On the ground floor there are offices and a small civil court. The main courtroom, which can accommodate up to six hundred people, stretches along the length of the first floor with the back of the public gallery to the main gable and its triple window facing out to the Mar and Drysdale Streets junction. The court was renovated in the 1990s but retains many original features including the open hammerbeam timber roof and the raked timber public gallery (with a sloped rather than a stepped passage to mount its height). There are niches on the wall to either side of the bench, and the Crown Coat of Arms is a stylized color frieze that sits high inside a cornice traversing the wall. Below the arms is a full-size portrait of Sheriff Tait by J. G. Gilbert, Royal Scottish Academy, who opened the building.

Arbroath

Urban Situation

Arbroath is an ancient settlement and is currently the largest town in Angus with a population around 22,000 although Forfar is the administrative center

for the district. Arbroath Abbey was founded and the town was made a royal burgh in 1178. It played an important symbolic role in the Wars of Independence. It grew as a center of production of flax and jute in the Industrial Revolution and was a large and important fishing port until the late twentieth century.

Architecture: Historic Scotland Listed Building, Category B

Arbroath sheriff court is housed across two contiguous buildings on the High Street, namely the town house and the Guildry building. It occupies the whole of the former building and only the upper floors of the second. The original sheriff courthouse was on the upper floors of a building a few yards along the road, at 80 High Street, but the sheriff court moved its business to the town house in the early 1970s and expanded into the Guildry building in 2000. The buildings are in the center of town and surrounded by commercial and retail activity on the High Street.

The town house is a two-story, three-bay neoclassical villa in gray stone, completed by David Logan in 1803. It originally housed the burgh chambers, has twinned Roman Doric columns flanking a Venetian window in the central bay of the piano nobile, and twinned pilasters at each end. There are blind parapets under the flanking windows, and an open parapet above with a solid wallhead containing a clock with drapes and swags above the entrance bay. The sandstone Guildry building has commercial use on the ground floor and an arch above the central bay on the first floor. The second floor has a sculpted panel in the middle bay below a diminutive pediment with a rotunda window. One of the two sculpted figures in this panel is Justice—but she was put there long before that part of the building switched from commercial to court use.

Interior

In the ground entrance hall is a floor mosaic of the Arbroath coat of arms underneath a heavy Scots Renaissance plaster ceiling. The courtrooms are on the first (of the town house) and second (of the Guildry building) floors. The main courtroom, court one, sits on a lateral axis across the main façade of the town house piano nobile, with light from all three windows there. The bench is to the north side (RHS facing the building), and there is an exceptionally large, colored crown coat of arms behind it. The jury box is to the interior (west) side of the court, and there is a disused balcony with a wrought iron balustrade above it. (This is a typical remnant from days as a council chamber.) The bar has glass panels separating the public gallery (which is not raked) from the well of the court. The courts were refurbished and opened in 2001 by Sheriff Principal R. A. Dunlop, Queen's Counsel.

Ayr

Urban Situation

Ayr commands an important position as an anchorage at the mouth of a river. It was made a royal burgh in 1205. In the nineteenth century it grew as

a fashionable seaside resort, and as the administrative center of the county it developed extensive suburbs. Its current population is around 47,000.

Architecture: Historic Scotland Listed Building, Category A

The sheriff courthouse is on Wellington Square, an area that is part of a Georgian new town development to the southwest of the original medieval town. It originally housed the county hall too, but the Ayr County council buildings were completed to the west side, facing the sea, by Alexander Mair in 1935.

The courthouse is a grand neoclassical two-story sandstone building facing the town across the vast square. It was completed in 1822 by Robert Wallace at a cost of £32,000. Its centerpiece is a tetrastyle portico, with a diastyle in antis as one enters the building. There is a balustrade on the wallhead and a stone dome with a lantern surmounting it. The jail just behind the building was demolished in 1931.

Interior

Inside the front door one is confronted by the staircase, a sandstone spiral inside an eight-column Doric peristyle, with a robust newel consisting of one smaller sandstone cylinder surmounting a larger and topped by a brass tripod and bowl. The staircase goes to the first floor under the coffered ceiling of the dome, with an oculus to the lantern, all set out like a mini-Pantheon. The courts are set out around the circular landing at this level with the two main courts to north and south, respectively, and modern courts three and four in an extension to the west. These modern courts are fitted out in cherrywood with black marble trim and have clerestory windows on the west elevation.

Court one, through a consoled door to the south, is an Ionic-columned oblong plan room (with six columns down its length) with a small oblong flat-roofed skylight. The bench is to the pilastered west with the Crown Coat of Arms against blue curtains and an armorial stained glass window on the north side. The main windows to the courtroom are on the main façade behind the public gallery, which is not raked.

Court two, to the north of the stairwell, is the former county hall with a similar skylight. It has coupled pilasters behind the bench on the west and a frieze at the east end behind the public gallery.

Banff

Urban Situation

Banff is an ancient established settlement but did not receive its charter as a royal burgh until 1372. It prospered through Hanseatic trade. There are many grand houses of the local aristocracy—including the splendid Baroque Duff House—who would winter in the town in centuries past. It has been described as Edinburgh in miniature by author and former Dundee United captain, Neil Paterson, who was raised in the town. Its current population is around four thousand.

Architecture: Historic Scotland Listed Building, Category B

The sheriff courthouse sits on Low Street, which is the civic and administrative center of the town and county. The council offices are at the opposite end of the street, as is the Mercat Cross. The court building sits on the site of the former house of Lady Gight (see the plaque on the courthouse wall). She was Byron's grandmother, and he often visited. Johnson and Boswell stayed in a hotel that formerly sat directly opposite.

The sheriff court is a grand two-story blond sandstone Italian palazzo completed in 1871 by James Matthews. The prominent three central bays containing the entrance are fronted by a twin Ionic-columned tetrastyle porch topped with a balustrade. There is also a parapet above the arched upper-floor windows.

Interior

The main courtroom sits on a lateral axis across the ground floor, with three windows along the elevation to the back of the building. It is thus on a north-south orientation, with the high bench to the left/south as one enters the courtroom. There are still charming original features in the court. The raked benches of the public gallery are inserted as one large timber piece of furniture onto the otherwise horizontal floor of the room. Thus, like court two at Perth, one has to mount a steep ladder/stair at the row end of each pew to access public seating. The witness box is of the high curved canopy type seen in the Court of Session and at other sheriff courts, such as Hamilton and Stirling. The coat of arms is set in front of pink drapes behind the sheriff.

Campbeltown

Urban Situation

Originally Kinlochkilkerran ("head of the loch by the kirk of Ciarán"), it was renamed Campbeltown since it became part of Campbell lands in the late seventeenth century. The town, created a royal burgh in 1700, later became an important port for fishing, shipbuilding, and exporting whisky. The main quays were built in the eighteenth century. The population rose

in the nineteenth century from 7,003 in 1801 to 9,749 in 1881. The quays were further extended in the late nineteenth century. The current population is around 4,800.

Architecture: Historic Scotland Listed Building, Category B

The sheriff court is at the top of Castlehill, which is a continuation of Main Street running uphill in a southwest direction from the central harborside area. Main Street, the principal shopping area, has several large hotels and hostelries, and the town house, originally completed in the mid-eighteenth century, with a tower and steeple, but much added to through the ages.

The courthouse is a two-story crow-stepped gabled gothic building in rough-faced red sandstone completed by David Cousin in 1871. Its front façade has three bays, with a central tower containing a gothic-arched entranceway, flanked with dwarf columns, and a machicolated belfry.

Interior

The interior was refurbished in 1989, and on the ground floor there is accommodation for the sheriff clerk and faculty offices and witness rooms. The courtroom is at the back of the building on a lateral axis, with the bench to the right (east) on entering. There is a paneled vaulted ceiling and three small clerestory windows above the bench. There are full-length windows on the elevation behind the jury box (north) and the public gallery. The same dark paneled timber is used throughout. There are four rows of public seats across the breadth of the court; they are not raked.

Cupar

Urban Situation

A central market town in Fife with a population of around nine thousand, Cupar was a site where the medieval government of the three estates sometimes sat, and it became a royal burgh in the fourteenth century. The town functioned as the market town for the surrounding farming country. The 1815 county buildings and sheriff courthouse in St. Catherine's Street were complemented by a classical-style jail built to a design of James Gillespie Graham at around the same time, which today functions as a restaurant in Coal Road. After eight hundred years as the seat of a sheriffdom, the last sheriff court case was heard on May 29, 2014 before the court shut its doors for good.

Architecture: Historic Scotland Listed Building, Category B
St. Catherine's Street is an important broad, early-nineteenth-century neoclassical thoroughfare leading directly into the heart of town. The sheriff courthouse is flanked on the terrace by the county buildings and the county buildings extension. The terrace ends with the leaden dome and cupolaed town hall (1817 Robert Hutchinson to a James Gillespie Graham design) at the Mercat Cross. Banks, hotels, and the corn exchange also front on this street.

The courthouse is a five-bay tenement with a rusticated ground floor, which was converted to courthouse premises by William Burn in 1836.

Interior
The courtroom sat on a lateral axis across the first floor, with the bench to the east wall and the five windows along the side of the jury box and public gallery. It had a paneled segment-vaulted ceiling and anta-pilastered walls.

Dingwall

Urban Situation
A small market town with a vantage to sea-trading for its hinterland of Highland Glens, Dingwall was made a royal burgh in 1226. With a population of

5,500 it is the biggest town in the massive extent of the former County of Ross and Cromarty.

Architecture: Historic Scotland Listed Building, Category B

The sheriff courthouse sits on the east side of town, on the road leading to the harbor built by Telford in 1815–1817. This must have been an important situation on the main trade transport route. The railway arrived in town fifteen years after the court was completed, and its path cut the courthouse off from the main part of town (with a bridge running over the tracks) and the east-west lying High Street.

A castellated blond sandstone Tudor pile on the north side of Ferry Road, Dingwall sheriff court was completed by Thomas Browne Jr. in 1845 and originally used as the county buildings. The main tall gable housing the courtroom is flanked by smaller gables, each with two-story bay windows with finials above. Public entrance is by a door in the nearest of the two towers on the west side. The prison block of 1843 behind the court has been converted to housing.

Interior

The interior contains offices and auxiliary rooms on the ground floor. The main court sits on a longitudinal axis on the first floor, with the bench against the elevation of the main external gable. The court is striking in its many original features—bench, public gallery, jury box, and so on. The vaulted ceiling is impressive with its open timbers. While the room is not—unlike Inverness and Inveraray—in a semicircular plan, the public gallery is set out at a rake as a series of diminishing curves retreating upward from the well of the court. The dark timber benches have individual carved timber armrests/separators along their length. The walls to the public stairways to the gallery were decorated with full-size framed portraits, but they were removed when the court closed down.

Dumbarton

Urban Situation

Dumbarton (population around twenty thousand) is currently the administrative center of West Dunbartonshire council and was formerly the county town of Dunbartonshire. It is an ancient settlement around the castle atop Dumbarton Rock, and the town became a royal burgh in 1222. In the nineteenth century its position on the Clyde River allowed for expansion as a center of shipbuilding, whisky, and glass manufacture.

Architecture: Historic Scotland Listed Building, Category B

The sheriff court is on Church Street, close to Dumbarton High Street. It is beside a main junction and a modern traffic roundabout that leads to Glasgow. Important civic buildings situated at this junction include the Edwardian Baroque library of 1910, by William Reid, the eclectic medieval municipal buildings of 1903 by James Thomson, and the police station. The building used to house the council offices, but they moved out in 1965. The original two-story blond sandstone Georgian mansion sheriff court still forms the core of this building, but it has been much extended over the years. The original façade has a piano nobile with twinned Ionic pilasters and a pediment. Entrance is through a Doric porch on the rusticated ground floor. The slightly lower wings with balusters were added in 1898 by William Spencer. Further extensions to the east, forming the two legs of a U-plan, reaching back toward the old prison, were built in 1895–1898 by D. McNaughtan. A black marble extension T-form plan was inserted into the nineteenth-century U-plan, making the whole into an oblong plan, at a cost of £6M by Aedas Architects, completed in 2009. This extension provides office, administrative, jury, sheriff, and High Court judge accommodation. The old prison to the east of this new extension was demolished in 1973, and only some fragments of the wall and an arched doorway, bearing Dumbarton's coat of arms, remain.

Interior

All five courtrooms are housed on the first floor. The main courtroom, court two, is on a north-south orientation in McNaughtan's 1898 south extension. The Venetian window on its north side, behind the public gallery, no longer looks to the outside but is now a public entrance from a corridor of the 2009 extension/insertion. There is glass atop the bar separating the public from the dock. There are round-topped windows to the exterior on the south wall on either side of the bench. There are brackets for a canopy above the bench and a bracket for the mace when the High Court is in session. Court one sits laterally across the front of the first floor, with windows on the façade. It is the former council chambers and is completely at a horizontal level, although there is a disused small railed public balcony at a higher level on the south wall behind the rows of public seating.

Dumfries

Urban Situation

Sitting on the River Nith, the market town of Dumfries (population about 31,000) is in a strategic position in the southwest. It became a royal burgh

in 1186, and with its rich agricultural hinterland has long been the center of local government—currently of Dumfries and Galloway council.

Architecture: Historic Scotland Listed Building, Category B

The sheriff courthouse at the edge of Dumfries' New Town is in Buccleuch Street. This street was laid out as an elevated approach to the New Bridge, which was built as the main route over the river and to the west in the 1790s. John R. Hume says of Buccleuch Street that it is "the most pretentious in Dumfries." Next door to the court is the procurator fiscal's building and besides various banks and churches, the municipal chambers and the post office are to be found there too. The courthouse completed by David Rhind in 1866 cost £13,715, of which £6,069 was paid by the government and £6,967 by the county council, which originally used the building for its meetings too.

The sheriff court is a four-story neo-Baronial building of squared red sandstone rubble. Three stories rise above the street level with a bridge to the arched entrance, which has a heavy rope molding around it (just like Rhind's court in Selkirk). It has an asymmetrical frontage with a tower rising from a corbel above the main door, two bays with gablets above the wallhead on the east side, and one bay with an open balustrade at the wallhead on the west. It is a full-blown Baronial style, with stringcourses, dummy cannons, corbelled turrets at the corners, and copper roofs on all the towers. To the rear, on the southwest, is a five-story square plan tower, also topped with a balustrade and a turret.

Interior

There is one small court on the entrance floor beyond the reception and offices, and the main court two is on the first floor. At the landing on the way up to the courtroom, there is a colored stained glass of the Crown Coat of Arms. The courtroom has a heavy ornate plaster ceiling with two ceiling lights. Most of the timber features and fixings for the courtroom are recent, as a renovation program was carried out in the 1990s—the public gallery is reinstated at a raked angle, although the balcony is closed. There is a glass barrier atop the bar across the breadth of the court. The courthouse sits on the old riverbed of the Nith, and by the 1980s traffic vibration from the street had caused the building to lean. The Scottish Court Administration carried out a program of stabilization and upgrading of the whole building between 1991 and 1994.

It is interesting that the planning requirements for the architects, David Le Sueur, included

- segregation of public circulation space from court staff and officials,
- secure entry and detention area for defendants held in custody, and
- upgrading all mechanical and electrical systems.

In the renovations a new steel-framed roof was erected over the old rafters, securing the plaster ceiling and transmitting the weight of the roof vertically to the wallhead. The courthouse was reopened by a local MP and government minister, Hector Munro, on September 12, 1994.

Dundee

Urban Situation

Dundee, with a population of 147,000, is the fourth largest city in Scotland. A royal burgh since the thirteenth century, it developed as an important wool-exporting port on the Firth of Tay, in trade with the Low and Baltic countries. In the eighteenth century whaling became an important industry and provided vital ingredients for the process of jute fabrication, which was in turn the most important nineteenth-century industry (along with printing and publishing). Whaling from Dundee carried on until 1912, jute production slowed in the middle years of that century, and shipbuilding died out in the eighties. Electronics, high-tech industries, and digital design and medicine have now become the mainstays of the Dundee economy. Since 2013 Dundee has been unique among the long-established cities of Scotland in not hosting sittings of the High Court.

Dundee sheriff court is in the West Bell Street at the west end of Dundee's business district. Bell Street was laid out as part of an 1820–1830s' extension

of new straight streets to the north of Old Dundee and was named after Provost Bell, whose family (as part of Bell & Balfour) were merchants and flax spinners. The 1970s' former British Telecom building across Court Square houses temporary civil courts, and further east along Bell Street are Abertay University, the Dundee High School, and nearby the former Royal Exchange.

Architecture: Historic Scotland Listed Building, Category A

The sheriff courthouse is a blond sandstone two-storied Roman temple–fronted building completed in 1863 by William Scott, possibly from an original design by George Angus in 1833 that was not fully carried out. The Roman Doric portico has the columns standing on plinths protruding from the channeled stylobate, with stairs on either side. It has a nine-bay frontage, with pilasters flanking the three bays on either side of the portico. The upper floor has arched and keystoned windows, and the Crown Coat of Arms carved in the tympanum bears the two English mottos—"Dieu et Mon Droit" and "Honi Soit Qui Mal y Pense"—rather than the Scottish ones. There are extensions to the east and west, with the justice of the peace court in the three-bay pilastered pavilion to the east, which has a newer extension behind by Gauldie, Wright, and Partners in 1981. The smooth-walled courtroom extension to the west, with clerestory windows, was completed in 1996 by Nicol Russell Studios.

Interior

In the interior there are five courtrooms, four on the ground floor and court five on the upper. The entrance to the main courtroom, court one, is opposite the main entrance. Court one reaches northward into the depth of the plot with entrance on the south side behind the gallery and the bench on the north wall. It is a double-height space, with tall arched windows around three sides—north, east, and west—and a first-floor gallery (now closed) supported on slender fluted-Doric columns over the entrance to the room. It has a compartmented ceiling with decorative plasterwork on the beams.

Most of the timber fittings to the room are modern, and the glass paneling above the bar extends across the full breadth of the dock. There is an original plaster band around the walls marking the separation of the two levels, with a series of stucco roundels bearing emblems of Dundee (a vase of lilies), Scotland (thistles and lions), and Justice (the scales). The bench has a canopy over it borne up by consoles on fluted pilasters, and there is a row of diminutive halogen lights set in its underside. The bracket that formerly held the High Court mace is still fixed to the bench wall.

Dunfermline

Urban Situation

A former royal town and a center of medieval pilgrimage, Dunfermline became a royal burgh in 1588. It grew as a weaving town in the eighteenth century, and in the nineteenth century the surrounding coalfields brought wealth. Although it is still the most important settlement in Fife, with a population around fifty thousand, it is largely a dormitory town for Edinburgh now.

Architecture

Dunfermline sheriff courthouse is low key and unobtrusive; it sits surrounded by car parks, sunken and isolated by traffic from the town center on the High Street and East Port, on the north side of the busy dual carriageway, Carnegie Drive. Its nearest neighbor on the east side is the 1973 police station by Fife county council.

The sheriff court was completed by Public Service Agency Architects in 1983. It is a single-story brown brick building with peripheral mono-pitched slate roofs. Its plan form is of a main oblong block with an L-shaped extrusion on the west enclosing a courtyard between it, the main block, and Carnegie drive. The building sits below the road so that entrance down a flight of steps from the road brings one to an enclosed, isolated courtyard, shielded further from general view by the shrubbery at the roadside. This design (see also Airdrie) is not only the inverse of the public notion of a court entrance as seen in American films—broad, open stairways leading up to the busy civic space on high and open to all—but it also transgresses all the common sense of defensible space. What if a witness, a jury member, or a member of the public encounters a violent, aggressive, upset, or angry accused in this enclosed space hidden from any general or natural surveillance from casual passing citizens? This poorly designed entranceway seems to prepare the user of the court less for trial by peers than for braving it with a step into the unknown.

Interior

This enclosed entrance contrasts with the open car-park spaces around the other three sides of the courthouse. Indeed, the Scottish Court Service claims that this court is one of the most efficient in providing vehicular access for prisoner escort and court custody service.

In the interior there are four courtrooms. One smaller one sits in the long arm of the L-branch, while the procurator fiscal's office is in the foot of that part. The three courts sit in series with their longitudinal axes parallel to Carnegie Drive and their benches at the east end. The largest courtroom—court one—is to the north. With timber paneling all around, a glass-topped bar the full width of the court, and exposed timber beams in the roof, there is an open Scandinavian feel to the space. There are eight rows of public seating, which rises only two broad steps in rake. The Crown Coat of Arms is set against a timber latticework, and there is one high window above it.

Dunoon

Urban Situation

Dunoon, with a population around eight thousand, is the largest town on the Cowal Peninsula of Argyll and Bute. It grew from being a small fishing center to become a tourist destination in the late nineteenth century because of its easy accessibility on the Firth of Clyde to steamers from the centers of population around Glasgow. It is also important as a center of public administration, and until 1991 a large American naval base was situated in the nearby Holy Loch.

Architecture

The sheriff court is in the narrow George Street in the town center. The court building, a two-storied Jacobean villa with dormers of an attic floor, was completed in whinstone rubble with red sandstone dressings by James McKissack in 1900. The off-centered entrance gable has a round arched entrance with keystones, a full first-floor height mullion, and transomed window with a balustrade balcony in front and is topped by a pediment with a carving of the Dunoon arms in the tympanum. The stained glass in the main window also contains a central pane with the galley of the coat of arms, with thistles in all the other panes around it.

Interior

The main first-floor courtroom sits on a lateral axis at the back of the building with a large arched window at the north end behind the six raked rows of the public gallery. There are also four windows on the west side behind the jury box and to the side of the public gallery. The court has many of its original timber features intact, including an open timber roof with three beams and the coat of arms held on a chamfered timber panel behind the bench. The dock now has glass panels separating it from the public gallery. There is a postwar extension leading to the disused prison at the rear of the building.

Duns

Urban Situation

Duns (population around 2,500) is an ancient market town that has also intermittently—in the seventeenth and again in the twentieth century (until 1975)—been the county town of Berwickshire. It was created a burgh of barony in 1490, and it became the location for holding the sheriff court.

Architecture: Historic Scotland Listed Building, Category B

The sheriff courthouse sits on Newtown Street, a broad thoroughfare that sits to the north of Old Market Square and runs roughly east-west. The courthouse shares a building with the council (Council Contact Center) and is next door to the police station of 1895. The town library, Free Church, and former British Linen Bank are also to be found among the fine sandstone buildings on Newtown Street.

The sheriff court is a two-story blond sandstone Jacobean building completed in 1855. It has three bays with triple light windows—both upper and lower floors in each bay—apart from the central bay entranceway. There are gables with louvered attic openings above each end bay and a gablet over

the central bay. All the gables are stepped at the base, and the doors and windows have hood moldings. There is a 1970 extension to the east, which has the entrance to the council accommodation.

Interior

The main courtroom is on the first floor to the rear of the building, with the axis running south-north longitudinally into the plot. The bench is to the north wall. Entrance from the southeast is at the back of four horizontal rows of public seating. The courtroom is modern with no original features, and there are four windows along the west side.

Edinburgh (Sheriff Court)

Urban Situation

Edinburgh is the second largest city in Scotland (population around 490,000), but as a former royal city and the location of the centers of the national church, legal system, education system, and government, it has for several centuries been the capital city of the country.

Architecture

The sheriff court, first established in Edinburgh in the twelfth century, has been held in numerous locations throughout history, including the Castle; the tolbooth from the fourteenth century; Parliament House from the 1800s; and more recently, the purpose-built Lawnmarket courthouse, now converted for High Court use only. (See Edinburgh High Court of the Justiciary.) The current sheriff courthouse is in the heart of the old town. Built on lands formerly owned by Heriot Watt University between Chambers Street and the Cowgate, it reproduces the closed courtyard view of the Parliament House/Court of Session from George IV Bridge, albeit in a more utilitarian fashion.

Edinburgh sheriff courthouse has an eight-story sandstone façade in an eclectic mix of Scots medieval and Renaissance and classical details with a French-style mansard roof and was completed in 1994 by the Property Services Agency. Fitting to the irregular, tight site in the old town, it is in an inverted F-plan form, with both arms pointing backward to George IV Bridge (and forming that visible courtyard mentioned above between them), the entrance in the underside of the lower arm across a setback courtyard from Chambers Street, and the top of the F sitting along the Cowgate. It cost £47 million to build and is the second busiest court in Scotland.

Interior

Entrance from Chambers Street is through brass gates to the courtyard, and then through channeled stone archways under curved glass roofs one comes in at the fourth level because of the height differences between the Cowgate and Chambers Street. Descent from the foyer to the third level then brings one to the base of the long, thin spine of the plan with its right angle. This spine is a full-height glass ceiling's atrium, which in appreciation of both the narrow footprint and the historic site, has been designed as a reproduction of an old Edinburgh close. Thus, external materials—sandstone and polished granite—have been used here in the interior of the atrium, and its tall walls have overhangs and oriel windows, just as one would have seen in the closes. The materials and the bare uncluttered spaces (with no unfixed furniture) are reminiscent of the simple geometry of public circulation in the Glasgow sheriff court—but not as opulent.

There are sixteen courtrooms in the building. Three of the four main jury courts are on level five and one on level six; all are accessed by bridges across the atrium. The courtrooms have light-colored timber fittings, and the galleries are either on the horizontal or only slightly raked with two or three broad steps. Again, like Glasgow sheriff court, some courtrooms have stucco-encircled Crown Coat of Arms (e.g., court three), while others have the more usual color relief fixed to the wall (see courts ten and four). The courtrooms on the upper floors (levels five and six) have no natural light, while on level three there are small windows on either side of the sheriff on the wall behind the bench. Some of the courts have glass paneling atop the bar.

Elgin

Urban Situation

Elgin is an ancient settlement that has been a royal burgh since 1130. The now ruined cathedral was begun in the same century, and the medieval town was an important religious center with Dominican and Franciscan houses established. It became an important administrative and commercial center in the nineteenth century, and the railways arrived in 1852.

Architecture: Historic Scotland Listed Building, Category B

The sheriff court building sits in the heart of Elgin at the east end of the High Street. It sits beside the administrative buildings of Morayshire council.

The court building was completed in 1866 by A. & W. Reid. It is a two-story, five-bay blond sandstone Italian *palazzo*. McKean (p. 26) opines

that while "baronial" was the fashionable style in Scotland at that period, neoclassicism "quite rightly" still ruled in Elgin. The lower-story façade is of channeled stone, with the main public entrance on the central bay. The upper has tetrastyled, paired Ionic columns supporting a wallhead above with paired dwarf Ionic pilasters. The vermiculated quoins at each end emphasize the foursquare regularity of the building.

Interior

On the interior there are clerks' offices on the upper floor. The main courtroom is on the ground floor with entrance opposite the main door. The courtroom is on a longitudinal axis leading into the depth of the building. It is a light double-height space with arched windows at the upper level—three behind the bench on the south side and four on the long elevation to the west. There are many original features in the courtroom and the bench; the public gallery and witness, press, and jury boxes are all of one timber. The walls on the lower level are also timber paneled, and the eight rows of public timber benches are raked at a low gradient. The most striking feature in the room is the canopy above the sheriff's chair, which is crowned by a very delicate type of rococo fretwork pediment.

Falkirk

Urban Situation

Falkirk, with a population of around 35,000, is the largest town in the former central region. It developed early as an important center for production of iron and steel when both the Union and Firth and Clyde Canals were built in the eighteenth century. Recently, it was deindustrialized but remains a significant retail and administration center.

Architecture

Courts of justice have historically been held in various locations in the town, including the Red Lion Inn on the High Street, Wilson's building opposite the steeple, and a Temperance Hotel in Bank Street. The first purpose-built sheriff court was completed on the corner of Hope Street in 1868. The police station is next door, but the sheriff court is now occupied by a funeral undertaker's business. The new sheriff courthouse is now on Main Street outside the suburb of Falkirk in Camelon.

The sheriff courthouse is a long, two-story, red sandstone building extruding a central entrance rotunda, with an aggregate concrete colonnade along the ground floor (as a peristyle in the rotunda). It was completed in 1990 by Robert Matthew, Johnson-Marshall and Partners, and sits back from the street raised above a flight of steps. It has a series of string courses running the length of its main first-floor façade.

Interior

The four courtrooms are laid out on a lateral axis along the back of the building with a broad corridor to the street side. The public galleries have a very low rake of two broad steps, and light is brought into the courtroom by clerestory windows. There is glass paneling across the top of the bar and the walls are wood paneled to a height of around three meters. The first floor is accessed by a marble staircase. There is a public café in the rotunda on the first floor. A plaque on the wall commemorates the May 1991 opening of the building by government minister Lord James Douglas Hamilton.

Forfar

Urban Situation

The county town of Angus (formerly Forfarshire), with a population of around 14,000, originally became a royal burgh in the twelfth century. It

became a weaving center in the early Industrial Revolution and became known for production of jute. The railway arrived in 1839 from Arbroath, and although there is currently no railway station in Forfar, its football club, Forfar Athletic, plays at Station Park.

Architecture: Historic Scotland Listed Building, Category B

The sheriff court sits on Market Street in the leafy suburbs of the town to the north of the center. The former sheriff courthouse, built in the 1820s sits in the center of town beside the town and county hall.

The two-story plus attic eclectic Baronial/Tudor sheriff court of squared sandstone rubble was completed in 1871 by Brown and Wardrop (see Stranraer). It is on a shallow U-plan with crow-stepped and crocketted gables at each end and a gablet above the central entrance. From its prominent high position it looks south over the town. The wall of the Baroque staircase up from the street bears a distinctive memorial plaque to the Polish Army, which was in Forfar in World War II. The main entrance to the building has buttresses and consoles supporting a balustrade balcony with quatrefoil openings to the central window on the first floor. The windows have squared hood moldings, there are stringcourses between the floors, and gryphons sprout from the high corners of the end pavilions.

Interior

The sheriff clerk's office and small civil court two are on the ground floor. The main courtroom, court one, sits on the first floor laterally across the building with the high timber paneled bench to the west side and the windows of the main façade on the south. There are many original features to the courtroom, including the timbering and the flat hammerbeam roof. The seating in the slightly raked public gallery is a more modern insertion. The Crown Coat of Arms is mounted against purple drapes and surmounted by a timber cornice above the bench. The door to the balcony above the main entrance is between the jury box and the public gallery. The sheriff's seat has the date 1870 carved on it, and there is a Forfar armorial panel on the bench wall.

Fort William

Urban Situation

A strategically placed settlement in the battle of various regimes and dynasties for the control of the West Highlands, Fort William is the only major settlement between Oban and Inverness. The railway arrived in 1894, and the population is currently around ten thousand.

Architecture

The sheriff court stands at the south end of the High Street. All the commercial, tourist, and administrative facilities are found on this street, which ends with a railway station at its north end.

The courthouse is a two-story, chunky gothic building of blond sandstone rubble completed by Matthews and Lawrie (see also Lochmaddy and Portree) in 1877. Entrance is on the ground floor of a three-stage corner tower, with a steep slated roof surmounted by ironwork railings and finials. There are stringcourses on the facades and hood moldings around the windows. The molding on the main doorway is terminated at each end with carvings of royal heads.

Interior

The main courtroom is on the first floor occupying the length of the building, with the three main windows on the main north façade behind the four rows of the public gallery (at a slight rake of only two steps). The Crown Coat of Arms is etched onto the middle window of the southern façade. The bench in front of it is the only original fitting that remains after refurbishment in the 1980s and again in the 1990s. It is in a dark-stained Gothic paneled wood with quatrefoils and other carvings.

Glasgow (Sheriff Court)

Urban Situation

Glasgow is the largest city in Scotland with a current population of around 600,000. A former center of fishing, it grew in the nineteenth century with shipyards, iron, steel, print, and locomotive works. In its postindustrial age it is now a center of media and culture, administration, education, and finance.

Until 1986 Glasgow sheriff court business took place in the former county buildings and courthouses, where it had shared accommodation with the county offices and the Merchants' House. This building, completed in 1841 by Clarke and Bell has been much extended and adapted over the years and finally occupied a full block between Wilson and Ingram Streets in the center of the city. A sandstone Greek Revival building, it has a hexastyle Ionic portico on Wilson Street with a frieze on the stylobate by Walter Buchan that depicts a jury trial in a classical era.

Architecture: Historic Scotland Listed Building, Category B

In 1986 a new freestanding sheriff courthouse was completed by Keppie Henderson and Partners on a riverside location, 1 Calton Terrace, in the

Gorbals on the opposite (south) bank from the city center. The Gorbals was a largely Victorian residential suburb, reworked in the postwar period as a working-class housing estate, and currently undergoing a third regeneration. The courthouse is easily accessible by bridges—vehicular and pedestrian—from the city center, and a subway station is nearby at Bridge Street. There are twenty-one courtrooms in the building, and folk legend has it that the courthouse is the busiest in Europe, but the provenance or accuracy of that assessment is not clear.

The sheriff court is an oblong plan building sitting up on its own plinth from the river and obscured on south and east sides by surrounding plantings. It is clad in Durham Cat Castle blond sandstone, and its in-situ concrete frame is expressed on the exterior by a framing in polished deep brown Danish Moselokke granite. Despite the restriction on height due to the neighboring listed three-story Georgian terrace, the courthouse manages to dominate the surrounding area. The building cost £30 million and was the first postwar court facility in the country to be given listed status.

Interior

The entrance is in the middle of the frontage facing onto the Clyde and leads into a full-height 10-meter-broad atrium, which runs laterally through the breadth of the building and has bridges crossing on the upper floors. A semicircular reception area in the atrium faces the entrance and sits below Jake Kempsall's sandstone bas relief depicting St. Mungo and the social history of justice in Scotland. The interior is clad in Hopstonwood and Wirksworth limestone and polished marble. The ceilings in exposed coffered concrete are painted to blend with the honey color of the limestone. It is no surprise given that the architects are professional descendants of the office for which Charles Rennie Mackintosh worked. The building was completed at the height of the "Mackintosh" style years, and much of the interior detailing in terms of gridded timber screens, black lacquer work, clocks on the first floor, and even the general formal tension between the circular voids and square patterns evidence a distinct Mackintosh influence. The atrium stairwells and public spaces have no moveable furniture, but rather fixed marble benches, which together with the height and polished surfaces, imparts a clean, bold geometrical ambience to the interior.

There is a hierarchy of position and dimension in the spatial organization of the courtrooms throughout the building. The principal and largest jury courtrooms are double-height spaces reaching longitudinally north-south into the building on the entrance and the first floors, with the benches at the southern end. The fixtures of the courts—the bar, jury and witness boxes, and dock—are set out in boxy orthogonal forms in Wenge (a dark hardwood from Zaire), while the benches are also made from that timber or from marble. Other materials include limestone and white rendered plaster walls. In some courtrooms the Crown Coat of Arms is a stucco relief in an enclosing circle on the wall behind the sheriff—as in courtrooms seven and nine—while on others a more usual three-dimensional color version hangs on the wall—as seen in the appeals court on the second floor. The courtrooms on the second floor are arranged in two halls that both sit on the same longitudinal axes as the main courts below. There are six courtrooms to each of these halls, three each side, leading off on a lateral east-west axis. The halls themselves are fitted out in limestone, and each courtroom has a freestanding marble doorframe marking its entrance. The courtrooms in the basement have a slightly cramped feeling due to their lower ceilings. The public galleries at Glasgow sheriff court are either at the horizontal or at a very gentle rake (one or two broad steps). None of the courtrooms have natural light.

Greenock

Urban Situation

Greenock's first major expansion came as a port in the Atlantic trade after the Union of 1707. It thrived in the nineteenth century and grew wealthy with several harbors, shipyards, and engineering works. New populations flooded into the town from the Highlands and Ireland, and new gridded sub-

urbs were built by the middle classes beyond the original center. Its current population is around 44,000.

Architecture: Historic Scotland Listed Building, Category B

The sheriff court was originally held in the town hall before moving to Bank Street. The current sheriff court sits on Nelson Street, a broad thoroughfare at the edge of the West End, which began to be built up from around the

1830s (despite original planning in the 1770s). There are several other fine nineteenth-century buildings on this street, including the St. George's North Church, the Old Kirk, and a fine modernist building in the 1973 eight-story-tall former James Watt College.

The courthouse, completed in 1867 by Peddie and Kinnear, is a bulky blond sandstone Baronial building with a central tower flanked by symmetrical three-story wings. The building is decked out with an assortment of carved baronial paraphernalia—corbelling, crow steps, bartizans, and arched windows. The four-stage tower is topped by a pyramidal roof with a lantern and has a bartizan corbelled out at each corner. The main entrance is on the base of the tower. Each three-story wing has three gablet dormers and a bartizan at the end corner. The side elevations show two crow-stepped gables ending the twin roofs. A single-story modern extension housing court two was added to the north by PSA Architects in 1980–1981, in plain blond sandstone with a cubist style proliferation of vertical and horizontal cutaway corners and chamfered sills. The court was reopened "following Major Refurbishment and Extension" by Lord Fraser of Carmyllie, Queen's Counsel and Minister of State for the Scottish Office on October 17, 1994 (brass plaque). The prison formerly adjoining the court was used until 1910.

Interior

There are four courtrooms in Greenock. The principal courtroom, court one, sits laterally across the back of the building on the ground floor. The public entrance to the courtroom is at the southwest corner behind the public gallery. There are several original features in the courtroom. The public benches, in four rows at a slight rake, are dark timber and sit below a disused first-floor balcony, which is supported by two slender Doric columns from the front pew. There are two tall arched windows behind the bench, and there is a timber canopy over the sheriff's seat.

Haddington

Urban Situation

A burgh and a market town, receiving its burgh status in the mid-twelfth century and with a population around nine thousand, Haddington is the main administrative center for East Lothian. It played a role as an important urban center in medieval Scotland.

Architecture: Historic Scotland Listed Building, Category A

The modern-day sheriff courthouse is on the south side of Court Street, a broad square-like street leading west from the apex of the medieval High Street. The town house of 1748, at the angle of the High Street, was built to a plan by William Adam and housed the original sheriff court, council chambers, and jail. The modern-day sheriff court is part of the county buildings, with administrative offices, and the police station is farther west along Court Street.

The county buildings are a two-story blond sandstone Tudor building with mullion and hood-molded windows completed in 1832 by William Burn. The entrance through a depressed archway is marked out on the façade by a corbelled oriel window on the first floor surmounted by a gable. The main staircase rises in this bay. A brass plaque on the outside wall tells us the site was once occupied by a royal palace and that King Alexander II was born there on August 24, 1198.

Interior

On the ground floor are council offices and entrance to a marriage suite under a panel with the names of past conveners, county clerks, chairmen, and chief executives of East Lothian county council. The stairwell to the first-floor sheriff court accommodation is decorated by full-size portraits: Walter George Hepburne Scott, Baron of Polwarth and Lord Lieutenant of East Lothian, 1937–1944; Sir Archibald Buchan Hepburn, convener of the council, 1909–1929; and George Hay, Eighth Marquess of Tweeddale and Lord Lieutenant of Haddingtonshire (1787–1876). There is also a bust on a pink granite column of James Andrew Broun-Ramsay, First Marquess of Dalhousie and MP for Haddington, and a plaque of the arms of Dunbar from the HMS *Dunbar*.

The main court, court one, sits on a lateral axis at the back of the building on the first floor. It has windows on its south side, and the high bench is on the west side with the Crown Coat of Arms on wood paneling behind. The fixtures are modern with glass between the dock and the horizontal seating in the public gallery. Prisoners coming to the dock are brought from a door on the east wall behind the public gallery, along a passage cutting between the gallery and the south wall. The small no-jury court two on the west side of the building has an unusual public entrance point at the side of the bench on the south wall, where the small public gallery is against the north, hard by the front windows.

Hamilton

Urban Situation

Although not the eponymous county town of Lanarkshire, Hamilton, population around 48,000, derives its regional importance from its long period as the seat of one of the premier noble families of Scotland, namely, the Dukes of Hamilton. Indeed, the Duke of Hamilton was appointed the first sheriff of

Hamilton in 1455 by James II. Originally a market town and later a weaving center, Hamilton grew in the nineteenth century as successive dukes developed coal mining on their land.

Architecture: Historic Scotland Listed Building, Category A

The main sheriff court building is at the junction of Almada and Beckford Streets. This situation is around one kilometer to the northwest of Hamilton town center, but important civic institutions in this area include the council buildings (opposite), a campus of the University of the West of Scotland (farther along Almada Street), and the railway station Hamilton West. Hamilton is said to be the third busiest sheriff court in Scotland. This main building is used only for criminal business, while civil business takes place at Birnie House (built 2006) situated in a nearby business park (on Caird Park). The main building formerly housed both the sheriff court and county hall. When Lanarkshire County council built the modernist skyscraper opposite in the early 1960s, the sheriff court took over their accommodation in Beckford Street. The former entrance to county hall is now the main public entrance to the sheriff court. The entrance on Almada Street is now closed.

The two-story sandstone Greek Revival Hamilton county hall and sheriff court was completed by John Lamb Murray and his assistant Henry Francis Kerr in 1882. The two conjoined nine-bay blocks have central tetrastyle Ionic porticos and bays on either side separated by Roman Doric pilasters.

The block facing Beckford Street was formerly county hall, and that on Almada Street, the original sheriff court.

Interior

There are seven courtrooms in Hamilton sheriff court, with two main rooms, courts one and two, on the first floor. Entrance through the portico on Beckford Street brings one into a foyer with stained glass on the north and south walls. The north glass shows the Lanarkshire constabulary coat of arms, and the south window, Saint Kentigern as a child. On the stairs to the first floor, there are two more stained glass windows at the half landing: another of Saint Kentigern with his iconography and one of the coat of arms of Airdrie (a shield bearing a double-headed eagle). There is also a portrait of Allan Graham Burns Graham, Esq., of Limekilnburn, convener of the County of Lanark, by J. Coutts Michie, Royal Scottish Academy (October 1908).

Court one is the original sheriff court. It sits with its longitudinal axis pointing out to Almada Street, with the bench at that south end. There is no rake to the public gallery, and the original timber fixings throughout have a distinct dark hue. The high bench has the Crown Coat of Arms behind it contained in a panel with an aedicule bearing the date and initials of the monarch: "18VR87." The witness box has the distinct old-style curved canopy above it, as seen in the Court of Session.

Court two, the former chambers of the county hall, sits laterally across the first floor above the Beckford Street entrance. The oak timbers in this court are lighter in hue than in court one. The splendid deep relief stucco ceiling and cornicing with swags, fasces, relief coat of arms, and gold leaf detailing was uncovered from above a 1960s' lowered ceiling and restored by Oberlanders Architects as part of their £2M refurbishment in 1992. There is also a bust of Queen Victoria in the cornicing above the false balcony gallery opposite the bench. The public gallery is not raked.

Inverness

Urban Situation

Inverness has a population of around 54,000 and is the administrative center of the Highland region and has had city status since 2000. It was created a royal burgh by 1214. Its strategic position at the mouth of the River Ness means it has been at the center of much historic upheaval in Scotland, with battles fought and sieges carried out in the fourteenth-century Wars of Independence, the seventeenth-century religious wars, and the eighteenth-century Jacobite risings.

Architecture: Historic Scotland Listed Building, Category A

The sheriff court occupies a hill—on Castle Street—dominating the town, which had been the site of a medieval castle and fort. The castle was destroyed in 1746 by Charles Edward Stuart.

The sheriff court is housed in two castellated forts built on the hill where the former castle stood. The main building, in ashlar stone housing the sheriff court, is farther south, and the northern building, in rubble stone, is on the town's center side and houses the sheriff and district courts.

The main two-story building with its four corner towers with machicolated parapets (the southwest tower is round planned and the other three, square) was completed in 1835 by William Burn. It has arched windows on both floors and a smaller round plan tower on its east side near the current public entrance. There is a statue of Flora MacDonald, 1899, by Andrew Davidson, outside the mainly disused formal front entrance on the south. The three-story north building was originally completed as the jail by Thomas Brown in 1848. It has a proliferation of towers on its northwest side, with two octagonal plan towers, one with machicolations to its parapet, the other without, and a tall slender circle planned tower. The wall linking the two buildings, replete with bartizans and these towers, was designed by the civil engineer Joseph Mitchell.

Interior

There are three courtrooms in the south building and two in the north. The main courtroom, court one, is on the ground floor of the south building. The public side entrance to the building ruins the promenade that would have been experienced by entry from the original main south entrance to the arcaded foyer at the foot of the imperial stairway rising up under a coffered tunnel vault ceiling. In a niche at the center of the landing, erected in 1852, is a bust on a pink granite column of William Fraser Tytler, Esq. (1777–1823), lieutenant and convener of Inverness County council. The main courtroom is underneath the stairs to the north. The courtroom is hemicircular in form—unique in Scotland since Inveraray sheriff court closed in 1954—with the bench at the north side and the public pews curving concentrically with the walls. There are many original features in the court including the Tudor Gothic canopy above the bench. The courtroom underwent a refurbishment that included the installing of carved oak gable ends to the public benches. The work won a 1985 Carpenter's Award for the very best in British furniture making. There are three clerestory three-light windows, one above the bench and one on either flank over the disused balcony.

Jedburgh

Urban Situation

Jedburgh, with its population of around four thousand, is the former county town of Roxburghshire. It is an ancient settlement, which being only ten miles from the English border was of strategic national importance. It was a religious settlement from early on, with an Augustinian community, and the abbey was built in the twelfth century. The town became a royal burgh by 1214. The town was a center for cereals and flour milling and later for textile production. Much of the textile making ceased in the 1950s, and the railway line closed in 1964.

Architecture: Historic Scotland Listed Building, Category A

The sheriff courthouse sits on the central square, Market Place, and turns the corner into the old main street of Castlegate. Next door on Castlegate is the police station, and the library is farther up the hill. Some houses from the seventeenth and eighteenth century remain. Next door to the courthouse on the square is the impressive Newgate with its 36-meter-high pink ashlar tower with a clock face, a broad spire, and a weather vane. The lower stages of the building are harled and have a pend through to the courtyard with "Entrance to Bridewell Jail" inscribed above, then a sign "Newgate 1755"

and a colored armorial panel with the date 1720 set in the wall. The building dates from the 1750s and served as the county and remand prison for the court until it was replaced by the castle jail (still at the top of Castlegate) in 1823. The Newgate was also formerly used for the court, and it communicates with the first floor of the current courthouse.

The Jedburgh courthouse was originally built on Market Square on the site of the older county buildings in 1812. The court was then extended in 1862 by David Rhind. It is a two-story blond sandstone (quarried from the abbey) Greek Revival building. The current public entrance is in the middle of the three Doric pilastered bays to Market Square. The former and more obvious entrance was by the arcaded porch on the Castlegate. The original courtroom was on the first floor, marked by the three arched windows. Rhind added the three similar Doric bays to the south (next to the police station), which is where the current court is (although these three bays do not light it—it only has windows to the rear (or east) facing the abbey). There is a plaque on the Market Place wall to Walter Scott by Alexander Carrick, set in 1937. Scott made his first court appearance as a defense lawyer in Jedburgh in 1793.

Interior

On the ground floor is the sheriff clerk's office, and on the first floor the main court is at the south end. The courtroom has the bench to the west and windows only on the east side facing the abbey. There are many original timber features in the diminutive courtroom, including an upper-floor public gallery (now shut), raked timber pews on the lower level, and the dock with a timber railing surround. There is a large press box on the sheriff's left hand (the north wall), and above it is a full-size portrait. A black and white photo of James Paterson (1928–2010), who was sheriff in Jedburgh, Selkirk, and Duns, 1963–2000, also hangs on that wall. The decorative plaster ceiling to the courtroom has two long skylights, which compensate for the lack of windows.

Kilmarnock

Urban Situation

Kilmarnock grew as a weaving town through the eighteenth and early nineteenth centuries. A plentiful supply of coal in the surrounding area made the town into the industrial center of Ayrshire later in the nineteenth century, and the railways arrived in 1843. It has a current population around 46,000 and is the second largest town in Ayrshire after Ayr itself.

Architecture

The current sheriff courthouse sits on the corner of Dundonald Road and St. Marnock Street, opposite the former sheriff courthouse, a Greek Revival Temple of Corinthian order of 1864 by William Railton (now the procurator fiscal's office). The court is next door to St. Marnock's Church completed in 1836 by James Ingram, with the 1970s' police station next again.

The sheriff court was completed and opened by Sir Malcolm Rifkind in 1987. It was designed by David N. Gregory for the Property Services Agency. It is a modern oblong plan building clad in red sandstone with one of the smaller elevations set back from St. Marnock Street containing entrances. The western side is elongated along Dundonald Street to the south and north so that an entrance courtyard is formed to St. Marnock Street. The fenestration is contained within full-height voids on the entrance façade and down Dundonald Road. The façade bears aloft at the second-floor level a large brass version of the Crown Coat of Arms alongside the words "Sheriff Court House."

Interior

The entrance leads past the sheriff clerk's office to a slate-floored foyer area. Of the six courtrooms in this courthouse, there are three on this floor—two reaching farther south from the foyer and one on the west side. The two main jury courts—courts one and two—are on the first floor, accessed by the open stairwell in the middle of the foyer. These courts also penetrate deep into the south of the building with the bench at the south end. There is no natural light to these two main courts. Public entrance is at the north from the back of the public gallery, which has several rows of seats at a slight rake (two steps). The courtroom is wood paneled around the sides, and the Crown Coat of Arms behind the sheriff is in brass like the one on the outside of the building, with no coloring, which makes it difficult to distinguish details, apart from the distinctive outline.

Kirkcaldy

Urban Situation

Kirkcaldy has a population around fifty thousand and was an important trading port since the sixteenth century, having become a burgh in the 1320s. The major town of the central Fife area, it industrialized in the nineteenth century with linoleum becoming its principal product.

Architecture: Historic Scotland Listed Building, Category B

The sheriff court is on Whytecauseway on the southern edge of the great civic square, which has David Carr's Scandinavian-style town house of

1937 design (completed 1956) on its east side. This civic nexus is on the southwest edge of the commercial center of town, and the Whytecauseway itself joins with the High Street at the opposite (eastern) end from the courthouse.

The sheriff courthouse is an eclectic Baronial sandstone building completed by James Gillespie in 1894. A central balustrade tower with an octagonal turret houses the no longer used main entrance at ground floor and is flanked by a hexagonal pavilion like a baptistery on the east and a two-story gabled block on the west. The latter block is crow stepped with a carved lion at its apex, and it has a double-height Tudor window marking the situation of the main courtroom. Entrance is now through the angular concrete-walled extension completed by Property Services Agency in 1979. The wall of the extension with its pattern of projecting stones appears to be a modernist attempt to reproduce the massing effect of a medieval castle, and the tall full-height glazed stairways with curved copper roofs echo the turret on Gillespie's original building.

Interior

Kirkcaldy is the fifth busiest sheriff court in Scotland, and there are four courtrooms. The original courtroom, court two, is in the double-height space on the first floor of the nineteenth-century building. The large Tudor window is behind the horizontal public gallery, and the bench is against the wall on the south side. The courtroom has been renovated and retains few original features. The bar is of original timbering, though it is now topped with security glass.

There is an interesting use of space and material in the courtrooms in the extension to the courthouse. In all courtrooms there has been an attempt by the designer to utilize the same timber continuously flowing from bench to witness and jury boxes, dock and bar, such that through varying dimensions, positions, and height, the participant or viewer can easily read a coherent timber language of hierarchy and right. It is an interesting evocation and reproduction of the full-coherent timber nineteenth-century courtroom as still seen in court one at Perth or in the Court of Session. Court three is an oblong plan oriented on the diagonal, with the bench sitting in the southwest corner, the bar reaching from southeast to northwest diagonally across the room with the lozenge-shaped dock at its midpoint, and the public gallery against the east and north walls. Court one has a more normal four-square orientation, but entrance on the northeast corner leads to a diagonal timber-barred passage between the press box (on the east) and the gallery (on the west) directly to the dock.

Kirkwall

Urban Situation

In the medieval world the bishops and earls of Orkney, being distant from the power of Edinburgh—or Scandinavia—had quite a degree of independence. Kirkwall became a royal burgh in 1486. A typical stone-built Scottish town, with a population now around 8,500, was laid out in a herringbone pattern with perpendicular closes leading off a long main street/market place.

Architecture: Historic Scotland Listed Building, Category B

The sheriff courthouse constitutes the south side of Palace Gardens, an effective square formed between it, the ruin of the seventeenth-century Earl's Palace on the east, the ruin of the thirteenth-century Bishop's Palace on the west, and St. Magnus Cathedral across Palace Road on the north (and first constructed there in the twelfth century). These gardens originally formed the enclosure known as the "New Wark of the Yairds." In 1849 the intention was to move the jail, courthouse, and county buildings from the former town hall and renovate the Earl's Palace to accommodate them. David Bryce drew up plans to carry this out (his survey drawings formed the basis for McGibbon and Ross's "Reconstructed Perspectives"; see pp. 12 and 14 Burgher). There

were objections to the plans from the treasury on the grounds of excessive cost, but at any rate the project was dropped when the Prison Authority declared it "incompetent and beyond the powers of the Home Secretary" to allow a new prison to be accommodated in the new building.

A new building was thus designed by David Bryce, who died in 1876, and was completed in 1877 under the supervision of his nephew John Bryce. The two-story building has an asymmetrical façade with two crow-stepped gables to the east, one corbelled out over the projecting entrance bay, and two dormer windows to the west. On the west elevation is a large three-light window to the first-floor court. The front façade is finished in square-necked blond stone and the facades in squared rubble with ashlar dressings. Older armorial stones from elsewhere in Kirkwall have been reset into the walls bearing the crests of local bishops. The plan of the building is of an oblong court block with the adjoining police station and cells in an L-plan appended to the south.

Interior

In the interior there are sheriff clerks' and procurator fiscals' offices on the ground floor. The stairway to the first floor is marked on the exterior south-west corner where the L-block joins the court with a round tower. On the stair wall there is a framed photograph of Sheriff Alistair A. MacDonald and a gouache sketch of Lord Birsay, sheriff of Caithness, Sutherland, and Orkney. On the wall on the landing is a painted portrait of Andrew Gold, fifty-three years the chamberlain of the earldom of Orkney.

The court of the first floor sits laterally across the front of the building with the bench to an interior east wall. Much of the interior still has its original features, including the bench, witness and jury box, dock, and public gallery all in a light stained timber. The jury box sports inkwells for its members. All the timber-seating features—except the bench—are lower height than in the typical Scottish courtroom, giving overall a somewhat "dinky" feeling. There is a vaulted ceiling, a large three-light window on the west behind the public and three individual windows along the north side. The colored Crown Coat of Arms is interesting for its oversized carved timber form in heavy relief.

Lanark

Urban Situation

The county market town of Lanark (population nine thousand) became a royal burgh in 1140. It has a large agricultural hinterland. With the industrial development of towns in the north it lost its importance in the county.

Courts were originally held in the tolbooth of the High Street. The current sheriff courthouse is on Hope Street, next to the police station and nearby municipal library.

Architecture: Historic Scotland Listed Building, Category B

The sheriff courthouse consists of two buildings built at different dates, joined together. The northern part is a two-story seven-bay neoclassical building with a channeled stone ground floor and projecting central bay topped by a pediment with four engaged Doric columns on the first floor. It was completed in 1835 and housed offices and the main council chamber/ballroom on the first floor. The court shared facilities here and the prison was at the back. The southern building has five bays with similar cornice lines and channeling and a similar projecting section with arched windows at ground level, but it has a basement, a balustrade instead of a pediment, and pilasters instead of columns on the first floor. This building was completed in 1868 by John Johnstone. It housed the courtroom and sheriff court facilities and cost £2,654. In 1877 the cells were demolished as the Prisons (Scotland) Act 1877 resulted in all prisoners going to Glasgow.

In 2003 the sheriff court took over all business in the building and bought out South Lanarkshire council's interest. The architects, Oberlanders, carried out a renovation to the cost of £3 million. New circulation—stairs and lifts to the first-floor courts—was inserted. The first-floor entrance to the foyer outside the courts is from a glass-roofed landing through a sandstone archway. This feature was the former tender entrance to the fire station, which operated from the rear of the building between 1939 and 1957.

Interior

There are now two courtrooms in the building. Court one is the former council chamber and sits laterally across the first floor of the 1835 building with windows to the street. It has simple timber-paneled furniture, the colored Crown Coat of Arms is against the plain yellow painted walls, and the high ceiling has three roses and distinct cornicing. The original courtroom in the 1868 building is now the smaller court two.

Lerwick

Urban Situation

Lerwick, with its population of 7,500, has been a town only 350 years. It was founded as a fishing town. The nineteenth century saw great growth as

a herring fishing port. The discovery of oil offshore brought unprecedented growth to the town and Shetland in general, from the 1970s onward.

Architecture: Historic Scotland Listed Building, Category B
Courts were formerly held in the Lerwick tolbooth of 1767 on Commercial Street, and then moved to the former Fort Charlotte in 1837. From the 1860s onward Lerwick's rapid growth meant that there was no possibility of needed expansion in its overcrowded fisher-town closes, and a new town was planned on the hill above. The sheriff court and police station were one of the earliest

buildings in the new town. In the history of the town a rivalry with Orkney in civic terms is noted when the county buildings are cited, along with the Union Bank, post office, and Commercial Bank as examples of fine buildings without compare in Kirkwall's "street" (Thomas Manson "Lerwick during the last half-century," Lerwick 1923, p. 35). At the opening of the new courthouse in April 1876, there was a grand procession formed in the following order:

> Town Band, volunteers, Good Templars, Odd Fellows, Masonic Bodies, Police Commissioners, Town Clerk, Superintendent of Police, Burgh Officer, Sheriff Clerk of the County and His Depute, Sheriff of the County, Minister of the Parish, and Honorary Sheriff Substitute, Members of the Bar, Clerk of Works, Commissioners of Supply.
>
> A dinner was held in the Queens hotel that evening. (*Shetland Times* 1/4/1876, p. 3)

The court building on King Erik Street sits atop the hill in the new town opposite Alexander Ross's 1884 town hall. The 1970s' library is just along Hillhead. The courthouse presents a proliferation and variety of crow-stepped gables and gablets to the King Erik Street facade, with one gablet and three larger size gables, one with a chimney head, one with a finial (over the entrance), and one sporting a globe. The three main windows to the first-floor courtroom can be seen to the elevation on Market Street, below the slate roof with ironwork cresting across the ridge. To the north, along that street, is the slightly lower and bulkier range of similarly gabled buildings of the prison and the police station. The prison originally contained six cells each for male and female criminal prisoners, and one apartment each for male and female civil prisoners.

Interior

In the interior there are offices and administrative facilities on the ground floor. On the first floor the longitudinal axis of the courtroom is north-south, with the bench to the south. Original timber features are still present throughout. There are three rows of seats to the public gallery with no rake. Windows on the east and north sides bring much light into the room, prompting the *Shetland Times* to comment in 1876, "The room is handsome and well lighted and seems admirably fitted up for the purpose for which it is intended" (1/4/76, p. 3).

Livingston

Urban Situation

Livingston, planned in 1962, is the only Scottish new town with a sheriff court. With a population of 56,000, the town is the biggest settlement in the region and the administrative center of West Lothian.

The sheriff court shares a large new building, the West Lothian Civic Center, with the police and council offices. As such it recreates the common nineteenth-century practice of council and sheriff courts occupying the same premises. Livingston is a sprawling town, but the civic center is in the approximate center in Almond Park. The main shopping center is a short walk to the south, over a pedestrian bridge on the River Almond. The building is at the center of a network of footpaths, which also access the local hospital and theater.

Architecture

The West Lothian Civic Center is a vast freestanding sandstone, glass, and copper-clad building in open parkland, which was completed in 2009 at a cost of £53 million by Building Design Partnership. The entrance to the building is marked by a full-height copper rotunda and a porch. Immediately inside is a full-height broad atrium, which the architects call an "internal civic space." The sheriff court is on the top floor along the north side of this space. It is marked out by a silver panel bearing the lion rampant and "In Defens" motto beside its opaque glass front.

Interior

There are seven courtrooms in Livingston sheriff court. Six of them are laid out three to each side of the building: one, three, and five are accessed from the corridor running on the west side, and two, four, and six by the corridor on the east side. Courts one and two at the farthest north point in their respective corridors have brackets for the mace when the High Court is in session there. All the courts are horizontal with no rake for the public gallery. Courts three and four have an unusual orientation, with the public gallery stretching along the long side of the court between the bench and the dock (rather than behind the dock as is found in all other courts except Aberdeen High Court of Justiciary—another recently completed courtroom). This orientation of the dock at the extreme end of the courtroom is often found in England. The docks and benches in these two courtrooms are back under an inset, where the rest of the courtroom is double height. This orientation was chosen because—according to the Scottish Court Service—these courtrooms were originally intended to have "secure docks" (i.e., completely enclosed by glass screening). In the final fitting, however, the "secure" design was not fully carried through.

Lochmaddy

Urban Situation

Lochmaddy, with its population of around three hundred, is the principal town and the ferry port on the island of North Uist, and the most important administration center for all the outer isles south of Harris.

One history points out that "many of the village's finest buildings are linked to the law" (MacGregor p. 23). In fact, it specifies, "In the nineteenth century many large, grand buildings were built here, the base for a largely English-speaking professional class of fiscals, factors, sheriffs and sheriff clerks, solicitors, policemen and bankers" (p. 4).

The village of Lochmaddy is set out across a broad coastal area, and the sheriff courthouse is a half mile or so from the pier, but it sits next to both the old courthouse and the new police station. The old courthouse was built in 1827 and the new one was completed in 1875, but the cells from the old courthouse remained in use until 1891.

Architecture: Historic Scotland Listed Building, Category B

The sheriff court was designed by Matthews and Lawrie and is an eclectic Gothic Renaissance villa with beige rendered walls and sandstone dressings. The castellated surrounds to the doorways and the windows have arches that somehow do not stretch up to the full gothic peak.

Interior

The main triple lancet windows on the east and west facades mark the length of the main courtroom through the building. On the ground floor is the sheriff clerk's office and administrative accommodation. There is original timber paneling at the interior doorways. All signage is bilingual English-Gaelic.

In the main courtroom the bench is to the east with the triple lancet window behind. There are three windows along the north side with the jury box below. The court still retains the original light stained timber features, with a large dock, a Gothic arch pattern to the panels on the bench front, and four rows of pews on a low gradient rake for the public.

Oban

Urban Situation

Oban as a town came into being with the planning of a harbor in 1758 and the arrival of the customs house in the late eighteenth century. Its most rapid period of growth was the late nineteenth century, when it grew threefold between 1851 and 1891, along with the arrival of the railways in the 1880s and became a tourist destination. Its current population is 8,500 but can reach 25,000 at the height of the summer season.

Architecture: Historic Scotland Listed Building, Category B

The Oban sheriff courthouse stands on Albany Street, which runs off the main town square leading to South Pier. The long gray granite terrace of the

police station is next door on the south, and the blond sandstone Italianate palazzo of the former municipal buildings faces it across the street. Both these buildings were constructed in the same period, 1880–1890s, as the courthouse. Also on Albany Street, nearer the square, is the original post office building built 1910.

The courthouse itself is a two-story blond sandstone Italianate villa, which makes a handsome corner block with Campbell Street, completed by Ross and Mackintosh in 1888. It has a channeled ashlar ground floor and double-height round-headed windows on the piano nobile under a heavy parapeted cornice. The central entrance is marked out by a prominent blind balustrade with urns atop. Bilingual Gaelic-English signage throughout the building reflects the West Highland heritage of the clientele.

Interior

On the ground floor are administrative offices and the small modern courtroom. The main courtroom occupies the full piano nobile volume, sitting laterally to Albion Street with the bench at the south and public gallery to the north side. Entrance to the courtroom is unusual in that there are glass panes on the door and in the partition wall separating the first-floor landing from the courtroom itself. Thus, a certain part of the proceedings can be observed from without. The courtroom was renovated circa 1990 but has retained the dark wooden bench with Greek anthemion pattern and corresponding timber on the jury box and dock. Together with the tall round-topped windows on the sides, the high coved ceiling, and the egg and dart cornicing a certain Victorian ambience persists despite the renovation. The dock has glass paneling on three sides, and the public gallery is now at the horizontal with the three rows of blue cushioned seating.

Paisley

Urban Situation

In the hundred years from the late eighteenth century on, Paisley saw an expansion in size and population unparalleled in Scotland. Between 1735 and 1821 alone its population increased almost sevenfold as it became a major center for weaving and thread and textile mills. The current population is 76,000.

Architecture: Historic Scotland Listed Building, Category A

The sheriff courthouse is in James Street, in the North End, cut off from the historical and main commercial and administrative center of Paisley by the Glasgow to Greenock Railway.

The current sheriff courthouse consists of a series of adjoining buildings built at different periods by different architects. The original sheriff court was completed by Clark and Bell in 1885 and cost £22,000. It is a two-story blond sandstone palazzo with two Ionic pilastered pavilions joined by a recessed balconied Roman Doric loggia with a balcony. The court absorbed the next-door county buildings on the corner of St. James and Love Streets in 1979 after the county council (Renfrewshire) was abolished some years earlier. This building was also built by Clark and Bell, completed in 1890 for Renfrew County council for £32,000. It has a first-floor Ionic portico with a pediment on a channeled ground floor. Inside the portico, above the first floor is a stone frieze by F. W. Pomeroy. There are three parts to the frieze, with groups of allegorical virtues, mostly female—such as Charity, Justice, Law, and Order—gathered around the central figure of the county. The tenemental extension to the county buildings along Love Street was built by T. G. Abercrombie in 1910. The modern extension in red sandstone and brick

to the rear, facing Love and Glen Streets, was completed in 1997 by Baxter, Clark, and Paul at a cost of £9M.

Interior

There are nine courtrooms at Paisley sheriff court, five on the ground floor, three on the first, and one on the second. Entrance via the original sheriff court door brings the public into a large double-welled atrium with a staircase rising to the right (legend has it that it used to rise in the opposite direction). At the top of the stairs is a marble bust of landowner Archibald Campbell of Blythswood (1809–1868) dating from 1890 by local sculptor James Fillans (1808–1852).

The main courtroom, court one, is on the ground floor, reaching into the depth of the plot on a longitudinal axis. Public entrance from the atrium takes one immediately into the back of the public gallery. The court is a double-height space with Georgian windows around three sides (two times longitudinal and behind the bench) at first-floor level. The courtroom is fitted out in the original dark timber. The public pews in that timber are raked at a low gradient. The witness and jury boxes and bench are all of that same timber, but glass panels now separate the dock and the gallery. Behind the bench the timber paneling has four pilasters and a pediment above the sheriff so that she or he effectively sits in an aedicule. There is also a bracket attached to this timber to hold the mace when the High Court is in session.

Court eight is also notable in its delightful design features in having been the council chambers (before absorption of that building into the sheriff court). It sits inside the Ionic portico, and around the three interior walls above the dado runs a bronzed plaster frieze by John Rhind (1826–1892). It is in six sections, two feet high, forty feet in total length, with seventy human figures in scenes representing agriculture, the thread industry, justice, mining, boat building, and assorted other activities. There is a timber-lined ceiling with a rose in the center, doubled timber half Ionic columns stemming from giant socles around the walls, and the coat of arms in an aedicule bears the Renfrew County motto "Avito, Viret Honore"—"Flourishes in an Honourable Ancestry."

After major refurbishment the courthouse was reopened in 1997 by Lord Rodger, the Lord President of the Court of Session.

Perth

Urban Situation

At a strategic, navigable point on the River Tay, Perth, with a population around 47,000, became a burgh by 1130. It was an important center of religion, with Dominican, Carmelite, Franciscan, and Carthusian monasteries, as well as being a royal city with precedence over all towns, apart from Edinburgh. At the heart of a fertile agricultural hinterland, it had long been a wealthy town. Industry, commerce, and finance flourished after the railways arrived in 1848, and it has had city status since 2012.

Architecture: Historic Scotland Listed Building, Category A

The sheriff court is on Tay Street along the bank of the river in the heart of town. Tay Street was built up as a boulevard on an embankment in the nineteenth century, and many grand buildings—churches, hotels, and insurance offices present grand stone facades to the riverfront.

The sheriff courthouse is a long, low sandstone Greek Revival building with a frontage of thirteen bays, comprising two pavilions, north and south, flanking a Doric octostyle central portico. It is on an E-plan (with legs reaching to the west) and was completed by Robert Smirke in 1819. The building cost £32,000, and the portico itself between £300 and £400. The courtrooms were originally in the north end of the building and the county hall, or assembly rooms, in the south. This hall was also originally used for public functions like balls and although it is now converted to court offices, it still has original features like the white marble mantelpiece supported by fluted Doric columns topped by eagles. The jail to the rear of the courthouse was shut in 1968.

Interior

The main courtrooms are still on the ground floor on the north side of the building. Court one, on an east-west axis running deep into the plot was an oblong redesign of Smirke's semicircular room completed by David Smart in 1867. The courtroom retains most of those 1860s' features. It is double height with a coffered ceiling with decorative plasterwork and high arched clerestory windows around three sides. There is a balcony now closed to the public supported by iron leaf-capital columns. Otherwise, the court is furnished with pews and other fixtures in light-colored timber. The bench is on the west side with the seating in a broad arched recess under a canopy that reaches across the breadth of the court. The color Crown Coat of Arms sits under the overhang of the canopy.

Court two sits farther to the north also on an east-west axis, with the bench to the west wall in an arched niche flanked by pilasters. The original steep raked public gallery is a one-piece wedge-shaped furniture that has effectively been installed on an otherwise horizontal floored courtroom. Access to each pew is by a type of steep stair/ladder at the end of the row (see also Banff).

Peterhead

Urban Situation

Peterhead was established as a fishing port in the sixteenth century. It still operates as such but was given a great boost as a port by the North Sea oil industry from the 1970s onward. It is the biggest town in Aberdeenshire, with a population around 18,500. Her Majesty's Prison Grampian—a replacement for Peterhead Convict Prison—is situated in the town.

Architecture

The courthouse sits on the corner at a busy junction of Queen Street and St. Peter's Street. Courts had formerly sat in the tolbooth on Broad Street in the heart of Old Peterhead. The situation of the current court reflects its construction in a period of expansion: a lifeboat station was established in 1865, the railway arrived, the prison was built and opened in the 1880s, and the south and north breakwaters were massively extended around that period.

The sheriff court comprises two distinct parts—an original building by William Smith in 1869 and an extension with the introduction of a new courtroom, foyer spaces, offices, and toilets completed by LDN Architects in 2002. Smith's building to the east is a suburbanized Baronial construction, with crow-stepped gables and dormer windows. The entrance wing on the main L-plan block has corbelling, a balcony with wrought iron railings in front of the main first-story windows, and a stringcourse. The flat-roofed modern extension turns the corner southward in a stepped section with extensive glazing to the street frontage.

Interior

Public entrance to the court is now made only through the new building, flanked by a large glass panel etched with the Crown Coat of Arms. The new building is light and open, and a stairway leads directly to office and administrative facilities on the first floor.

Both main courtrooms are on the ground floor, the new one contained within the modern extension. The large criminal court sits laterally behind Smith's original frontage in an east-west orientation. It is entered from the rear (west), at the back of the public gallery on the north side. There is no natural light to this large, open courtroom. There are four rows of low raked public seating that sits behind the broad dock with glass panels, which has stairs leading down to the cells. The courtroom has wooden paneled walls and an unusual artex plastered ceiling, the latter giving it a "seventies" feel. The bench also has an unusual "modern" aspect because it is freestanding and built from squared stone blocks finished with a timber tabletop. It is the only stone built bench in Scotland. The sheriff sits in a slightly curved inset in the wall behind the bench.

The smaller civil court, added in the 2002 extension, runs north-south with the bench against the wall to Queen Street. It has similar timber and glass fixtures as the first court but makes interesting use of light from a clerestory looking to Smith's old building, and a vertical full-height translucent pane that joins the old and new parts of the building facing Queen Street; this glass is also etched with the Crown Coat of Arms.

Portree

Urban Situation

The planned village of Portree, now the main town on Skye, was built circa 1820 around the wharf and pier planned by Telfer. It has a population of around 2,500.

Architecture: Historic Scotland Listed Building, Category B

The sheriff court sits on the south side of Somerled Square, which is still the public heart of the town. The court sits next door to the two-story vernacular police station, and other public buildings on the square include banks, churches, and the masonic hall, as well as a hotel and a café. A war memorial of 1922 in the form of a traditional Scots mercat cross aims at enhancing the civic ambience.

The sheriff court is a two-story plain blond sandstone Italian villa completed in 1865 by Matthews and Lawrie. It has three bays to the square frontage, with a small pediment to mark entrance by the central bay. Urns

top the corners of the parapet. The building is much deeper than it is broad, and a former cell block adjoins it to the rear, fronting onto the street. The vehicular entrance to a courtyard formed between the courthouse, jail, and police station is also from that street.

Interior

On the ground floor are offices and administrative rooms. The main courtroom sits laterally across the breadth of the building, spanning the second two bays on the side elevation. There are thus two windows behind the bench on the east wall and two behind the public gallery on the west. The court was refurbished in 1994–1996 and reopened by the then sheriff principal on June 25, 1997. There is thus modern seating throughout the courtroom; the public gallery has four rows of unraked seating, and the jury box is on the south side against the wall. The court wall is timber paneled and the long Crown Coat of Arms on the wall behind the bench is set against a timber panel with a curved top. Signage in the court is bilingual English-Gaelic.

Selkirk

Urban Situation

Selkirk (population around 5,700) is an old town that has been a royal burgh since the sixteenth century. Originally known as a town of shoemakers, it expanded when textile mills proliferated in the nineteenth century, especially after the building of the railway in 1856.

One of the earliest purpose-built sheriff courthouses was completed on Market Square in 1804. Walter Scott served there during his period as sheriff of the County of Selkirk 1799–1832. That building and courtroom still exist and are currently refurbished as a museum. A new sheriff courthouse was completed by David Rhind in 1870 and is situated around the corner from the main square with the old court and town house. The prison of 1803–1804 was originally attached to the new courthouse by an underground passage below Ettrick Street. That former prison is now the local lending library.

Architecture: Historic Scotland Listed Building, Category A

The 1870 courthouse is a baronial building of bull-faced sandstone rubble, which with its heavy-rope-molded archway entrance (the hangman's rope?) and full-blown tall castellated style is very reminiscent of Rhind's Dumfries courthouse. There are three broad bays to Ettrick Street and a double-height oriel window above the doorway. There is a proliferation of corbelled bartizans and tourelles with pepper-pot roofs, chimneys, and crow-stepped gables, and a great circular plan five-story donjon with a pierced parapet rises on the northwest corner.

Interior

There are offices and a small civil court (modernized) on the ground floor, accessed by a bridge over the basement void to the entrance from Ettrick Street. The main double-height courtroom is on the first floor on the west side, with windows on that wall above the drop to Forest Road.

The courtroom has most of its original features including a fine open timber roof and a cast-iron fireplace. The bench is on the north side, and the jury box against the west wall. The door on the sheriff's right leads to the donjon, which at this level forms a circular jury room. In front of the dock there is a lozenge-plan delicate balustrade that surrounds the stairwell to the cells below. There are six rows of steeply raked seating in the original timber public gallery, now closed. There is a full-length portrait of the Duke of Buccleuch on the wall behind the bench and a portrait of his wife, the Duchess of Buccleuch on the wall behind the public (both from 1806), and on the east wall are portraits of Sir Walter Scott with his dog and Lords Napier and Ettrick.

Stirling

Urban Situation

Stirling is an ancient settlement clustered around a hillfort. Important geographically as a strategic site on the Highland-Lowland border, Stirling has been a significant town since medieval times. It was an important religious and royal center containing a royal palace and became a royal burgh in 1130. It is a market town (but with city status since 2002) and administrative center for local government with a population of around 45,000.

Architecture: Historic Scotland Listed Building, Category B

The original Stirling courthouse and jail were built next to the tolbooth in the early nineteenth century. The current courthouse is on Viewfield Place at the bottom of the hill near the main routes out of town and near the railway station.

The current sheriff courthouse, a three-story sandstone Baronial building with a piended platform roof topped by ironwork cresting was completed in 1876 by Wardrop and Reid to original plans (of 1864) by Thomas Brown. Two projecting wings with crow-stepped gables enclose the five-bay main block, which is surmounted by French dormer windows with segmental aedicules. There are stringcourses and hood moldings, and Scots Renaissance strap work atop the piano nobile windows on the wings. The central Gothic entrance porch has a depressed arch doorway and supports a balcony at the first-floor window. A small extension in copycat style was built to the north in 1912.

Interior

There are four courtrooms in the interior, with the main one on the lateral axis across the entrance on the first floor. It retains many of its original timber features, including a single timber open hammerbeam roof modeled on the sixteenth-century roof of the Great Hall at Stirling Castle, a canopy over the (south end) bench with the carved color Crown Coat of Arms perched in profile at the edge, a canopied witness box of the Court of Session type, eight rows of steep raked dark timber pews in the public gallery, and a curved bar (again like the Court of Session) of the same timber separating the public from the well of the court. Behind the public gallery there are three paintings on the wall. The largest central portrait is of Queen Victoria. The one on the east side is of Alexander Graham Speirs of Culcreoch (convener of the County of Stirling) by Sir Daniel MacNiece in 1878. There is also a painting of Sir Ralph Abercrombie of Tullibody, 1734–1801, who was MP for Clackmannan, on the east wall above the press box.

Stornoway

Urban Situation

Stornoway grew from the sixteenth century around a sheltered natural harbor. It is the biggest town in the Western Isles with a third of the total population. Twelve thousand live in the town, and it is the administrative center for the islands' council "Comhairle nan Eilean Siar." It is also a fishing port with an important maritime industry.

Architecture: Historic Scotland Listed Building, Category B

The courthouse sits in Lewis Street on the Victorian grid layout in the center of the town. Important commercial and administrative facilities are situated in this area.

The sheriff courthouse is a broad two-story sandstone Tudor building completed in 1843 by Thomas Brown Jr. (see Dingwall and Stirling). It presents four gables to the street with machicolated chimneys and a bellcote on the one farthest south. The central entrance porch has a hood-molded doorway.

Interior

The courtroom is on the first floor occupying the two gabled blocks to the south. There is an unusual orientation of the space and fixtures in this room. Public entrance is by a door on the north at midpoint in the length of the courtroom. The bench is against the west wall with the color Crown Coat of Arms hung against the middle windows, which face out to the street. The dock is against the east wall opposite the bench. The four rows of public gallery are on the north side (to the left or east of the door on entering) and thus have a lateral view of the entire well of the court from the bench to the dock. The jury box is against the south wall across the well from the public gallery, and the witness box is against the bench.

Stranraer

Urban Situation

Stranraer, with a population around ten thousand, is the biggest town in Wigtonshire. It is important even if it is isolated from other urban settlements. It

is the administrative and local government center, as well as a main ferry port on the route to Ireland. It was created a royal burgh in 1617.

Architecture: Historic Scotland Listed Building, Category B

The sheriff courthouse is on Lewis Street, a long nineteenth-century thoroughfare leading from the center of town to the main route to Portpatrick. Besides a terrace of Victorian houses, there are several churches on this street. The 1920 bronze War Memorial of a Fusilier on a Creetown granite plinth sits front and center of the building.

The sheriff court is a two-story Tudor villa in red Galashiels sandstone with blond Hexham stone dressings completed in 1874 by James Maitland Wardrop of the Edinburgh firm of Brown and Wardrop at a cost of £7,000. It has two main gables at the north and south ends and three gablets across the main façade, all crow stepped, and a spire with an octagonal belfry to the northwest. The central bay has a porch entrance with an open balustrade balcony above the main floor. There are corbelled chimneys topping the north and south gablets and a lion rampant on the middle one.

The building was formerly shared with the county council, and the main interior space, laterally spanning the first floor and formerly used as council chambers, for receptions, and as a ballroom, now has a lowered ceiling and is used for the small-sized court two and as office space. The disused balcony is hidden above the lowered ceiling.

Interior

The main courtroom, court one, is also on the first floor, and runs laterally through the building at the rear. It has an open beam ceiling, and there is glass above the bar to the well of the court. The public gallery is not raked.

The prison block at the rear of the courthouse was converted to other uses in 1882.

Tain

Urban Situation

Tain is a small, compact market town that became a royal burgh in 1066. It has a population of around four thousand.

Architecture: Historic Scotland Listed Building, Category A

The courthouse sits on the High Street right in the center of Tain. It abuts the tolbooth built in 1708 but which in style appears much older. The sheriff court replaced the former eighteenth-century council chamber.

Completed in 1849 by Thomas Brown Jr. it is in a two-story Scottish neobaronial castle with its bartizans, castellations, and corbelling. Yet its horizontality and general proportion import something of a Tudorish feel from Brown's recently completed Dingwall sheriff court.

Interior

There are offices and other administrative facilities on the ground floor. The main courtroom sits perpendicularly to the High Street, with the bench against the main façade. There are two pairs of long arched windows behind the sheriff and two single-arched windows behind the public benches. The court has been renovated, and there is now a very gentle rake to the public gallery. There is a coved ceiling with slender biomorphic cornicing, a ceiling rose, and two ceiling quatrefoils. All seating, apart from that at the bench, has dark green cushioning to match the lime green walls above the timber paneling.

Wick

Urban Situation

With a population of around 7,900, Wick is slightly smaller than Caithness's largest town of Thurso. It has been a royal burgh since 1589. It grew to its present size after Thomas Telford planned the original Harbour Bridge, new harbor, and new town. It became the largest herring fishing port in Europe, and the railway arrived in 1874.

Architecture: Historic Scotland Listed Building, Category A

The sheriff courthouse is on Bridge Street next door to the classical town hall and tolbooth of 1826–1828 by Robert Reid (see Court of Session) with its domed tower. The original Harbour Bridge was replaced with a three-span concrete bridge by Blyth and Blyth in 1939.

The sheriff court was completed by David Rhind in 1866 at a cost of £6,000 (half paid by the county) in an eclectic mix of an Italian Renaissance palazzo, with windows copied from the Vendramini Palace in Venice, and a French town house. The three-bay Italianate façade has heavy quoins and a balustrade across the double windows at the first-floor level. The wallhead dormers are in French style with a high slated mansard roof on the middle bay, topped by cast iron railing work and finials. The main arched doorway is flanked by twin squared Doric pilasters.

Interior

The main sheriff courtroom is on the first floor's west side (right-hand side) reaching from the front windows (covered with salmon pink curtains) into

the depth of the building on a longitudinal axis. The public gallery backs up to those covered windows, and the bench opposite is in the depth of the building. There are original timbers, and the whole court sits below a corbelled and coved corniced ceiling with a large skylight. A glass screen doubling the height of the bar separates the five rows of low raked pews from the well of the court. The Crown Coat of Arms sits on a stepped series of timber panels on the wall above the older and more original timber panels of the bench. There is an interesting open timber-framed witness box.

Aberdeen High Court of Justiciary and Sheriff Court Extension

Architecture: Historic Scotland Listed Building, Category A

A former Bank of Scotland on the Castlegate opposite the town and county buildings, it was completed in 1801 by James Burn as a three-story white granite Italian palazzo with giant Tuscan pilasters running through the two upper floors, topped by a balustrade, and with a rusticated ground floor. It was converted to a courthouse in 2004 by David Murray Associates and received an Aberdeen Civic Society commendation in 2005.

Interior

The pastel color painted and Corinthian columned and corniced ground floor—formerly a spacious banking hall—houses the reception and a new insertion of an opaque glass walled area as a "witness point." A new glass-encased lift has been inserted in the stairwell and cells in the basement.

The main coffer-ceilinged courtroom on the first floor has an unusual lateral orientation of the plan, with the bench on the long south side of the room, the public on the long north side (with windows to the Castlegate), and the glass panel topped bar running longitudinally across the room east-west, with the dock in the middle. The jury box is at the east end. The public in the horizontal gallery space is thus afforded an unusually broad panorama of the goings-on in the well of the court.

Edinburgh High Court of Justiciary

Urban

This building was originally constructed as the Edinburgh sheriff court on the Lawnmarket, two-thirds of the way up the Royal Mile. It is at the heart of the political, civil, and cultural center of Edinburgh Old Town. Situated across the High Street from the Advocates Library, Parliament Hall, and the Court of Session, it also faces St. Giles High Church across the square. It sits at one of the busiest junctions in the town where the nineteenth-century George IV Bridge meets the High Street. It is diagonally opposite the site where the headquarters of the Lothian council was formerly located, and the national headquarters of the Bank of Scotland sits on the Mound behind it.

Architecture: Historic Scotland Listed Building, Category B

The current Edinburgh High Court of Justiciary, a heavy, freestanding neo-Georgian building in gray sandstone was completed in 1937 by A. J. Pitcher and J. Wilson Paterson of H.M. Office of Works. It has a typical 1930s' simultaneous hypertrophy and flattening out of classical motifs, as seen in its giant cubist keystones above the ground floor windows and doorways (especially on the east side) and in the squared Roman Doric order on the first floor. The ground floor is of heavy channeled stone, and the main entrance on the High Street is under a tetrastyle pediment with Roman Doric piers. There is a sculpture of Lady Justice, flattened out in thirties style, with sword and scales centered in symmetry, completed by Alexander Carrick in 1937.

Interior

The sheriff courthouse was originally converted to the High Court of Justiciary from 1992–1994 after the new sheriff courts were opened in Chambers Street in 1993. A new entrance and atrium with light, airy T-plan barrel-vaulted aluminum standing seam roof was completed in 2011 at a cost of £1.2 million by McLean Architects. The stem of the T-plan roof sails high above the entrance and the main stairs moving north into the building. The east-west oriented foyer at the first-floor level sits under the bar of the T-plan.

Four panels of a tapestry "In Camera" by Alice Kettle (1997) hang on the north wall depicting scenes from court procedure. There are six courtrooms in the building, and courts one and two (the original courts) are at the lower level below and to the north of the entrance, off a marble-walled and stone-benched entrance hall. All the other courts are on the upper floor. The "early Georgian style woodwork" of which Gifford et al. write as existing in Edinburgh sheriff courtrooms (courts one and two) in 1990 is now gone. All courtrooms have been refitted with light timber paneling with a heavy curved cornice/lip at two-thirds height up the wall. There is a very low rake of broad steps to the public galleries.

Edinburgh Court of Session

Urban

Edinburgh, the second biggest settlement in Scotland, with a population of around 495,000, has been the capital city of the country since the fifteenth century. It was the principal seat of royalty and government, and even since the 1707 Union, when much political power was transferred to London, it has continued as the national center for civil, political, and religious life in Scotland.

Parliament House and the Court of Session are just off the High Street, which, together with the collinear Canongate, form the principal thoroughfare of Edinburgh Old Town, namely the Royal Mile. The Royal Mile extends from the royal Edinburgh Castle at the topmost west end of the ridge on which the town is built to the royal palace at Holyrood. Other important civic and national institutions housed on the Royal Mile include the Parliament House's next-door neighbor, the High Church of St. Giles, the center of national church government in the National Assembly rooms at the Mound; the city chambers of Edinburgh city council; and the new Scottish Parliament building (completed in 2003) facing the Palace of Holyrood. Just as in many towns across Scotland the sheriff court shared or still shares accommodation with local government, so in Parliament House the pre-1707 Scottish national government shared a building with the highest court in the land—the Court of Session.

Architecture: Historic Scotland Listed Building, Category A

Originally designed and constructed on the St. Giles Kirkyard in the seventeenth century by Sir James Murray to house the Parliament, Court of Session, and Privy Council, it was the Edinburgh town council who footed the £10,585 bill for this building. This original building was in a Scots

Renaissance style with bartizans, decorative strap work, pediments, and a pierced parapet. The Justice and Mercy statues by Robert Mylne in 1637 that adorned the east-facing doorway are now in a niche inside the building. It underwent many changes and adjustments over the years, including a "defacing" (Cullen p. 5) by Cromwell and the outbreak of fire twice in 1824. The current classical façade and rearrangement of buildings was constructed to a scheme by Robert Reid. The first part of his design on the west side was completed in 1803 with its characteristic channeled arcade on the ground floor, loggia with an Ionic colonnade running up through the two floors above, and wallhead balustrade with carved recumbent sphinxes. The design was extended around to the west when accommodation belonging to a bank was taken over there, and it was completed in 1838 wrapping around three sides of Parliament Square, with an Ionic temple frontage on the east side.

Interior

The historical centerpiece of the whole complex is the Parliament Hall with its Danish oak hammerbeam roof supported on carved stone corbels, as completed by John Scott in 1639. Court cases were formerly heard here—many concurrently—until the 1844 completion of the Outer House courtrooms (now courts ten, eleven, and twelve), with some benches against niches in the walls. Currently, statues fill these niches, such as the 1752 statue of Duncan Forbes in full judicial action by Louis Francois Roubiliac. There are many other statues throughout Parliament House, including Walter Scott by John Greenshields in 1835 and Lord Cockburn by William Brodie in 1862, plus busts and numerous portraits, especially of former judges, such as Sir William Nairne, Lord Dunsinane (1731–1811), by Henry Raeburn. The large arched Great Window on the south side of the Hall was designed by Wilhelm von Kaulbach and executed by Maximilian Ainmuller in 1868. It depicts James V founding the Court of Session in 1532. In the foyer between the Hall and the Outer House courts, Mylne's statues of Justice and Mercy are framed together in a niche.

The courtrooms are disposed around Parliament Hall along corridors and arms of the irregularly shaped building (as are the Advocates' and Signet Libraries). The principal courtrooms—courts one and two, or the First Division and the Second Division of the Inner House—sit to the east of Parliament Hall. These courtrooms, completed by Robert Reid in 1835, are both double height with arched windows on the upper level and first-floor balconies (now closed) supported by slender fluted Corinthian columns. They both have red felt topped curving benches and original timber fixtures throughout, which include the first two rows of benches for advocates and their instructing solicitors, then five rows of raked public benches accessed by a steep, narrow stair at the end of the pew (see Perth and Banff also). Court one has a colored Crown Coat of Arms on the wall behind the bench with the English ("Dieu et mon droit") rather than the Scottish motto on it. Court two has its very large colored Crown Coat of Arms with the usual Scottish motto, mounted on the cornice above the judge. Both courts have ribbed ceilings, and court one also has very prominent pendants. Court one is presided over by the Lord President, and court two, by the Lord Justice Clerk.

Along a corridor to the east, court three is the former High Court of Justiciary, although only rarely is it used for criminal trials nowadays. It has a coved ceiling with skylights and arched windows down one side. The bench is framed between twin gold-leafed Corinthian columns with pilasters on the wall behind. Farther east court four also has Corinthian columns and a coved ceiling with pendants. Court five is a utilitarian 1950s' court in dark timber with entrance from the domed circular hall of the former bank on the east side of the building.

At the south end of Parliament Hall are courts ten, eleven, and twelve, smaller courtrooms with original timbering from the 1840s but horizontal public pews. There are library shelves of books on the bench wall and a canopy over the bench rests on prodigiously extended consoles. All these courts have large oblong plan skylights in the ceiling but no windows. Court nine is on a corridor farther to the south, an impressive courtroom completely oak paneled to full height with Doric pilasters running around the walls. There is a splendid domed ceiling with skylights but there are no windows. Entrance to the court from the south-north running corridor is through a type of timber aediculed porch that runs into the east end of the courtroom behind the public gallery. That gallery consists of six rows of benches at a slight rake, with three rows for counsel in front of them. The bench sits back in a timber curved ceiling inset with three aediculed sets of library shelves behind. The unusual Crown Coat of arms sits in a segmental arch in the heavy timber cornice and has no lion or unicorn but instead is flanked by the royal initials E and R.

To the southeast of the complex is the four-story block containing courts six, seven, and eight, which was completed by W. Michael M. Normand of PSA Projects in 1992 and opened by HRH Anne, the Princess Royal, in 1993. The exterior of the block is of a heavy sandstone modern version of neobaronial, which sits on the Cowgate. The three courts have black onyx portals projecting into the foyer (an updated version of the entrance at court nine), which lead into the interior of the courtrooms. The courtroom design seems to owe much to the Glasgow sheriff court, with two-thirds height polished marble walls, no windows, white coffered ceilings diffusing light, and a full-height polished marble wall behind the bench. The public seating is not raked and is behind two rows of benches for counsel.

The Laigh Hall, completed in 1634, is on the floor below the Parliament Hall and has an ashlar arcade supported on octagonal piers. Until 1965 it housed a library, which was then transferred to the neighboring National Library of Scotland on King George IV Bridge. It is currently used by the Faculty of Advocates.

Glasgow High Court of Justiciary

Architecture: Historic Scotland Listed Building, Category A
The original courthouse at Jail Square, at the foot of the Saltmarket, of which only the Doric fluted hexastyle portico remains, was completed in 1814 by William Stark. The unfortunates who were sentenced to capital punishment in that court were hanged in the square opposite, "facing the monument" as the popular voice had it, as they would dangle with Glasgow Green and the distant obelisk to Nelson's victory stretching out before them. Stark had also designed the Signet Library at the Court of Session, and Walter Scott referred to him as having "genius." The High Court was redesigned and built by J. H. Craigie of Clark and Bell and opened again

with new pavilions containing courtrooms to the north and south, a hall between, and an entrance vestibule. Since the 1997 extension to the rear, entrance is no longer via the main steps and door on the Saltmarket.

Interior

Entrance instead comes via a stairway and corridors, in line with Clark and Bell's architectural drawings, to the hall, and subsequently the vestibule. The hall or atrium between the courts is glass roofed and has doors to the courtrooms for counsel and solicitors only. There are six classical plaster relief friezes on the walls. The vestibule (formerly accessed by the main doors from Saltmarket) is marble floored and has two rows of six onyx Ionic columns with sandstone capitals and socles.

The courtrooms on the north and south are both double-height spaces reaching longitudinally into the building in apsidal form at the bench end (west) and with many of the original 1913 features. There are tall windows between an Ionic colonnade at the upper level; the walls are light blue painted with the columns in white. The timber fixings throughout the courts—including the doors—is of dark staining, and the raked gallery sits under the disused balcony. There are glass panels atop the bar. The judge sits at the bench below a slightly curved soffit with a lintel above supported by lion carved consoles and topped by dwarf Doric columns.

The extension to the rear of the courthouse was completed in 1997 by TPS Consultants. It houses six new courtrooms and is entered via a sandstone tempietto with a Doric peristyle on polished granite plinths. Beyond this is the double-height columned atrium with marble floor and travertine walls, lit by the glass curtain east-facing wall. The curved reception desk sits below the balcony, which bears a frieze carved with texts. Artist Gary Breeze has carved overlapping excerpts from three books that he believes "speak about the compassion and wisdom in the formation, not merely of a system of justice, but of our society as a whole" (pamphlet published by GHCJ). The texts represent "The Law" in classical Roman style intaglio lettering with excerpts from Baron Hume's *Commentary on the Law of Scotland* (1797); "The Word of Man" in humanist italicized handwriting style intaglio with excerpts from David Hume's *Enquiry Concerning the Principles of Morals* (1777); and "the Word of God" in a grit blasted relief lettering with an excerpt from the biblical Book of Solomon. This extension is limited to the height of the 1913 building and is built with a steel-frame roof structure over a reinforced concrete frame on pile foundations. The new courtrooms have natural light drawn through a roof glazing integrated into the coffered ceiling. There is a very low, broad stepped rake to the public galleries. The walls are paneled with pear wood and feature plain pilasters and a brass dado with Celtic knot patterns.

In the foyer of the old court a text on the wall describes the centenary celebrations of the opening of the court in 2013, as led by Lord Gill. In the description the Lord Advocate, Frank Mulholland, is cited describing the courthouse as "Scotland's Old Bailey." There is also a description of the pageantry that formerly accompanied the opening of sessions in this court.

Until the 1960s at the offering of prayers, new sittings of the High Court were heralded by state trumpeters.

Bibliography

Aquinas, Thomas. *Summa Theologiae*. Oxford: Oxford University Press, 2014. Originally published Paris, 1273.

Asimow, M., S. Greenfield, G. Jorge, S. Machura, G. Osborn, P. Robson, C. Sharp, and R. Sockloskie. "Perceptions of Lawyers: A Transnational Study of Student Views on the Image of Law and Lawyers." *International Journal of the Legal Profession* 12 (2005): 407–36.

Bankowski, Z., N. Hutton, and J. McManus. *Lay Justice*. Edinburgh: Edinburgh University Press, 1987.

Barty, A. *The History of Dunblane*. Stirling: Eneas Mackay, Stirling, 1944.

Bissett, Andrew. *History of the Commonwealth of England*. London: John Murray, 1867.

Black, Jeremy, and Anthony Green. *Gods, Demons, and Symbols of Ancient Mesopotamia: An Illustrated Dictionary*. London: University of Texas Press and the Trustees of the British Museum, 1992.

Blackie, J. "Judges and Parties in the Provincial Courts in the First Half of the Nineteenth Century." In *Judicial Case Management and Efficiency in Civil Litigation*, edited by C. H. Van Rhee. Antwerp: Intersentia, 2008.

Bowen, Edward F. *Review of Sheriff and Jury Procedure*. Edinburgh: Independent Review of Sheriff and Jury Procedure, 2010.

Browning, Reed. *Political and Constitutional Ideas of the Court Whigs*. Baton Rouge: Louisiana State University Press, 1982.

Burgher, Leslie, "Kirkwall Sheriff Court and Prison," unpublished typescript produced for seminar 'Architecture in Society' at Edinburgh College of Art/Heriot Watt University. Kept at Kirkwall Sheriff Court.

Burman, Michele. *Criminal Justice Responses to Rape and Sexual Assault*. Glasgow: Scottish Centre for Crime and Justice Research, 2012.

Burman, Michele, Lynn Jamieson, Jan Nicholson, and Oona Brooks. *Impact of Aspects of the Law of Evidence in Sexual Offence Trials: An Evaluation Study*. Edinburgh: Scottish Government Social Research, 2007.

Cairns, John. "Historical Introduction." In *A History of the Private Law in Scotland*, edited by K. Reid and R. Zimmermann, 14–184. Oxford: Oxford University Press, 2000.

Carlen, P. *Magistrates' Justice*. London: Martin Robertson, 1976.

Carloway, Lord. *The Carloway Review*. 2010. www.gov.scot/About/Review/CarlowayReview.

Cavanagh, K., C. Connelly, and J. Scoular. *An Evaluation of the Protection from Abuse (Scotland) Act 2001*. Edinburgh: Scottish Executive, 2003.

Clark, B. *Lawyers and Mediation*. Edinburgh: Edinburgh University Press, 2012.

Clark, B., and C. Dawson. "Scottish Commercial Litigators and ADR: A Study of Attitudes and Experience." *Civil Justice Quarterly* 26 (2007): 228–49.

Cockburn, Henry, Lord. *Memorials of His Time*. Edinburgh: Blackie, 1856.

Colvin, H. *A Biographical Dictionary of British Architects 1600–1840*. New Haven, CT: Yale University Press, 1997.

Committee on Petition of Royal Burghs of Scotland respecting the Providing of Jails (1818) 346.

Commissioners for Municipal Corporations (Scotland) (1835) Local Reports of the Commissioners Part II from Glasgow to Wigton.

Commissioners on the Courts of Justice. *11th Report*. London: HMSO, 1832.

Contioso, T. *Mediation and Divorce in Spain*. RCSL Conference, Andorra, 2016.

Cook, C., and J. Stevenson. *The Longman Handbook of Modern British History 1714–1987*. London: Longman, 1883.

Cooper, Lord. "The Central Courts After 1532." In *An Introduction to Scottish Legal History*. Edinburgh: Stair Society, 1958.

Cotterrell, R. *The Sociology of Law*. Oxford: Oxford University Press, 2005.

Cruft, Kitty, John Dunbar, and Richard Fawcett. *The Buildings of Scotland: Borders*. New Haven, CT: Yale University Press, 2006.

Cullen, W. Douglas. *Parliament House: A Short History and Guide*. Edinburgh: Scottish Courts Administration, 1992.

Davie, G. *The Democratic Intellect*. Edinburgh: Edinburgh University Press, 1961.

de la Casiniere, N. "A Nantes, le style du palais sévèrement jugé." *La Liberation*, July 10, 2000. www.liberation.fr/societe/2000/07/10/a-nantes-le-style-du-palais-severement-juge_332632.

de Montaigne, Michel. *Shakespeare's Montaigne: The Florio Translations of The Essays*. Translated by John Florio. New York: New York Review of Books, 2014.

Douglas-Robinson, W. *The Younger Goethe and the Visual Arts*. Cambridge: Cambridge University Press, 1981.

Duncan, I. "Urban Space and Enlightened Romanticism." In *The Edinburgh Companion to Scottish Romanticism*, edited by Murray Pittock. Edinburgh: Edinburgh University Press, 2012.

Eyre-Todd, George. *Famous Scottish Burghs: Their Romantic Story*. London: Heath Cranton, 1923.

Fenton, Clive. "Edinburgh University and the Monumental Tradition." *Edinburgh Architecture Research* 26 (1999): 29–76.

Fine, Bob. *Democracy and the Rule of Law*. Caldwell, NJ: Blackburn Press, 2002.

Finnis J. *Natural Law and Natural Rights*. Oxford: Oxford University Press, 1980.

Flood, John. "Transnational Lawyering: Clients, Ethics and Regulation." In *Lawyers in Practice: Ethical Decision Making in Context*, edited by Lynn Mather and Leslie Levin. Chicago: University of Chicago Press, 2012.

Flood, John. "Institutional Bridging: How Large Law Firms Engage in Globalisation." *Boston College Law Review* 54, no. 1 (2013): 1–35.

Flood, John, and Peter Lederer. "Becoming a Cosmopolitan Lawyer." *Fordham Law Review* 80 (2012): 2513–39.

Forfarshire Commissioners of Supply. *Forfarshire Court Houses Committee Minute Book*. Forfar: Angus Archives, Hunter Library, Restenneth, Forfar, 1820–1939.

Foster, Hal. *The Art-Architecture Complex*. London: Verso, 2011.

Foucault, Michel. *Discipline and Punish: The Birth of the Prison*. Translated by A. M. Sheridan Smith. Harmondsworth: Penguin, 1991.

Freeman, M., ed. *Lloyd's Introduction to Jurisprudence*. London: Sweet and Maxwell, 2014.

Friedman, Lawrence. "Law, Lawyers and Popular Culture." *Yale Law Journal* 98 (1989): 1579.

Fuller, Lon. *The Morality of Law*. New Haven, CT: Yale University Press, 1969.

Gifford, John. *Dundee and Angus: The Buildings of Scotland*. New Haven, CT: Yale University Press, 2012.

Gifford, John, Colin McWilliam, and David Walker. *The Buildings of Scotland: Edinburgh*. London: Penguin, 1991.

Gill, Lord. *Scottish Civil Courts Review: A Consultation Paper*, 2007. www.scotcourts.gov.uk/docs/default-source/civil-courts-reform/scccompleter-(2)7CDD54ABAE89.pdf?sfvrsn=2.

Gill, Lord. *Report of the Scottish Civil Courts Review*. Edinburgh: Scottish Civil Courts Review, 2009.

Glendinning, Miles. *The Architecture of Scottish Government: From Kingship to Parliamentary Democracy*. Dundee: Dundee University Press, 2004.

Graham, Clare. *Ordering Law: An Architectural and Social History of the English Law Court to 1914*. Farnborough: Ashgate, 2003.

Grant, Lord. *The Sheriff Court*. Edinburgh: Scottish Home and Health Department and HMSO, 1967.

Greenfield, S., G. Osborn, and P. Robson. *Film and the Law: The Cinema of Justice*. Oxford: Hart, 2010.

Greig, J. *The Letters of David Hume*. 2 vols. Oxford: Clarendon Press, 1932.

Griffith J. *The Politics of the Judiciary*. London: Fontana, 1975.

Gunningham N. *Pollution, Social Interest and the Law*. London: Martin Robertson, 1974.

Halliday, S. *Introduction to the Study of Law*. Edinburgh: W. Green, 2012.

Hart, H. *The Concept of Law*. Oxford: Clarendon, 1961.

Harvey, David. *Social Justice and the City*. London: Edward Arnold, 1973.

Harvey, David. *Consciousness and the Urban Experience*. Oxford: Basil Blackwell, 1985.

Harvey, David. *Spaces of Hope*. Edinburgh: Edinburgh University Press, 2000.

Harvey, David. "The Right to the City." *New Left Review* 53 (2008): 23–40.

Hay, Douglas, Peter Linebaugh, John Rule, E. P. Thompson, and Cal Winslow, eds. *Albion's Fatal Tree: Crime and Society in Eighteenth-Century England*. London: Pantheon, 1975.

Hay, George. *The History of Arbroath to the Present Time*. Arbroath: Thomas Buncie, 1876.

Historic Scotland. *Scottish Courts: Preliminary Report*. www.historic-scotland.gov.uk/scottish-courts-preliminary-report.pdf, 2014.

Houser, R. E. *The Cardinal Virtues: Aquinas, Albert and Philip the Chancellor*. Toronto: Pontifical Institute of Mediaeval Studies, 2004.

Hunter, R. *Impact of Mediation on Divorce*. RCSL Conference, Andorra, 2016.

Irvine Smith, J. "The Transition to the Modern Law 1532–1660." In *An Introduction to Scottish Legal History*. Edinburgh: Stair Society, 1958.

Jackson, A., M. Robertson, and P. Robson. *The Operation of the Matrimonial Homes (Family Protection) (Scotland) Act 1981*. Edinburgh: Scottish Office, 1988.

Jacobs, Jane. *The Death and Life of Great American Cities*. New York: Vintage Books, 1961.

Judicial Office for Scotland. *Principles for Provision of Access to Justice*, 2012. www.scotcourts.gov.uk/docs/default-source/scs-consultation-court-structures/statement_of_principles.pdf.

Kelsen, H. *The Pure Theory of Law*. Berkeley: University of California Press, 1960.

Knox, J. *The Works of John Knox*, edited by David Lang. Edinburgh: Wodrow Society, 1855.

Knox, James. *Airdrie: A Historical Sketch*. Airdrie: Baird and Hamilton, 1921.

Lefebvre, Henri. *Le Droit a la Ville*. Paris: Anthropos, 1968.

Lefebvre, Henri. "Reflections on the Politics of Space." Translated by M. Enders. *Antipode* 8 (1976): 30–37.

Lefebvre, Henri. *Writings on Cities*. Cambridge, MA: Blackwell, 1996.

Linebaugh, Peter. *The London Hanged: Crime and Civil Society in the Eighteenth Century*. London: Allen Lane, 2006.

Lipman, Alan. "The Architectural Belief System and Social Behaviour." *British Journal of Sociology* 20, no. 2 (1969): 190–204.

Lockhart, J. *Memoirs of the Life of Sir Walter Scott*. Cambridge: Cambridge University Press, 1846.

Lord Chancellor's Department. *Modernising Justice: The Government's Plans for Reforming Legal Services and the Courts*. Vol. 4155 of Cm Series. London: Stationery Office, 1998.

Lowrey, J. "From Caesarea to Athens: Greek Revival Edinburgh and the Question of Scottish Identity in the Unionist State." *Journal of the Society of Architectural Historians* 60, no. 2 (2001): 136–157.

Macaulay, Stuart. "Images of Law in Everyday Life: The Lessons of School, Entertainment and Spectator Sports." *Law and Society Review* 21 (1987): 185.

MacGregor, M. *Between Two Worlds, Lochmaddy 1600–1995*. North Uist: Taigh Chearsabhaigh, 1996.

MacKecknie, A. *Scots Court Architecture of the early 17th Century*. PhD thesis, Edinburgh, 1993.

Mackintosh, C. R. "Scotch Baronial Architecture." In *Charles Rennie Mackintosh: The Architectural Papers*, edited by Pamela Robertson. Wendlebury: White Cockade, 1990.

Mahood, L. "'Give Him a Doing': The Birching of Young Offenders in Scotland." *Canadian Journal of History* 37, no. 3 (2002): 439–57.

Malcolm, C. "Sheriff and Other Local Court Records 1386–1935." In *An Introductory Survey of the Sources and Literature of Scots Law*. Edinburgh: Stair Society, 1936.

Marks, A. *What Is a Court?* London: JUSTICE, 2016.

Mays, R., and B. Clark. *Alternative Dispute Resolution in Scotland*. Edinburgh: Scottish Office Central Research Unit, 1996.

McGibbon, D., and T. Ross. *The Castellated and Domestic Architecture of Scotland from the 12th to the 18th Century*. Edinburgh: James Thin, 1971.

McInnes, John. *The Summary Justice Review Committee: Report to Ministers*. Edinburgh: Scottish Executive, 2004. www.gov.scot/Publications/2004/03/19042/34181.

McKean, Charles, *The District of Moray: An Illustrated Architectural Guide*. Edinburgh: Scottish Academic Press, 1987.

McKenzie, Ray. *Public Sculpture of Glasgow*. Liverpool: Liverpool University Press, 2002.

McMullan, R. *Environmental Science in Building*. London: Macmillan, 1983.

Melville, R. D. "The Use and Forms of Judicial Torture in England and Scotland." *Scottish Historical Review* 2, no. 7 (1905): 225–248.

Milne, Isabel. "The Sheriff Court before the Sixteenth Century." In *An Introduction to Scottish Legal History*. Edinburgh: Stair Society, 1958.

Ministry of Justice. *Transforming Our Justice System*. London: HMSO, 2016.

Montgomery Hyde, H. *Judge Jeffreys*. London: Butterworth, 1948.

Moody, D. *Scottish Towns: Sources for Local Historians*. London: Batsford, 1992.

Morton, Graeme. *Unionist Nationalism: Governing Urban Scotland 1830–1860*. East Linton: Tuckwell Press, 1999.

Mulcahy, Linda. *Legal Architecture: Justice, Due Process and the Place of Law*. London: Routledge, 2011.

Mulcahy, Linda. "Back to the Future? The Challenge of the Past for the Courthouses of Tomorrow." In *Architecture and Justice*, edited by N. Temple, J. Simon, and R. Tobe Farnborough: Ashgate, 2013.

Mulcahy, Linda. "Putting the Defendant in Their Place: Why Do We Still Use the Dock in Criminal Proceedings?" *British Journal of Criminology* 53, no. 6 (2013): 1139–56.

Munro, R., and J. Munro. *Tain Through the Centuries*. Edinburgh: Birlinn, 2005.

Muzio, Daniel, and John Flood. "Entrepreneurship, Managerialism and Professionalism in Action: The Case of the Legal Profession in England and Wales." In *Handbook of Research on Entrepreneurship in Professional Services*, edited by M. Reihlen and A. Werr, 369–86. Cheltenham: Edward Elgar, 2012.

Newman, Oscar. *Defensible Space*. London: Architectural Press, 1973.

Nicholson G. *The Sheriff Court at Edinburgh*. Edinburgh: Scottish Courts Administration, 1994.

Ormond, W. *Lives of the Lord Advocates of Scotland*. Edinburgh: Green, 1883.

Paterson, A. *The Law Lords*. Oxford: Socio-Legal Studies, 1980.

Paterson A. *Final Judgment: The Last Law Lords and the Supreme Court*. Oxford: Hart, 2013.

Paton G. "The Eighteenth Century and Later." In *An Introduction to Scottish Legal History*. Edinburgh: Stair Society, 1958.

Perthshire Commissioners of Supply. *Perthshire Public Buildings Committee Records Minute Book*. Perth: AK Bell Library Archives, 1807–1820.

Perthshire Commissioners of Supply. *Perthshire Public Buildings Committee Records Minute Book*. Perth: AK Bell Library Archives, 1815–1928.

Perthshire Committee for Sheriff Court Houses and County Buildings. *Minute Book*. Perth: AK Bell Library Archives, 1862–1889.

Philipopoulos-Mihalopoulos, Andreas, ed. *Law and the City*. London, Routledge, 2007.

Pryde, George. *The Burghs of Scotland: A Critical List*. Oxford: Oxford University Press, 1965.

Quick, Estelle. *Tain Tolbooth*. Tain: Tain and District Museum Trust, 1998.

Radbruch, G. "Rechtsphilosophie." In *Gesamtausgabe*, vol. 1, edited by A. Kaufmann. Heidelberg: C. E. Müller Verlag, 1987.

Rapping, Elaine. *Law and Justice: As Seen on TV*. New York: New York University Press, 2003.

Refrewshire Council Department of Planning and Transport. *Paisley's Public Sculptures*. Paisley: Refrewshire Council Department of Planning and Transport, 2001.

Resnik, Judith, and Dennis Curtis. *Representing Justice: Invention, Controversy, and Rights in City-States and Democratic Courtrooms*. New Haven, CT: Yale University Press, 2011.

Resnik, Judith, Dennis Curtis, and Allison Tait. *Constructing Courts: Architecture, the Ideology of Judging, and the Public Sphere*. Dordrecht: Springer, 2014.

Robertson, Marie, and Peter Robson. *The Matrimonial Homes (Family Protection) (Scotland) Act 1981: The First Six Months*. Glasgow: University of Strathclyde, 1983.

Robson, Peter. *Housing and Judiciary*. Glasgow: University of Strathclyde, 1979.

Robson, Peter. "Lawyers and the Legal System on TV: The British Experience." *International Journal of Law in Context* 2, no. 4 (2007): 333–62.

Robson, Peter. "The Portrayal of the Corporate Lawyer on TV: The US and British Models from *L.A. Law* to *Trust* and *Suits*." *Journal of the Oxford Centre for Socio-Legal Studies* 1, no. 3 (2017).

Robson, Peter, and Jennifer Schulz. *A Transnational Study of Law and Justice on TV*. Oxford: Hart, 2016.

Robson, Peter, and P. Watchman, eds. *Justice, Lord Denning and the Constitution*. Farnborough: Gower, 1981.

Rodger, Johnny. *Contemporary Glasgow: The Architecture of the 1990s*. Edinburgh: Rutland Press, 1999.

Royal Commission on the Ancient and Historical Monuments of Scotland. *Tolbooths and Town-houses: Civic Architecture in Scotland to 1833*. Edinburgh: HMSO, 1996.

Royal Incorporation of Architects in Scotland. *Buildings at Work*. Edinburgh: RIAS, 1983.

Ryrie, Alex. *The Origins of the Scottish Reformation*. Manchester: Manchester University Press, 2006.

Schotz, B. *Bronze in My Blood*. Edinburgh: Gordon Wright, 1981.

Scott, W. *Sir Walter Scott's Journal*, edited by D. Douglas. Edinburgh: Douglas, 1891.

Scottish Civic Trust. *Historic Buildings at Work: A Guide to the Historic Buildings of Scotland Used by Central Government*. Edinburgh: Scottish Civic Trust, 1983.

Scottish Court Service. *Shaping Scotland's Court Services*, 2013. www.scotcourts.gov.uk/docs/default-source/scs-consultation-court-structures/response_to_the_consultation_and_recommendationspdf.pdf.

Scottish Government. *Scottish Government Response to the Report and Recommendations of the Scottish Civil Courts Review*. Edinburgh: Scottish Government, 2010. www.scotcourts.gov.uk/docs/default-source/civil-courts-reform/scottish-government-response-to-the-report-and-recommendations-of-the-scottish-civil-courts-review.pdf?sfvrsn=2.

Scottish Government. *Making Justice Work: Courts Reform (Scotland) Bill—A Consultation Paper*. Edinburgh: Scottish Government, 2013.

Scottish Government Social Research. *Courts Reform (Scotland) Bill: Analysis of Consultation Responses*. Edinburgh: Scottish Government, 2013.

Scottish Home and Health Department. *The Sheriff Court*. Edinburgh: HMSO, 1967.

Sherwin, Richard. *When Law Goes Pop*. Chicago: University of Chicago Press, 2000.

Skolnick J. *Justice without Trial*. Berkeley, CA: Wiley, 1966.

Soja, Edward. *Seeking Spatial Justice*. Minneapolis: University of Minnesota, 2010.

Stuart, James, and Nicholas Revett. *The Antiquities of Athens and Other Monuments of Greece*. London, 1762.

Susskind, Richard. *The Future of Law: Facing the Challenges of Information Technology*. Oxford: Clarendon Press, 1996.

Susskind, Richard. *Transforming the Law*. Oxford: Oxford University Press, 2000.

Susskind, Richard. *The End of Lawyers?* Oxford: Oxford University Press, 2008.

Turnock, David. *The Wheatley Report: Local Government in Scotland*. Oxford, Blackwell, 1970.

Walker, David. *A Legal History of Scotland, Volume V: The Eighteenth Century*. Edinburgh: T & T Clark, 1998.

Walker, David. *A Legal History of Scotland, Volume VI: The Nineteenth Century*. Edinburgh: T & T Clark, 2001.

Walker, Frank. *The South Clyde Estuary*. Edinburgh: RIAS, 1992.

Watkin, D. *Athenian Stuart: Pioneer of the Greek Revival*. London: George Allen & Unwin, 1982.

Whetstone, Ann. "The Reform of the Scottish Sheriffdoms in the Eighteenth and Early Nineteenth Centuries." *Albion: A Quarterly Journal Concerned with British Studies* (The North American Conference on British Studies) 9, no. 1 (1977): 61–71.

Whetstone, Ann. *Scottish County Government in the 18th and 19th Centuries*. Edinburgh: John Donald, 1981.

Willock I. *The Origins and the Development of the Jury in Scotland*. Edinburgh: Stair Society, 1964.

Wilson, John. *Not Proven*. London: Secker and Warburg, 1960.

Woolf, Lord. *Access to Justice*, 1996. webarchive.nationalarchives.gov.uk/+/http:/www.dca.gov.uk/civil/final/contents.htm.

Young, George. *Reminiscences of Glasgow Sheriff Court*. Glasgow: William Hodge, 1907.

Youngson, A. *The Making of Classical Edinburgh*. Edinburgh: Edinburgh University Press, 1993.

Index

About the Authors

Peter Robson, LLB (St. Andrews), PhD (Strathclyde University), is a poverty lawyer and professor of Social Welfare Law who teaches at the University of Strathclyde in Scotland. He is a solicitor and judge in Her Majesty's Court and Tribunals Service. He is author of *Homeless People and the Law* (1996, third edition), *Housing Law in Scotland* (2011), and *Residential Tenancies* (2012, third edition). He also works in the area of popular culture and was coeditor of *Law and Film* with Stefan Machura in 2001; coauthor with Steve Greenfield and Guy Osborn of *Film and the Law: The Cinema of Justice* (2010), updating the influential first edition; and coeditor with Jessica Silbey of *Law and Justice on the Small Screen* (2012) and with Jennifer Schulz of *A Transnational Study of Law and Justice on TV* (2016). Recent essays include *British TV Lawyers* (2009) *Teaching Law and Popular Culture*, *Law in Modern Popular Fiction* (2014), *Law and Theatre* (2015), and *Vigilantes in Film* (2016).

Johnny Rodger is a writer and critic, and professor of urban literature at the Mackintosh School of Architecture at the Glasgow School of Art. He is editor of the *The Drouth*, a quarterly literary/arts journal. His published books include literary fiction, such as *The Auricle* (1995), *g haun(s) Q* (1996), and *redundant* (1998), and scholarly works, such as *Contemporary Glasgow* (1999), *Gillespie Kidd & Coia 1956-87* (2007), *Tartan Pimps: Gordon Brown, Margaret Thatcher and the New Scotland* (2010), and *The Red Cockatoo: James Kelman and the Art of Commitment* (2011). His latest book, *The Hero Building: An Architecture of Scottish National Identity*, was published in September 2015.

Lightning Source UK Ltd.
Milton Keynes UK
UKHW021254090223
416759UK00009B/205

9 781683 930884